## BY WAYNE GARD

*The Great Buffalo Hunt* (1959)
*Fabulous Quarter Horse: Steel Dust* (1958)
*The Chisholm Trail* (1954)
*Frontier Justice* (1949)
*Sam Bass* (1936)
*Book Reviewing* (1927)

# THE
# GREAT
# BUFFALO
# HUNT

# THE GREAT
# BUFFALO HUNT

BY

# WAYNE GARD

*with drawings by*

## NICK EGGENHOFER

A BISON BOOK

UNIVERSITY OF NEBRASKA • LINCOLN/LONDON

Library of Congress Catalog Card Number 59–11049
Copyright © 1959 by Wayne Gard
All rights reserved
International Standard Book Number 0–8032–5067–3

*First Bison Book printing:  August, 1968*

*Most recent printing shown by first digit below:*
6     7     8     9     10

*Bison Book edition published by arrangement with Alfred A. Knopf, Inc.*

# FOREWORD

LIKE THE HARDY New England whalers of an earlier day, the hunters of the buffaloes were mighty men. On the bleak Western plains they outlasted blizzards and sandstorms and, in most instances, outshot or outwitted the redskins who wanted their scalps. Usually the hunter was a young but grizzled and uncouth fellow, itchy from tiny crawlers out of the piles of hides about his camp. Yet he knew how to dodge the charge of a wounded buffalo bull, and he used his heavy rifle with a precision that even a Prussian field marshal would have admired. At the bar of a frontier outpost, when his work was done, he could outdrink even the thirstiest cowpuncher.

Rightly the buffalo hunter has taken his place among the heroic figures of the early West. He was so pictured by John Steuart Curry in his striking murals in the Kansas Capitol and by Harold D. Bugbee in his equally impressive ones in the Panhandle-Plains Historical Museum at Canyon, Texas.

This stubbly-faced rifleman was one of a long line of rugged pioneers who tamed the West. He followed the missionary, the explorer, the fur trader. He went ahead of the cowman and the settler. By clearing the plains of their almost boundless herds of shaggies, he made way for the ranchman with his cattle or sheep. By depriving the hostile plains Indian of his chief source of food, garb, and shelter, he starved him into submission to the whites.

Of course, the buffalo hunter didn't give a hoot for the stockman or for those who wanted to solve the Indian problem. His interest was in acquiring a great stack of buffalo hides that would bring him a dollar or so each. He didn't care how many tons of meat were left on the prairie each day to rot or to be devoured by ravenous wolves. All that mattered was those smelly hides.

Although the hunting of buffaloes for robes, meat, or sport had been going on longer than anyone could remember, the era of the professional hide men was brief. It began after tanners learned how to make good leather from buffalo skins. It lasted only a dozen years, 1871–83, seldom more than four years in any given section of the plains. Yet that was long enough to slaughter the enormous herds that had darkened the broad grazing lands of the West and to almost wipe out the species. The killing left the prairies whitened with bones that pioneer farmers in need of a few dollars would pick up and haul to the nearest railroad town.

The hide hunters were recruited from adventurers who had drifted west for various reasons. One of the most successful was a young man of Vermont birth who had been a streetcar conductor in Chicago and a carpenter's helper in a small Illinois town. Others were former soldiers or railroad construction workers who sought an exciting and lucrative life. Still others had left Eastern homes to avoid the sheriff or the outraged father of a trusting girl.

When the butchery was done, those hunters who had survived Indian scalpers dispersed as quickly as they had come together. Some, like the former streetcar conductor, became successful cattle ranchers. Many hired out as cowhands or found security in the Army. The more restless turned to cattle rustling or horse thieving and soon tangled with vigilante law.

This book describes the great hunt of buffaloes for their hides as a factor in the conquest of the West. Its introductory chapters on the habits of the buffalo, on what the animal meant to the plains Indians, and on hunting for sport are included only as a backdrop for the dramatic action by the gatherers of hides.

I have talked with as many of the surviving buffalo hunters as I could find, and I have studied the memoirs of others. I have crossed several states to search early newspaper files and other contemporary accounts. I have visited the sites of some of the more important incidents described.

Research for the book was supported in part by a grant from the American Philosophical Society. I am grateful for that and for the help given by many librarians, archivists, and fellow historians. Information, advice, and the loan of source materials have been volunteered by friends over a wide area.

Special acknowledgment goes to Dr. H. Bailey Carroll, director of the Texas State Historical Association; Nyle H. Miller, secretary of the Kansas State Historical Society; Agnes Wright Spring, State Historian of Colorado; Miss Louise Mooar of Marietta, Georgia; J. Frank Dobie of Austin, Texas; J. L. Baughman of Rockport, Texas; Ramon F. Adams, Dan Ferguson, and Leon C. Jackson, all of Dallas; and my wife, Hazel D. Gard. All opinions and errors my own.

W. G.

*Dallas, Texas*

# CONTENTS

# ILLUSTRATIONS

# THE
# GREAT
# BUFFALO
# HUNT

# — 1 —

# MONARCH OF THE

# PLAINS

**M**ost paintings of buffalo hunts stem from an era when half the making of a hero was to mount him on a fiery charger. The artist portrayed a stirring scene in which horseback hunters, Indian or paleface, attacked a surging mass of buffaloes. Riding their sturdy and carefully trained steeds into the herd, the men began downing the shaggy beasts with rifle or six-shooter, lance or flint-tipped arrow.

Such scenes did take place in the early days of hunting, but they hardly were typical. Even the Indians usually found ways to kill the buffaloes with less effort, less danger to horses and men, and less frightening away of the game. The white hunters, in the years in which they slaughtered the buffaloes for their hides, quickly learned that the best results came from hunting afoot.

The hide hunter, with a rifle too heavy for easy use on horseback, crawled toward the herd against the wind and lay or crouched behind a rock or bush. Often he stuck in

the ground a Y-shaped stick, on which he rested the barrel
of his rifle for better aim. From the distance made possible
by his long-range weapon, he might down several scores of
the animals before the others became alarmed and fled to a
safer part of the prairie.

As the surviving buffaloes turned up their short, tufted
tails and galloped off, the skinners drove up in their mule-
drawn wagon and began their arduous work. Usually they
took only the hides, leaving the carcasses to rot. One of the
hunters, Skelton Glenn, said he had seen the skinned bodies
so thick that they looked like tree trunks where a tornado
had passed through a forest. "If they were lying on a hill-
side, the rays of the sun would make them look like a hundred glass windows. The carcasses would lie there, drying up,
until warm weather. I have seen fifty or sixty in a pile where
the hunter made a stand. As the skinners began at the edge,
they would have to roll each carcass out of the way to make
room for the next. In the end the bodies would be rolled up
as thick as saw logs around a mill. A man could ride over the
prairie and pick out the camps that were making the most
money out of the hunt."

The buffaloes thus killed for their hides were numbered
not in mere thousands but in millions. Never before had such
a slaughter of wild animals by human hands been recorded
by a historian.

The buffaloes, whose skins had come to be in greater
demand than their flesh, had been regarded, only a few years
earlier, as in endless supply. Plainsmen were convinced that
no amount of killing could made a lasting dent in the herds.
Yet the great slaughter that began in 1871 alarmed not only
the Indians—who saw their main source of food, clothing,
and shelter vanishing—but many of the whites as well. Some
raised their voices in vain pleas to prevent the wiping out of
the herds.

The vast numbers of buffaloes on the Great Plains had

been a subject of comment by explorers and other travelers since Cabeza de Vaca described the "Indian cattle" he saw in Texas in 1533. Many of the stories sound like the tales of Paul Bunyan. They hardly would be credited by historians except that they were attested by many reliable eyewitnesses. Until about 1836, those who crossed the Great Plains between the Rocky Mountains and the Missouri River had large bands of buffaloes within view almost all the way.

Often the herds of shaggy beasts darkened the whole horizon. In 1832, after skirting the North Fork of the Platte River, Captain Benjamin Bonneville climbed a high bluff that gave him a wide view of the surrounding plains. "As far as the eye could reach," he reported, "the country seemed blackened by innumerable herds." In the following May, J. K. Townsend, while crossing the Platte Valley, stopped on the rise of a hill to view a similar scene. The whole region, he wrote, "was covered with one enormous mass of buffaloes. Our vision, at the least computation, would certainly extend ten miles; and in the whole of this vast space, including about eight miles in width from the bluffs to the river bank, there apparently was no vista in the incalculable multitude." [1]

Those accounts were matched by others that came from the high plains of northwestern Texas. One pioneer there described a herd which he said covered fifty square miles. Another reported that he saw between two and three million buffaloes at one time. A third told of herds that in his estimate held four million head. Many frontiersmen, like the Indians, thought there were enough buffaloes to last forever.

Sometimes the herds were so solid that they impeded travel. On the upper Missouri River in the summer of 1867 the steamer *Stockade*, in charge of Captain Grant Marsh, was held up while a snorting and bellowing herd crossed the stream. The buffaloes came so thickly that the boat could

[1] Washington Irving: *The Rocky Mountains, or Scenes, Incidents, and Adventures in the Far West*, I, 44; J. K. Townsend: *Narrative of a Journey across the Rocky Mountains*, p. 46.

not move, and the captain had to stop its engines. Many of
the animals became entangled with the wheel, while others
beat against the sides and stern, blowing and pawing. It was
hours before the whole herd had crossed and the boat was
able to continue its voyage.[2]

Railroad trains were no more immune to this type of barrier. In 1867 a Union Pacific train, traveling from Omaha to
Cheyenne, was stopped twice by buffaloes on the tracks. Two
years later, buffaloes were so thick in western Kansas that
a herd crossing the Kansas Pacific rails held up a train for
two hours.

In May 1871, Major Richard Irving Dodge set out in a
light wagon from Fort Zarah, on the Arkansas River in southwestern Kansas. His route took him along the river southwest
to Fort Larned. He reported that he drove at least twenty-
five miles through an immense herd of buffaloes that was
made up of many smaller bunches. The whole country, he
recalled, "appeared one mass of buffaloes, moving slowly
northward. Only when among them could it be ascertained
that the apparently solid mass was an agglomeration of innumerable small herds of fifty to two hundred animals."

This great herd, he added, "was about five days passing
a given point, or not less than fifty miles deep. From the top
of Pawnee Rock I could see from six to ten miles in almost
every direction. The whole space was covered with buffaloes, looking at a distance like one compact mass, the visual
angle not permitting the ground to be seen."

As late as 1874, after the hide hunters had begun to kill
great numbers, Texas drovers pointing Longhorn cattle up
the dusty Chisholm Trail sometimes found their route
blocked. More than a few had to stop in the Indian Territory
to let herds of buffaloes cross their path. The cowmen feared
that the buffaloes would cause their cattle to stampede and

[2] Joseph Mills Hanson: *The Conquest of the Missouri*, pp. 97–8.

that some of the Longhorns, and even the spare horses, might join the shaggies.

Buffaloes on the trail held back the progress of seven hundred big steers being taken to Kansas for W. H. Mayfield in 1870. Early one morning, just as the men were putting the herd on the trail, they were told that buffaloes were heading toward them. "I went to the top of a small hill and saw a black string," said one of the hands, W. R. Massengale. "It looked as though it were coming straight toward our herd. I went back, and we rounded our cattle so we could hold them; but the buffaloes passed just ahead of us. Our cattle got a little nervous, but we held them all right. It took the buffaloes two hours to pass." [3]

No one knows how many buffaloes roamed over North America before the white men came. The most carefully calculated estimates for the primitive period of Indian occupation range from sixty to seventy-five million head. As late as 1830, after gunpowder had begun to take its toll, an estimated forty million were left.

## II

The American bison or buffalo, the largest wild animal on the continent, was widely distributed in the Indian era. Although the great herds remained on the almost treeless plains of the West, smaller herds ranged from northern Georgia to Hudson Bay and from the Appalachians to the Rockies and beyond. In Canada and elsewhere the early French *voyageurs* called the strange animals *les bœufs,* meaning oxen or beeves. Hence came the English *buffle, buffelo,* and finally *buffalo.*

[3] Richard Irving Dodge: *The Plains of the Great West,* pp. 120–1; J. Marvin Hunter, editor: *The Trail Drivers of Texas,* p. 1023; Wayne Gard: *The Chisholm Trail,* p. 146. Major Dodge was the commanding officer at Fort Dodge, in southwestern Kansas.

The buffaloes that ranged over most of North America were not all exactly alike. Dominant in numbers was the prairie or plains buffalo, which became the victim of the hide hunters. The principal variant was the wood buffalo, found in small herds in eastern parts of the United States and Canada. The wood buffalo, which some called the Pennsylvania buffalo, was slightly larger than its cousin on the Great Plains. Although it grazed on the open prairies in the summer, it generally sought the protection of the woods in the winter. Another variant was the uncommon mountain buffalo of the Rockies and the Pacific Coast region. This was said to be a bit smaller and fleeter than the plains bison. Unfortunately, both the wood buffalo and the mountain buffalo became extinct before scientists could learn much of their appearance and habits.

The size, appearance, and grazing habits of the buffalo explain why early explorers referred to it as a cow. To the eye, it differed from the domestic bovine mainly in having a hump on its back, a larger head and front legs, and a mat of shaggy hair over its foreparts. But some hunters discovered in a wounded buffalo bull more ferocity than they had guessed.

The color of the buffalo's coat varied, as was noted even by Cabeza de Vaca, the first European to describe the animal. "Some are tawny," he wrote; "others black." If he had wandered farther north, he might have found an occasional blue or mouse-colored buffalo, or even a pied or spotted one. Rarest of all was the albino, which varied from dirty gray to pale cream.

Many of the Indians, especially the Mandans, set a high value on a white buffalo robe and were reluctant to sell it. A good one might be traded for ten to fifteen horses. One Cheyenne chief wore such a robe when he led his warriors into battle, believing that it would shield him from harm. Some of the medicine men used white robes in their cures.

In the day of the hide hunters, probably most of the animals that passed for white buffaloes were cattaloes, resulting from the mating of buffalo bulls with Longhorn cows.

The poor sight of the buffalo often gave him a reputation for being stupid, but he had a keen sense of smell and surprising speed. A Briton who had hunted in Texas before the Civil War wrote: "With their tails stuck right up on end, and shaking their shaggy manes, they rush off with a roll in their gallop which is likely to deceive the spectator as to the real pace they are going at, while the earth shakes as they thunder over it." After a hunt on the Kansas plains in 1871, Albert L. Green wrote: "They are built for speed, despite their big heads and heavy haunches. Their run is a heavy gallop, and it is not every horse that can come near matching them in speed." [4]

The need for grass and water kept the buffaloes on the move much of the time. After a herd had consumed the grass on one part of the range, it would move on to fresh forage. About every third day the animals would come to water, mostly at night, said Wentin A. Wilson, who hunted on the Canadian River in 1876. "When they leave the river and start up the canyon, the sound is like distant thunder and can be heard for miles."

Many early explorers believed that the herds made long seasonal migrations, from south to north in the spring and back in the fall. That was disputed to a degree by others who maintained that the herd movements were more nearly local. George Catlin, who went west in 1832 to study and paint the Indians, observed that the buffaloes were gregarious but not truly migratory. "They graze in immense herds and almost incredible numbers at times," he wrote. "They roam over vast tracts of country, from east to west and from west to east as often as from north to south."

[4] "My First Buffalo Hunt," p. 530; Thomas L. Green, editor: "Notes on a Buffalo Hunt—the Diary of Mordecai Bartram," pp. 219–20.

Lack of scientific data prevents any accurate charting of the movements of the herds. Yet the fragmentary evidence at hand suggests that their migrations, instead of being long ones like those of many birds, were mainly local. One early writer, J. A. Allen, found support for the view of Catlin. He noted that, while most of the buffaloes abandoned the hot Texas plains in the summer for those farther north, "it is improbable that the buffaloes of Saskatchewan ever wintered in Texas. Doubtless the same individuals never moved more than a few hundred miles in a north and south direction, the annual migration being merely a moderate swaying northward and southward of the whole mass with the changes of the seasons." [5]

Ordinarily the herd moved at a slow, leisurely pace, with each animal nibbling at tufts of grass as it went along. Yet any sudden fright could convert this movement into a terrifying and sometimes deadly stampede. A wind-blown leaf, the bark of a prairie dog, or the passing shadow of a cloud could set a whole herd in headlong flight. Too, the approach of a grass fire could send them running for many miles.

A stampede on the open plain might wear itself out without harm, but elsewhere it might leave scores or even hundreds of buffaloes dead. In their blind rush, many would be mired in the quicksands of a treacherous stream or would plunge to their death off a steep cliff. With others pushing from behind, the animals in front would be unable to sidestep the danger ahead. In 1541 some of Coronado's men saw stampeding buffaloes fill a ravine to the brim, so that the animals rushing from behind crossed on the trampled bodies of those that had been in front.

Near Great Falls, Montana, in 1805, men of the Lewis and Clark Expedition saw cliffs over which they were told buffaloes had been pushed into the Missouri River by the im-

[5] Wentin A. Wilson: MS.; George Catlin: *Letters and Notes on the Manners, Customs and Conditions of the North American Indians*, I, 248; J. A. Allen: *American Bisons, Living and Extinct*, pp. 59–61.

patience of those behind. In a later instance, a group of sixty
or seventy jumped off a bank of the Bow River, broke through
the ice, and were drowned. Still later, near the Blackfoot
Crossing of the same river, a large number, fleeing in a blind
rush from a raging prairie fire, plunged over the bank. In a
bellowing mass, they fell hundreds of feet to die on the rocky
shore.

A traveler who chanced to be in the path of a stampeding
herd would be in for moments of real terror. In crossing the
plains in 1848, George D. Brewerton and several companions heard one night, in the wake of a thunderstorm, a
strange rumbling of the earth. As the sound came nearer,
they discovered that their camp was about to be engulfed by
a herd of stampeding buffaloes. The dark mass, Brewerton
recalled, advanced across the prairie with the rapidity of a
horse at top speed, but remained compact. The tramping of
thousands of hoofs seemed to shake the ground.

Fortunately for the travelers, the leaders of the herd
swerved a bit in their course. As a result, the stampeding animals, instead of dashing against the wagons of the camp,
missed them by ten to fifteen yards. For nearly an hour the
buffaloes, with a roar of deep bellowings, swept past the
camp, leaving a cloud of thick, stifling dust.

In the fall of 1866, while trailing twelve hundred Longhorn steers across western Texas toward the Pecos River and
New Mexico, Charles Goodnight and his outfit encountered
a herd of stampeding buffaloes. They tore through the strung-
out cattle herd near its middle. Luckily, there were enough
men on each side of the buffaloes to round up the cattle.[6]

Major Dodge, in driving through the extensive herd he
found on the Arkansas River in 1871, had a hair-raising experience with a buffalo stampede. "When I had reached a
point where the hills no longer were more than a mile from

[6] George Douglas Brewerton: *Overland with Kit Carson*, pp. 246–9;
J. Evetts Haley: *Charles Goodnight, Cowman and Plainsman*, pp. 145–6.

the road, the buffaloes on the hills, seeing an unusual object in their rear, turned and stared an instant. Then they started at full speed directly toward me, stampeding and bringing with them the numberless herds through which they passed. They poured down upon me all the herds, no longer separated but one immense compact mass of plunging animals, mad with fright and as irresistible as an avalanche."

In this unpleasant situation, the major reined his horse, an old steed that was used to buffaloes. When the leaders of the plunging herd were within fifty yards, Dodge dropped a few of them with shots from his rifle. That action split the herd into two divisions that thundered on past the wedge made by the bodies of the leaders.

In western Texas in the fall of that year, an Army scouting party led by Captain R. G. Carter was camped at Cottonwood Springs, a few miles northeast of Double Mountain. About midnight the men heard the rumbling sound of stampeding buffaloes headed toward their camp. Not wishing to fire guns in Indian country, Carter had the guards dash out with their blankets, waving them and shouting in an effort to turn the herd. This stratagem worked. The dusty mass veered to the left and headed out into the darkness of the plains.

In the Staked Plains of Texas in the summer of 1878, the men of a surveying party heard a peculiar throbbing sound. Looking north, they saw what seemed to be a low rain cloud. Then they made out dark objects coming from the dust.

"Buffaloes!" cried one. "A stampede!"

Caught in the path of the stampeding herd, the men stood in single file, with their one saddle horse held behind them. Then, as the terrified animals came close, Oscar Williams, who had the only rifle, killed several of the leaders and thus divided the herd.

The opening made by the dead animals was only about

twelve feet wide. Williams felt as if he could touch the buffaloes on each side with the muzzle of his gun. An estimated fifty thousand of them thundered past. The rushing animals went on across a small tule-bordered creek, their great mass damming the stream and stopping the flow of water for a few minutes.

## III

Midsummer to dog days was the mating or rutting season of the buffaloes—or running season, as some of the plainsmen called it. Travelers two or three miles from a herd could hear the nightly bellowing of the excited bulls as they vied—and often locked horns in bloody duels—for the favor of the cows. In a large herd, many battles might be in progress at the same time. One of the fur traders, Alexander Ross, noted the ferocity of the mating bulls. "There is perhaps not an animal that roams in this or any other country," he wrote, "more fierce and forbidding than a buffalo bull during the rutting season. Neither the polar bear nor the Bengal tiger surpasses that animal in ferocity."

Confronted by a rival, the amorous bull became a bundle of rage. His stumpy tail swelled, his hair bristled, his eyes bulged with anger. He gave out deep guttural sounds and pawed the earth, tossing big chunks of earth with his horns and raising a dust.

Soon the pair were at each other head-on, each trying to bring the other to his knees or to push him out of the way. Heavy mats of hair, often full of bull nettles and sandburs, helped to keep skulls from cracking. But any bull that lost his footing might have his flank ripped open by the horns of his frenzied rival.

Alexander Majors, the freighter king of the West, witnessed a ferocious battle on a bluff of the Missouri River in the summer of 1859. In an open space, the two belligerents went through their preliminaries of tossing earth, lashing their short tails, snorting, and bellowing. Then they squared and made a great plunge for each other. The crash brought each to his knees, but in an instant they were up and locking horns again.

The cords stood out like great ropes on the bulls' necks, Majors noted. "The muscles on thighs and hips rose like huge welts. We could see the roll of their blood-red fiery eyes. They braced and shoved with terrible force. The froth began to drip in long strings from their mouths. They were both held panting, their tongues lolling out."

After a momentary pause for breath, Majors related, the bulls renewed the duel, sinking their hoofs into the sod. Then, like the crack of a breaking tree, the legs of one of the fighters crumpled. His opponent made a furious lunge. As he did so, the earth trembled, and both bulls began to reel. A whole acre of the bluff dropped out of sight, plunging both animals into the river. Majors was unable to learn whether the water cooled their rage or whether they resumed their battle on some bank farther down the stream.

Most of the fighting was done by the young bulls. The old ones stayed on the outskirts of the herd, avoiding tests of strength that they had no hope of winning. A bull that became too feeble to travel with the herd might go off and live alone in some sheltered and secluded canyon. There he might be safe as long as he could keep on his feet; but once he was down, the watchful lobo wolves would tear him to bits.

Sometimes several young bulls would gang up on an old one, tormenting and attacking him. Apparently they were intent on killing him, or at least driving him out of the herd. Matthew C. Field, who went with Sir William Drummond Stewart on his 1843 hunting expedition, described such an encounter.

Two of the party, in approaching a small herd, noticed an

unusual commotion. "Young bulls were goring the ground with their short horns and darting about, describing circles in a most furious fashion. One poor bull lay at bay in the midst of the band. The others were plunging at him and running around him in a desperate rage. The superannuated victim stood in one spot, lowering his huge head and presenting his horns to his assailants as he turned from one to another.

"The bulls crowded upon him, wounding each other in their awkward fury as they plunged about and throwing clumps of dirt and grass high into the air as they dashed their horns into the ground. Three of them ran against the old bull at once. It was pitiful and frightful to see the poor monster stagger away and fall. He rose and ran a few steps feebly, then stopped and turned again, bending his head as before to receive the assault. In this way the brutes pressed their unfortunate companion from one spot to another for fifteen or twenty minutes. The bull at last turned tail upon his enemies." [7]

During the winter the bulls and cows usually grazed in separate groups, with the calves following their mothers. But often there were a few bulls with the cows. They tended to form a protective rim around the whole herd, as if they were aware of their role as lookouts and defenders. On sniffing a strange scent, the bulls would look up inquisitively. Sometimes they would lead the herd in a headlong retreat, but on other occasions they might fail to recognize an enemy until it was too late.

In the calving season in the late spring, the bulls were more attentive to their fatherly duties. They were on guard to keep the wolves away from the tawny young calves that frisked about the herd. Occasionally, when a wolf came too close, a bull would toss him so high into the air that when

[7] New Orleans *Daily Picayune*, December 30, 1843; Alexander Ross: *The Fur Hunters of the Far West*, 1956 edition, p. 283; Alexander Majors: *Seventy Years on the Frontier*, pp. 194–200.

he hit the ground he was killed. An angry bull might also give a mortal wound to a raiding bear. Yet the wolves generally were more agile. They outwitted the bulls so often that some Indians estimated that wolves killed a third of the calves every year.

Often the buffalo cows were careless in looking after their offspring and would desert the calves when danger approached. On other occasions, though, they would defend them as fiercely as did the bulls. Where cover was available, they might be as wily as Longhorn cows in hiding their calves in the brush. Yet the calves themselves were slow to learn to seek protection in the center of the herd. Sometimes one would poke his nose into a bunch of grass, apparently assuming that this made him fully hidden. The calf would follow the mother for a year, after which a new one took his place.

The calving season was also the time for shedding old hair and acquiring a new coat. The hair came off in patches, leaving the animal extremely tattered and sometimes almost naked. This was an uncomfortable time for the buffalo, since the shedding put him at the mercy of swarms of mosquitoes, flies, and other insects.

To rid himself of such pests, and perhaps to speed the shedding, the buffalo indulged more than ever at this season in his habit of wallowing in mud or dust. For wallowing, the shaggy preferred a damp spot in which he could plaster himself with mud, or at least with moist earth. As such sites often were scarce, especially in the southern part of the range, many of the animals had to content themselves with dust baths. Even a covering of dust gave some protection.

The ordinary wallow that the buffalo bulls pawed and gouged out was eight to twelve feet across and about two feet deep. Some of the depressions, used by many animals in turn and scooped out by the winds, might be twenty feet or more across and considerably deeper than the small ones.

Occasionally a wallow was made around a boulder or group of boulders, against which the buffaloes rubbed.

Next to wallowing, the buffalo liked, in the shedding season, to rub his hide against a tree. This habit destroyed many trees and twisted others out of shape. When telegraph poles came to the plains, the shaggies rubbed down many of them. After protective spikes were added, the animals seemed to find the poles all the more delightful. They also wore down flagpoles at some of the frontier forts.

In later years, many a plainsman had reason to be thankful for the wallows that the buffaloes had left in the range country. Often early scouts and other travelers found in them enough water to quench the thirst that was about to drive them crazy. As cattle began to populate the plains from which the buffaloes had been cleared, the wallows helped to solve the water problem by catching and holding some of the rain. Pioneer ranchmen used to gauge a rain by how well it filled the wallows. After a good soaker, they would say contentedly that the wallows were full.

More than once a buffalo wallow gave handy refuge to parties attacked suddenly by Indians. At Downer's Station, in western Kansas, in November 1865, several stagecoach passengers and station hands were lucky in finding a wallow near by when a band of Indians attacked them. From the protection of this circular hollow, they held off the warriors until nightfall, after which the attackers withdrew.

One of the buffalo hunters, Billy Dixon, found similar use for a wallow in the Texas Panhandle in September 1874. At that time he was a scout for General Nelson A. Miles, in command of troops campaigning against marauding Indians. Dixon and another scout, with four soldiers, were carrying dispatches from a camp on McClellan Creek to Fort Supply.

At sunrise on the second day out, a band of savage Kiowas and Comanches attacked this small party near a divide between the Washita River and Gageby Creek. One of the six whites was mortally wounded, but the others were able to reach a buffalo wallow. There they defended themselves until afternoon, when a hard, cold rain caused the Indians to leave.

## IV

The life of the buffaloes was much less placid than might be assumed by those who saw them grazing on the lush grass of the plains. The wolves that lurked on the fringe of each herd were alert for every chance to make a kill. Often with them were the smaller coyotes, sometimes called prairie wolves. Except for man, the wolf was the most dangerous enemy of the buffalo. The pack would pounce on any calf that wandered from the herd, on an old bull that had strayed off to sulk, or on any animal weakened by wounds. When the buffaloes moved, the wolves followed. They fed largely on animals killed by accident and on those too poor or too fat to keep up with the herd.

An old or wounded bull, isolated from the herd, had little chance against a concentrated attack by militant wolves. George Catlin and a hunting companion happened on one such battle in its final stage. The bull "had made desperate resistance. His eyes were entirely eaten out of his head, the gristle of his nose was mostly gone, his tongue was half eaten off, and the skin and flesh of his legs were torn almost literally into strings. In this tattered and poor condition, the poor old veteran stood bracing up in the midst of his devourers."

A lone buffalo carcass left on the prairie by hunters would probably be eaten by wolves before the next daybreak. Occasionally a hunter would try to protect his meat by tying to the kill some article of clothing, such as a coat or a hat, to hold off the scavengers. Or he might stick in the ground beside it a branch, to which he tied a handkerchief or a blown-up bladder to flutter in the wind. Unusually hungry wolves, though, would not be deterred by such stratagems.[8]

Other enemies of the buffalo included the grizzly bear and the panther or mountain lion. Although neither was numerous enough to take a heavy toll from the herds, both were dangerous. A veteran hunter in Dakota once watched a huge male grizzly attack a small herd of buffalo cows protected by five or six bulls. As the bear approached, the bulls closed ranks and lowered their horns. When the bulls charged, the bear struck one of them so hard with his paws that he broke the back of the bull, killing him instantly. But the other bulls used their horns so effectively that soon the bear crawled off with mortal wounds.

Equally aggressive were the mountain lions. While returning home from an exploring trip into Kentucky in 1770, Daniel Boone and his elder brother witnessed a bold attack. The big cat, reported one of Boone's early biographers, "had seated himself upon the back of one of the largest buffaloes and fastened his claws and teeth into the flesh until the blood ran down on all sides. Plunging, rearing, and running were to no purpose." The panther retained his seat until Boone took careful aim with his flintlock rifle and pulled the trigger.[9]

Predators were only part of the hazards in the life of the buffalo. Sometimes a wind-driven fire raced so quickly across the prairie that the herd could not escape. Some of the panic-stricken animals would be burned to death and others smothered or trampled in the rush to get away. Of the survivors, many would be singed and some blinded.

When a buffalo herd swam a turbulent river, often rapids and quicksands claimed large numbers. Occasionally

[8] Catlin: op. cit., I, 257–8; Elliott Coues, editor: *The Expeditions of Zebulon Pike,* II, 426.
[9] Timothy Flint: *Biographical Memoir of Daniel Boone,* pp. 74–5; John Mortimer Murphy: *Sporting Adventures in the Far West,* pp. 163–4.

some of the calves, after crossing a stream on the backs of their mothers, would be unable to climb the steep bank and would be left to starve. More serious, in some instances, was crossing on treacherous ice in the spring. Buffaloes accustomed to walking safely over a frozen stream all winter would continue the passage after warmer weather had made the ice too thin to uphold their combined weight. With a great crash, they would plunge into the icy water to be trampled and drowned.

After a spring thaw, travelers often could see thousands of buffalo carcasses floating down a river or washed up on the banks. One trader, John McDonnell, counted 7,360 of them on the Qu'Appelle River in 1795. Another, Alexander Henry, saw them floating down the Park River in a continuous line for two days and nights in the spring of 1801.

Even though they were partly migratory, the buffaloes sometimes suffered from winter blizzards. An unusually severe storm might seal off their food with ice or heavy snow and thus starve some of those that escaped freezing. Unlike the Longhorn cattle, which turned their backs to the wind, the buffaloes habitually faced it, since they had more protective fleece in front than behind. Yet even this was not always enough to save them, although they could withstand cold weather better than could most cattle. Some of the bunches found shelter in canyons, creek bottoms, or woods, where they could scrape away the snow and reach grass. But in the open country a sudden howling norther sometimes left the plains strewn with bleaching skeletons in the spring.

Even a summer storm could be disastrous. A tornado might strike with such force that it would drive eyeballs out of their sockets and lacerate the backs and flanks of the animals. Ely Moore, who went on a buffalo hunt with the Miamis in southwestern Kansas in the late summer of 1854, described such a storm. He saw where the wind had stripped acres of sod and topsoil from the prairie. The party also found two dead buffaloes, completely denuded of hair and with their bones crushed. Apparently the twister had picked them up, carried them to a great height, and then dashed them to the earth.[1]

V

On the Great Plains, buffalo meat was standard fare. It was relished not only by Indians but also by explorers, fur traders, sportsmen, and railroad builders. "Bluffer meat ain't bad," a plainsman might say, " 'specially fat cow and hump ribs." The taste and tenderness varied, of course, with the age of the animal, the part that was eaten, and the skill with which it was cooked. In 1833, men on an expedition to the fur country found an old bull almost too tough to chew; but the cows were more palatable. Exercise in the open air helped to whet the appetites of Westerners for almost any kind of meat. They consumed big helpings of buffalo flesh and found it easily digestible.

Coarser, darker, and usually fatter than beef, the buffalo meat—especially that from the cows—suited most plainsmen. One Texas pioneer, Bill Crabb, recalled wistfully that even the meat of an old bull was tender and delicious. Major Zebulon M. Pike, on November 6, 1806, wrote in his journal: "The cow buffalo was equal to any meat I ever saw, and we feasted sumptuously on the choice morsels." John James Audubon, the naturalist, preferred buffalo meat to beef. George Catlin found it "of a delicious flavor, resembling and equaling that of beef." Horace Greeley, editor of the New York *Tribune*, who crossed the plains in 1859, didn't like buffalo meat, which he called "tough and not juicy." But Colonel Samuel J. Crawford, who served as Governor of Kan-

[1] Ely Moore: "A Buffalo Hunt with the Miamis in 1854," pp. 407–8.

sas, 1865–8, asserted that in the fall, when the animals were fat, buffalo meat was superior to corn-fed beef.

The hide hunters of the 1870's lived almost entirely on buffalo flesh. "I would not eat anything but buffalo meat if I could get it," said one of them, Dick Bussell. "I used to kill four or five big fat bulls, hang the hams high in a mesquite tree in the winter, and go back to get it about April. It would be fine. In using buffalo meat that had been dried, I would trim off about a quarter of an inch of the outside. It would be as nice and red as could be. Then I'd slice it and throw it in a skillet of hot grease and make a lot of gravy with it. It was surely fine." [2]

Of the various cuts of buffalo meat, the most often eaten was the tongue. It not only was tender but also was the easiest part to get at. Roasted over a slow fire of wood or buffalo chips, it made delicious eating. Often some of the tongues were salted for later use or for sale.

Next in popularity was the hump. Skelton Glenn recalled that the best humps were those that had been hung out until a crust was formed. Then they were sliced across the grain, salted, and fried in deep tallow. Enough of the marrow bones were cracked to provide a supply of "hunters' butter."

If more of the animal were needed, the liver and one or both hind quarters might be used. Those who wanted a supply of meat for future use could easily cure it by salting or smoking or by cutting it into strips and drying it in the sun or over a slow fire, as did the Indians. "I have seen meat jerkers," said Frank Collinson, "who could cut a whole hind quarter into one big sheet of meat." Many converted this dried or "jerked" meat into pemmican by pounding the strips into a flaky mass and interspersing layers of it with melted buf-

[2] Brewerton: op. cit., p. 254; Inez Baker: *Yesterday in Hall County, Texas,* p. 6; Samuel J. Crawford: *Kansas in the Sixties,* p. 14; Richard Bussell to J. Evetts Haley, Canadian, Texas, July 19, 1926, MS. transcript in Panhandle-Plains Historical Museum, Canyon, Texas.

falo fat. Pemmican, packed in bags made of buffalo skin, would keep for years and was a staple food for most of the fur traders.

The Comanches gave flavor to their pemmican by mixing in various nuts and partially dried berries and fruits. When fresh meat was plentiful, the pemmican was stored for later use. Yet it was eaten so commonly that some white visitors to the camps called it Indian bread. Sliced and dipped in wild honey, it was appetizing as well as nourishing.

## VI

Almost as useful as the flesh of the buffalo were his droppings. Over most of the Great Plains, where wood was scarce if not entirely absent, buffalo chips served as standard fuel for campfires. The chips, which French explorers called *bois de vache,* wood of the cow, were so commonly used that they gave rise to the saying "dead as a buffalo chip." This fuel, which remained dry inside even after a rain had wet the surface, burned slowly. It made a hot fire, with more glow than flame. It was ideal for cooking.

Coronado reported the use of buffalo chips by his conquistadors. Later explorers and emigrants soon learned the value of such fuel. Such eminent travelers as Meriwether Lewis, Francis Parkman, and Josiah Gregg noted the high quality of the chips. In a letter written near the junction of the North and South Platte on June 6, 1846, Mrs. George Donner of the ill-fated Donner party, headed from Illinois to California, reported: "Wood now is scarce, but buffalo chips are excellent. They kindle quickly and retain heat surprisingly. We had this morning buffalo steaks, broiled upon them, that had the same flavor they would have had upon hickory coals."

James Linforth, traveling across Nebraska with a party of English Mormons in 1855, welcomed the abundance of chips. "It is a common joke on the plains," he wrote, "that a steak cooked on these chips requires no pepper. Young ladies who, in the commencement of the journey, would hardly look at a chip now come into the camp with as many as they can carry. The chips burn fiercely and cook as well as wood." A dozen years later a sportsman who had crossed the plains in 1865 testified that "there is no better broiling fuel than a perfectly dry buffalo chip."

A plainsman saved from starvation by buffalo meat and kept from freezing by a fire of buffalo chips might also avoid death from thirst by drinking the contents of the paunch. One of the pioneer Santa Fe traders, Captain William Becknell, set out from Missouri in 1822 with twenty-one men and three wagons loaded with goods. After cutting off from the Arkansas River toward the Cimarron, the band ran out of water and came so near dying of thirst that they killed their dogs and slashed the ears of their mules to drink the blood. Almost frantic with despair and with visions of a horrible death, they finally discovered a lone buffalo. Fortunately, this animal's paunch was distended with water from the near-by Cimarron, which the travelers hadn't yet discovered. "The hapless intruder was immediately dispatched," wrote Josiah Gregg, "and an invigorating draught procured from its stomach. I have since heard one of the parties to that expedition declare that nothing ever passed his lips which gave him such exquisite delight as his first draught of that filthy beverage."

A decade later, J. K. Townsend found that some of the early hunters, when a long way from water, resorted to this source. One would kill a buffalo and plunge his knife into its stomach. The green and gelatinous juice that gushed out was welcomed as a tasty and wholesome drink.

Yet, except for the robes brought in by the fur traders, no one seemed to view the buffalo as a commercially valuable animal until the early 1870's. The white plainsman, like the Indian, lived on buffalo meat and cooked with chips. In a blizzard, he might even crawl into a freshly killed and still warm carcass to keep from freezing. But he would have snorted at any prediction that the hide of the buffalo would bring a higher price than his meat and would attract thousands of hunters to the ranges.

## 2

# MEAT FOR THE
# RED MAN

On the western plains the buffalo and the Indian were linked as closely as they would be later on a nickel coin. When the army of white hide hunters rode out in small groups, with their weatherbeaten wagons and their powerful Sharps rifles, Indian scouts noted almost every move. As buffaloes fell by the thousands, the bronze warriors showed unbelief, then chagrin, and finally vengeful rage. The buffalo was as important to them as the camel was to the Arabs.

For generations the plains Indian had lived off the buffalo herds. Buffalo meat had been the main item in his diet. Buffalo robes had been his bed and his cloak against winter blizzards. Smooth buffalo hides, sewed together and stretched over the poles of his tepee, had made a home to shield his family from sun, rain, and wind. Buffalo bones had provided tools, ornaments, and even toys. The warrior hoped that, when he died, he would go to a land abounding in buffaloes.

There had been many buffaloes for every Indian in North America. It seemed impossible that they could disappear. Surely the Great Spirit would not allow that. Yet the stinking carcasses and the white bones strewn over the prairies were not illusions. They bespoke an end to the red man's way of life.

That was true especially of the Comanches and some of the other roving plains tribes. In other parts of the country, many Indians had become used to planting crops and were less dependent on hunting. But most of the plains Indians were nomads who lived mainly on game. They varied their diet with the flesh of deer, antelope, elk, and occasionally bear; but buffalo—fresh or dried—was their staple. Now they saw this source of sustenance vanishing before their eyes.

The Indians had downed buffaloes with arrow and lance long before they had acquired guns. They had hunted them afoot for generations before they obtained their first horses from the Spaniards. They had bent their tribal ways to the coming and going of the great buffalo herds.

In hunting buffaloes, the Indians attained an expertness that only the best of the whites could equal. They used a large variety of methods, most of which could be grouped under four heads: running, still hunting, surrounding, and impounding—all of which were used both before and after the Indians acquired horses.

The running hunt became much more effective, of course, after the braves were mounted. Often it involved a spectacular chase. The Indians trained their fleetest horses to run close beside the buffaloes. Even after guns were obtainable, some of the red men preferred their bows and arrows for a close attack. Usually the bow was a short one of not more than thirty inches, so that it could be handled easily on horseback. Commonly it was made of cedar or of Osage orange. The French called the latter *bois d'arc*—wood of the bow. Often the warrior strengthened his bow by wrapping it with twisted sinews of deer. The arrows might be of dogwood or cane, tipped with flint or iron.

With aim that seldom erred, the Indian hunter could shoot arrows almost as fast as the ordinary white man could fire a Colt six-shooter. Usually he tried to pierce the buffalo behind the short ribs, with the arrow ranging forward and into the heart or—still better—the lungs. Sometimes his arrow would enter the animal with such force that it would be completely buried. Or, missing the bones, it might emerge from the other side and fall to the ground. If the arrow failed to penetrate deeply enough, the hunter might pull it out of the running buffalo and use it again. A hunter who put too many shafts into an animal would incur the laughs and taunts of the squaws who, in their butchering, retrieved the arrows, recognized them, and returned them to their owners.

Yet, exciting as was the chase, it was, for the men out after a winter's supply of meat, less efficient than some other hunting methods. The running might end with more winded horses than dead buffaloes. Even Indians who had outstanding mounts might stake them and approach the herd against the wind, crawling tediously through the high grass. In this still hunt, later favored by white hide hunters, each man might kill many animals before the others took fright and sought safety in flight. Occasionally a hunter might kill the nearest bull and use the carcass as a barricade. The Indian hunter, especially in winter when the grass offered little or no cover, might disguise himself in a buffalo robe or a wolfskin.

When the snow was deep enough to impede the movements of the buffaloes, the Indians sometimes went on snowshoes to kill them with lances. Those floundering in drifts in the ravines were easy prey to the hunters. Even Indians who didn't need meat often made such killings to obtain robes, since the buffalo's hair was thicker and longer in the winter.

The surround was a common and usually productive method of obtaining meat and hides. Approaching a small bunch from all sides, a band of Indians would close in with savage yells and kill as many as they could with arrows and lances before the frightened animals could escape from the cordon. After they obtained horses, the Indians could surround larger numbers.

A large party of several hundred hunters could surround a fair-sized herd. George Catlin, the artist, told of such a surround near the Teton River in the spring of 1832. "An immense herd of buffaloes showed themselves on the opposite side of the river, almost blackening the plains for a great distance. A party of five or six hundred Sioux on horseback forded the river about midday and spent a few hours among them. Recrossing at sundown, they came into the fort with 1,400 fresh buffalo tongues, which were thrown into a heap for a few gallons of whisky. Not a skin or a pound of meat, except the tongues, was brought in."

On another occasion, on the upper Missouri, Catlin accompanied a band of daring Minatarees who, armed with bows and lances, rode out to surround a herd. The Indians divided into two columns and went around the herd, about a mile distant, forming a complete circle. When the buffaloes scented the hunters, they began to flee in confusion. The hunters, with frightful yells, turned them back from one side of the circle and then from another. As the distracted animals hooked and climbed upon each other, the Indians closed in and began the killing.

Even for the hunters there was confusion and danger. As Catlin, with pencil and sketchbook, watched from a horse outside the circle, the battle raised a cloud of dust. Buffaloes, infuriated by painful wounds, "erected their shaggy manes over their bloodshot eyes and furiously plunged forward at the sides of their assailants' horses. Sometimes they gored the horses to death at a lunge and put their dismounted riders to flight for their lives. Some blinded horsemen, too intent on their prey amid the cloud of dust, were hemmed and wedged in amid the crowding beasts, over whose backs they were obliged to leap for security, leaving their horses."

Many bulls turned on their assailants, added Catlin, "and many warriors who were dismounted saved themselves by the superior muscles of their legs. Some who were closely pursued by the bulls wheeled suddenly and, snatching the part of a buffalo robe from their waists, threw it over the horns and eyes of the infuriated beast and, darting by its side, drove the arrow or the lance into its heart. Others suddenly dashed off on the prairie by the side of the affrighted animals which had escaped and, closely escorting them for a few rods, brought down their carcasses upon the turf."

As the Minatarees were short of meat, the chief sent out from the village several hundred women and children to skin the buffaloes and carry home the hides and meat. With them were what Catlin estimated to be at least a hundred dogs, eager to feast on the leavings of the butchers.[1]

This method of surrounding the buffaloes had many variations. When the grass was dry, the Indians might set it afire in a circle around the buffaloes to hinder their escape. The fire might singe the hair of the animals, thus spoiling their hides for conversion into robes; but it left the meat intact.

The method of impounding called for more preparation. It required the building of a strong pen, which might be of timber, piled brush, or any other material that was handy. From widely separated beginnings, two fences converged at the narrow opening of the corral. Where posts or brush were not obtainable, such wing fences might be made of stone, frozen buffalo carcasses, or even bones.

[1] George Catlin: *Letters and Notes on the Manners, Customs and Conditions of the North American Indians*, I, 199–202, 256.

Some of the corrals, which were used by Indians of many tribes from Canada to Mexico, were intended for permanent use. They served to trap elk and deer and other animals, as well as buffaloes, and to capture wild horses. Early in 1840, Thomas Simpson found that three camps of Assiniboins each had a separate buffalo pen into which the men drove forty to fifty animals a day. But when the buffaloes failed to come near one of the permanent corrals, the men sometimes built a temporary one near the herd.

In some places, where the lay of the ground was favorable, the guide fence led not to a corral but to a steep cliff, over which the Indians drove the buffaloes. This "jumping pound" was popular because it did away with the laborious work of building a pen. Often it provided more meat and hides than the hunters could use.

When the Indians found buffaloes near enough to the wing fences of their corral, they would drive them gently toward the opening. In some instances a brave dressed in buffalo robes would walk ahead of the animals to decoy them. In others a man on horseback would ride beside them. But usually there was more prodding from behind than decoying. As the buffaloes approached the opening, Indians who had been hiding beside the fences—sometimes behind buffalo robes—would come out and join those who had been driving the shaggies. Thus they strengthened the rear guard whose task was to keep the animals moving toward the pen and to prevent their escaping.

Once inside the corral, the buffaloes could be killed readily and with little risk. Of those driven over a cliff, many would be dead or crippled from their fall. In any event, the Indian women would be on hand to start the butchering, which was to be followed by the drying of hides and meat.

After they obtained the white man's guns, the Indians killed buffaloes with less effort and by more varied methods. In August of 1854, about four hundred braves and fifty squaws, most of them Miamis, went on their annual hunt in southwestern Kansas. Six weeks later they returned home with a winter supply of jerked meat and seventeen hundred hides, most of them to be made into robes. Ely Moore, who went along, described their method of hunting.

As the mounted Indians approached the herd, he wrote, "always keeping pace with the buffaloes, they shoot down several bulls. As a gap in the line is thus made, they dash their ponies through the breach, conforming speed and direction to that of the herd. Gradually working toward the center, they find the cows, calves, and two-year-olds, thus securing the finest robes and choicest meats. When their revolvers are empty, for only revolvers and bows and arrows can safely be used in this mode of killing, they gradually worm their way out of the herd in the same manner as they entered."

Despite the glaring eyes and sharp horns of the bulls, the four hundred Indian hunters met with only one accident in the six weeks. When one horse stepped into a prairie-dog hole and lost his footing, a wounded bull fatally gored him and injured the rider by tearing into the calf of a leg.[2]

Even those Indians who cultivated crops were likely to spend much of their time in hunting. The Pawnees, who lived mainly in Kansas and Nebraska, grew patches of corn, beans, and squash; but the men spent more months on the buffalo range than in their villages. In mid-June, after the corn had had its second hoeing, they would ride off on their summer hunt, returning in September to harvest their crops. In late October, with the crops stored, they would be off again on their long winter hunt, usually on the prairies between the Republican River and the Arkansas. They would stay until April, returning home in time to plant their corn.[3]

[2] Ely Moore: "A Buffalo Hunt with the Miamis in 1854," pp. 404–7.
[3] James C. Olsen: *History of Nebraska*, pp. 23–4.

## II

On their regular hunts, most of the plains tribes left the butchering mainly to the women, after the men had done some of the heavier preliminary work. The hunters would leave a cow lying on her side, but would heave the heavier bull over onto his belly, with his legs spread. The butchers would first slash across the brisket and at the neck and fold the hide back so they could cut out the forequarters at the joints. Then they would slit the hide down the middle of the spine, being careful to avoid cutting the sinews.

After peeling back the hide, they would disjoint and take out the hindquarters, leaving the rump attached to the back. Next they would cut the flank upward toward the stomach and remove it in one piece with the brisket. After taking out the entrails, they would break the rib steaks from the spine.

These operations left only the bare spine, the rump, and the head. The butchers would bag the meat in the hides and load it on packhorses to be taken to the main camp. There the women had the tedious work of slicing and drying most of the meat and of pegging, scraping, and tanning the hides.

Converting some of the choice winter buffalo skins into robes was even more laborious. Leaving the hair on, the Indian women spread the pelts or undressed hides on the ground, flesh up, and fastened them with wooden pegs. Then two or three squaws scraped the skins with sharp tools made of stone, elkhorn, or buffalo bone. Often a flint or steel blade was fastened into the bone. After completing this fleshing, the women dampened the hides with water in which they had steeped buffalo brains. Keeping the skins moist for ten days, they rubbed and kneaded them once a day until they became soft and pliable. The robes were not smoked as were the hides. Some of the robes that the Indians kept for their own use they decorated with gaily colored figures. In addition to those used as winter cloaks and bedding, some were cut up and made into caps, mittens, and leggings.

The red men found use for virtually every part of the buffalo. The animal provided them with much besides food and warmth. The tanned hides were used not only for the walls of tepees but also for moccasins, saddlebags, and winding sheets for the dead. The raw or green hides were stretched to make shields for battle and were sewed together and fitted over the wooden frames of canoes. Narrow strips of rawhide were plaited to make lariats and tethers. Strong sinews from the neck and back provided thread, bowstrings, and the webs for snowshoes. The hair was woven into ornaments or twisted to make belts or ropes. The bladder might become a container for marrow.

The Indians converted the bones of the buffalo into spears and tools of many kinds. The Shoshones spliced two ribs, wrapping them with sinew, to make a bow. Often the shoulder blade served as a crude hoe, while smaller bones were used to scrape skins. In the north, youngsters would make a toboggan of a backbone with a few ribs attached. The horns provided drinking vessels, spoons, and containers for carrying coals of fire. Many Indians used the animal's back fat as hair grease. From the gall they made yellow paint for ornamental use. And, of course, the Indians used buffalo chips for fuel as readily as did the white plainsmen.[4]

To attract buffalo herds within easy reach or to guide their hunters to the nearest herds, the western tribes used a great variety of rituals. In the upper Missouri Valley, the Blackfeet and others had special songs believed to make the buffaloes approach. Some had dreamers who would tell where the buffaloes were most plentiful. The Mandans, after completing a meal, would present a bowl of food to a

[4] Ernest Wallace and E. Adamson Hoebel: *The Comanches: Lords of the South Plains*, pp. 60–1.

mounted buffalo head in the belief that this would attract
the living animals. The Mandans also prayed to the Great
Spirit to send them meat, and sometimes they addressed a
deity of the herds: "Hooee! Great bull of the prairie, be
thou here with thy cow."

The medicine men of the Sioux, the Assiniboins, and the
Pawnees used buffalo skulls in rituals to entice the herds.
Some tribes engaged in ceremonial dances before and after
the hunts. The Comanche hunters, although they depended
more on scouts than on rituals to locate the herds, sometimes sought the aid of their medicine men. On other occasions they would find a horned toad and ask it where the
buffaloes were. They believed the toad would scamper off in
the direction of the nearest herd. Or they would watch a
raven that circled over their camp and cawed, thinking it
would fly off toward the animals.

Usually the Comanches held a hunting dance before
the men left the main camp to look for buffaloes. In the light
of a campfire or of an autumn moon, drummers, singers, and
dancers would perform until midnight. After the hunt came
the buffalo-tongue ritual and feast. In the morning the
women would roast fresh tongues over an open fire. Then,
at noon, the men would seat themselves in a half-circle about
the fire, with the women on the other side. A medicine man
would light a pipe and blow puffs of smoke toward the sun,
the earth, and the four directions. As the pipe was passed,
the other men would go through the same routine. When all
had finished, a woman of unquestioned virtue would be called
on to serve the tongues.[5]

## III

The dependence of the plains Indians on the buffaloes
for food, clothing, and shelter made them all the more

[5] Ibid., pp. 61–2.

alarmed over the reduction of the herds by white men. Even before the hunting for hides commenced, whites shooting for meat, robes, or sport had made marked incursions into the herds. When the railroads began reaching across the plains, the Indians knew that more white hunters would come to kill the buffaloes.

Concern over their meat supply was a basic motive in the Indian attacks on the whites on the Great Plains in the middle and late sixties and the early seventies. Some of the attacks centered on the railroads that were bringing in new settlers, and others sought out the white hunters. The Indians attacked isolated cabins, traders' wagons, and parties engaged in railroad construction. In August of 1867 a band of Cheyennes wrecked and plundered a Union Pacific freight train, killing several men. As a result of many outrages and depredations, the government sent a peace commission to make a new treaty with the plains Indians. The meeting was held at a camp on Medicine Lodge Creek, in southern Kansas, in October 1867.

In its motives and in its results, this treaty had direct bearings on buffalo hunting. Represented at Medicine Lodge were five of the hunting tribes—the Cheyennes, the Arapahoes, the Kiowas, the Comanches, and the Apaches. The whites, besides the seven commissioners, included Governor Samuel J. Crawford of Kansas and other officials. Among the newspaper writers was Henry M. Stanley of the *Missouri Democrat*, who later attained fame as an explorer in Africa.

The commissioners and their friends arrived on October 2, escorted by troops. The Indians were slow to gather, especially those who had just been on the warpath. After all had arrived, Governor Crawford estimated their numbers at more than five thousand, including the women and children. In plain view was a great stack of boxes containing presents to be given to the Indians after the signing of a new treaty.

N. G. Taylor, Commissioner of Indian Affairs, headed the peace commission and did most of the talking for the whites. George Bent, half-blood son of the famous trader William Bent, was interpreter for the Cheyennes and the Arapahoes. Jesse Chisholm, the veteran Scotch-Cherokee trader who had posts on the Arkansas and the North Canadian, interpreted for the Kiowas and the Comanches.

Neither side believed the other would keep promises it might make. But the Indians at least looked forward to gaining amnesty for their recent crimes and to taking home presents and supplies that, along with their buffalo meat, would carry them through the winter months ahead. They did not want to be shunted to reservations or to give up their hunting grounds.

Governor Crawford had provided the commission with a written recital of recent atrocities by the Indians, but the chiefs preferred to talk about the wrongs their tribes had suffered from the whites. After the negotiators had assembled in a large tent, shaken hands, and smoked the pipe of peace, the oratory began. The commission wanted the Cheyennes and Arapahoes to quit hunting in Kansas and Colorado lands which they already had sold to the whites, and to retire to a reservation in the Indian Territory. But the six-foot Cheyenne chief Bull Bear held that the Indians still owned those lands. He insisted that no more railroads be built through them to scare away the buffaloes.

Chief Ten Bears spoke eloquently for the Comanches, insisting that his roving people could not live in houses on a reservation and give up buffaloes for sheep. Chief Santana of the Kiowas threw a scare into the assembly by making a vicious speech in which he insisted that his children grow up wild and in which he boasted of his atrocities. Then he suddenly walked out, followed by some of the other chiefs. Army officers prepared for a possible surprise attack, but the council was resumed the next day without incident.

The commissioners signed a treaty with the Kiowas, Comanches, and Apaches on October 21 and one with the Cheyennes and Arapahoes a week later. The initial pact gave the three tribes a large reservation north of the Red River, on lands formerly owned by the Choctaws and Chickasaws. The Cheyennes and Arapahoes, in exchange for lands they claimed in Kansas and Colorado, were given a reservation of about three million acres in the Cherokee Outlet, in the Indian Territory.

For the government, the commissioners were said to have agreed orally that henceforth no white hunters would be allowed to roam south of the Arkansas River, which flowed east across southern Kansas. Neither side seemed aware that such a promise could not apply to the broad buffalo range in northwestern Texas. In joining the United States, Texas had retained her public lands. As that state was not a party to the Medicine Lodge treaties, the pacts and their side pledges had no validity in Texas.

After the signing, the whites distributed the presents. The gifts included quantities of food, clothing, blankets, guns, and ammunition. There was so much material that the Indians were unable to carry all of it away, but had to leave piles on the prairie. As it was, all the Indians had to depart afoot, since they were using all their horses as pack animals.

On the probable effects of the treaties, Governor Crawford was cynical. Having raged ruthless war in Kansas in the summer, he said, the Indians "were now ready to return to their winter haunts on the Red River and indulge in sports and war dancing around the scalps of their victims until the weather was propitious for another raid in Kansas. The peace commission had granted them amnesty for past offenses and given them food, clothing, arms, ammunition, and other supplies for the winter; and that made them docile for the time being."

Taking a similar view was the correspondent of the *Rail-*

*way Advance* in the new village of Hays City on the Union
Pacific. "The grand powwow on Medicine Lodge Creek is ex-
ploded," he wrote. "The Indians have left with their booty,
and the commissioners with empty wagons. Until spring,
when the ponies will be fat, the Indians will attack no trains
nor molest any large bodies of persons; but if they can lift
the hair of one or two men, they will do so." [6]

Thus, the result of the palaver on Medicine Lodge Creek
was a truce rather than a peace likely to last. Few of the
Indians understood what the chiefs had signed with their
marks. If the white hunters of buffaloes would stay north
of the Arkansas River, there might not be much trouble. But
if an army of them should sweep down into the southern
ranges, which the Indians claimed as their own, and begin
a wholesale slaughter of the shaggies, violence might erupt.

---

[6] Record copy of the Proceedings of the Indian Peace Commission Appointed Under the Act of Congress Approved July 20, 1867, I, 104; Hays City
(Kansas) *Railway Advance*, November 9, 1867; Samuel J. Crawford: *Kansas in the Sixties*, pp. 263–81; George Bird Grinnell: *The Fighting Cheyennes*, pp. 254–6. The texts of the Medicine Lodge treaties, although often
cited as doing so, did not restrict the white hunters.

---

━━━ ◄ 3 ► ━━━

# TRADING IN ROBES

**B**efore tanners learned how to make serviceable leather from buffalo hides and thus set off the great hunt, thick-furred buffalo robes had given winter warmth to several generations of Americans. Whether one went by buggy, surrey, wagon, sleigh, or sled, the buffalo robe would help keep him from arriving with frozen toes. It was an essential to winter courting.

A fine robe brought several times the price of a tanned skin from which the hair had been removed. For decades the trading of such robes was the principal means by which tribesmen on the Great Plains obtained the white man's goods.

From the day of the early explorers, *voyageurs,* and mountain men, the buffalo robe had been a staple article in the fabulous fur trade of the West and Northwest. Jacques Marquette noted in his journal that the wealth of the Illinois Indians consisted of buffalo robes. In January 1675 he reported that three robes obtained for a cubit of tobacco were useful for winter comfort. In 1682 René Robert Cavalier,

Sieur de La Salle, referred to the valuable trade in buffalo robes in what later became Wisconsin.

Hardy French and French-Canadian traders had taken the lead in penetrating the western wilderness to obtain furs from the Indians. But English rivals, after obtaining from Charles II in 1670 a charter for the Hudson's Bay Company, entered this profitable field. Other groups followed, chief among them the North West Company, formed by Scotch traders and Montreal merchants.

American interest lagged until after the Lewis and Clark Expedition of 1804–6 had opened the Northwest and stirred the imagination of the adventurous. New Orleans-born Manuel Lisa, of Spanish ancestry, led his first trading expedition up the Missouri River in 1807 and, with others, formed the Missouri Fur Company. A year later German-born John Jacob Astor founded the American Fur Company, which later became dominant in the Northwest and the largest United States business firm of its day.

The fur trade, which had been pursued on a much smaller scale all through the 1700's, had its most flourishing period from 1807 to 1843. Trapping beavers and trading with the Indians for buffalo robes and lesser furs attracted many rugged mountaineers. Among them were William Bent, Jim Bridger, Kit Carson, Joe Meek, and Jedediah Smith. For the American trade, which used the Missouri River and the Santa Fe Trail as its principal avenues, St. Louis was the chief outfitting point and market.

The earlier traders dealt mainly in the smaller pelts that were in stronger demand, most of all in beaver. But continued trapping made that animal scarce, and the beaver hat went out of style in the early 1830's. Gradually the buffalo robe replaced the beaver pelt as the main item in the fur trade. It became the chief cargo of the steamboats that came down the treacherous Missouri to St. Louis.

The Indians would rather hunt buffaloes than trap bea-

vers. Their hunting kept them in meat; and their trading of
robes supplied them with whisky, beads, and bits of iron for
tipping their arrows and spears. Only the Indian women had
the patience to convert the raw winter pelts into soft furs
that would bring top prices from the traders. In this art the
Crow women were especially expert.

Buying buffalo robes with goods rather than with money,
the fur traders took every advantage they could of the Indians. They profited especially from the red men's thirst for
whisky and other intoxicants. Whisky was one of the chief
articles of trade, recalled James P. Beckwourth. "Four gallons of water were added to each gallon of alcohol, and a pint
of the stuff was traded for a buffalo robe worth five dollars."
Charles Larpenteur did even better when he obtained two
hundred fine robes from the Crees for five gallons of alcohol.

In 1822, Congress considered a drastic bill to ban the
carrying of liquor into the Indian country. Strongly opposed
were the fur merchants, including John Jacob Astor, whom
furs had made the country's wealthiest man. Spokesmen for
the pelt dealers declared that this bill would ruin them. If the
United States fur traders on the upper Missouri were denied the use of alcohol, they argued, all the business would
be lost to their rivals, the Hudson's Bay Company.

Congress enacted the measure anyway, but the traders
found ways to violate it. They hid kegs of whisky or alcohol
in their bales of goods and thus smuggled them into the Indian country. Some of them even concocted firewater in the
wilderness. For years Fort Union, at the mouth of the Yellowstone River, had an illicit still that turned out drink used in
the fur trade.

The traders had no qualms against either watering their
drink or adding flavors that made it seem more potent. One
early recipe called for a quart of alcohol, a pound of rank
black chewing tobacco, a handful of red peppers, a bottle of
Jamaica ginger, a quart of black molasses, and as much wa-

ter from the Missouri River as was needed. The trader poured all the ingredients into a big kettle and boiled the mixture until all the strength was drawn from the tobacco and the peppers.

The mountain men not only used whisky as an article of trade but also dispensed it to put the Indians in a jovial mood and thus gain an advantage over them in bargaining. In 1809, when Manuel Lisa stopped at an Arikira village, the chiefs demanded thirty rifle loads of powder and lead for each buffalo robe. But the next day, after Lisa had given out whisky and presents with a free hand, they reduced their price by one third.

Traders also profited by acquiring robes through the exchange of blankets, tobacco, axes, beads, hand mirrors, and other items. In the early days a trader could obtain a robe for a bead necklace that cost him only sixteen cents. The Crow women were especially partial to a kind of pale blue beads that they used in embroidering. If the white man's supply of trinkets ran out, he could trade his food. On the upper Missouri, in the early period, a trader could obtain a robe for three cups of coffee, six cups of sugar, or ten cups of flour. A three-point Mackinaw blanket was worth three robes.[1]

The Indian's interest in colors might lead him to swap more robes for a blanket whose color he liked than for another that was just as good. James H. Bradley recorded in his journal that a striped blanket would bring seven to nine robes, while a red one of the same quality would bring only six robes, a purple one five, and a white one three. An Indian would give eight robes for a red coat trimmed with gold or silver lace, but only six for a blue coat with red or white braid.

Barter went on slowly on the upper Missouri because some of the Indians would trade for only one commodity at a time. An Indian would come into the trading post, followed by

[1] *Prose and Poetry of the Live Stock Industry of the United States*, p. 292; Charles Larpenteur: *Forty Years a Fur Trader on the Upper Missouri*, I, 189–95; Peter Koch: "Life at Musselshell in 1869 and 1870," p. 298.

his wife, who staggered under a load of robes. The hunter would throw one robe on the counter and tell what he wanted for it. Only after the coffee or sugar was measured or some other specified item handed over would he throw down the next robe. Of course, if he wanted a saddle or a blanket, he would have to lay down several robes at once. At the completion of the swapping, he would expect the trader to give him a present of some sort as a bonus.

In other places a trader might make an Indian think he was getting a better bargain by offering him several small items for a single robe. One would set out a cup of sugar, a yard of calico, and a string of beads or a little red paint. If the robe were extra fine, he might throw in a plug of tobacco.

Later, as the Indians began demanding higher prices, trading terms became more nearly uniform. For years a saying prevailed across the Northwest that "ten cups of sugar make one robe; ten robes make one pony; three ponies make one tepee." Trading goods took on a wide variety. For his business in the winter of 1840–1, one trader, Pierre Chouteau, ordered from an English firm 6,000 pairs of French blankets, 300 guns, 300 dozen butcher knives, 9,000 pounds of blue and white chalk beads, 500 pounds of pigeon-egg beads, and a quantity of cloth goods.

In exceptional cases a trader might pay a price much higher than average for a buffalo robe of unusual color or outstanding quality. The type most eagerly sought was the rare white robe; few of these ever came into the hands of traders. On the Montana range in 1882 a trader paid two hundred dollars for one.

Next in scarcity was the beaver robe, so named because its color was like that of beaver fur. It was especially prepared by the Indian women, who took out the occasional coarse hairs, leaving the fur unusually soft and silky. Another type, the blue robe, with long, fine fur of bluish cast, also brought a premium. Among the twelve hundred robes he bought in 1882, James McNaney found only one beaver robe and a dozen blue ones. He obtained $75 for the beaver robe and $16 each for the blue ones.

More common, but worth a slight extra price, was the black robe of the mountain buffalo, sometimes called the black and tan robe. The ordinary robe that made up the great bulk of the trade was sometimes called the buckskin robe because of its tan color. In 1882 a robe of this type was worth about $3.50.[2]

In his camp or at a convenient fort, the trader would bind his buffalo robes into bales of ten or twelve each. Usually he paid little attention to quality except that, if he had several poor robes, he would avoid putting more than one of them in the same bale. Packhorses would carry the robes to the nearest boat-landing on the river.

The buffalo robe did not become an important item in the nation's commerce until the early 1800's. In 1803 only about 850 robes, valued at $5.50 each, were shipped down the Missouri River. But by 1815 the cargoes had reached an average of 26,000 robes a year. Traders had bought the robes at about $1.50 each and had sold them for twice that amount. Some of the robes were reshipped at St. Louis by boat to Pittsburgh, while others were sent down the Mississippi to New Orleans.

Trade in buffalo robes rose much higher in the 1820's. The Crescent City received 184,110 robes in 1825, though only 77,400 the next year. That city counted 134,120 robes in 1827 and 199,870 in 1828, its peak year. Thereafter the New Orleans trade declined, with 159,870 robes received in 1829, 30,610 in 1830, and smaller numbers in most later years. The last big year for robes was 1844, in which 54,450 were received in New Orleans, at an average price of $4.43. Later, as robes became scarce, the price gradually rose,

[2] Lyman E. Munson: "Pioneer Life on the American Frontier," p. 117; Hamlin Russell: "The Story of the Buffalo"; William T. Hornaday: *The Extermination of the American Bison*, p. 444.

reaching $7.50 in 1852 and a peak of $8.00 two years later. The last recorded sale there was in 1855.

During this period the American Fur Company was active in building trading posts on the upper Missouri. The largest was Fort Union, which Kenneth McKenzie built at the mouth of the Yellowstone River in 1828 to tie together the routes of the mountain trails and the rivers. In July 1831 the steamboat *Yellowstone* arrived back in St. Louis from its first trip into the fur country. It had a full load of buffalo robes and other pelts, along with a thousand buffalo tongues. On its second trip, a year later, it brought down several hundred packs of robes.

Despite the decline in shipments to New Orleans, the trade in buffalo robes continued until the outbreak of the Civil War. For the decade of 1833–43, an official of the American Fur Company estimated that his company had acquired about 70,000 robes a year, the Hudson's Bay Company 10,-000, and other companies 10,000. In this period Fort Benton, on the upper Missouri far above Fort Union, became an important rendezvous. About 2,000 robes changed hands there in 1834. By 1841 this number had risen to 20,000, and it remained at almost that level for two decades.

Meanwhile Fort Union continued to ship large cargoes of robes down the river. On April 2, 1835, D. Lamont and other traders arrived there with the yield of their season's barter. Besides the pelts of small animals, they had 4,200 buffalo robes, 390 buffalo tongues, 3,500 pounds of salted and 3,000 pounds of dried buffalo meat. Other robes were brought to Fort Union from Fort McKenzie—210 packs in the spring of 1835, 2,100 packs in 1841, and 20,000 robes in 1847. The robes made regular cargo for the Missouri River fur fleet. In August 1842 seven boats from the Yellowstone arrived at St. Louis with 20,000 robes for the American Fur Company.

Other robes, in smaller quantities, were floated down the

shallow Platte River, usually with difficulty. In the spring of 1840, Louis Vasquez and Andrew Sublette brought down a thirty-six-foot boat with a cargo that included 700 robes and 4,000 buffalo tongues.

## II

Not all the robes came from the Missouri River country. Another productive area was that drained by the remote Red River of the North and its tributaries. For the North West Company, Alexander Henry led a band of *voyageurs* and hunters to the forks of the Red River in the summer of 1800. He built a trading post where the Park River entered the Red, since the salty water there attracted buffaloes and other game. Early in the following January the surrounding plain, as far as anyone could see, was covered with buffaloes.

In May of 1801, Henry was able to send to Grand Portage thirty-one robes and five thousand pounds of pemmican. That summer he built a permanent post on the Pembina River, a tributary of the Red. From that and other trading posts in the Red River country of Canada, his company obtained large shipments of robes and pemmican in the next eight years.

But before long, opposition appeared in this northern wilderness. In 1812, a year after buying a vast tract from the Hudson's Bay Company, Thomas Douglas, the fifth Earl of Selkirk, planted a colony of Scottish Highlanders on the Red River two miles below the mouth of the Pembina. Until they could grow crops, the settlers hunted buffaloes. This activity alarmed the North West Company, and a controversy ensued. When the head of the colonists seized six hundred bags of pemmican from the traders, his action set off the bloody Pemmican War. This conflict lasted until the North West Company was merged with the Hudson's Bay Company in 1821.

In an effort to profit further from the still abundant buf-

I    BULL IN THE NATIONAL MUSEUM

2    BULL THAT SAVED HIS HIDE

faloes, the Red River settlers formed in 1821 the Buffalo Wool Company. Their purpose was not only to build a tannery for buffalo hides but also to manufacture cloth from the buffalo fleeces, to be sold in Europe. The company sent samples of the cloth to London and other cities and raised more than thirty thousand dollars from the sale of stock. But production costs proved so high that a year later the company failed. Soon afterward the same farmers shipped more than four hundred thousand pounds of buffalo tallow to England; but the transportation cost was so high that this venture, too, was abandoned.

For more than two decades, beginning in 1820, the Selkirk colonists, French-Canadian fur hunters, and half-blood Indians went on an annual buffalo hunt into the Pembina country. Usually several hundred persons made up the party. The hunt began about the middle of June and lasted through August.

Each hunter or pair of hunters took along what came to be called a Red River cart. This sturdy two-wheeled vehicle resembled the country cart of France, the *charette,* except that it had no iron parts. Its wheels were about five feet high. The box of the cart, held together with wooden pegs, would carry about a thousand pounds of freight.

The Pembina hunts grew in size until that of 1840, which started on June 15, embraced 1,630 persons and 1,210 carts. Each hunter, besides having an ox or a draft horse for his cart, took along a saddle horse trained in chasing buffaloes. Jean Baptiste, chosen leader of the 1840 hunt, commanded ten captains. Each captain had ten soldiers under his direction. There also were guides who took turns in directing the travel and locating and arranging the camps. Each evening the camp was formed in a circle of tents and carts, with the horses and oxen inside. When a flag was raised early in the morning, the hunters started to load up for the trail. An exception was Sunday, when no hunting was allowed.

Members of the party were kept under strict discipline. Each captain patrolled his section of the camp to see that the rules were enforced. A violator might have his saddle and his bridle cut into bits for the first offense. For the second, he might have his coat taken from his back and shredded into strips; and for the third, he might be flogged in public.

The big hunt of 1840 ranged southwest through the Dakota country to and beyond the Missouri River. Much of the killing was done on the plains around Fort Union. Each morning, as soon as the priest had said Mass, the four hundred hunters lined up to hear their orders. Then they rode off and cautiously approached the herd. Each waited for the leader to signal the start of the attack by shouting "Ho!"

The Pembina hunters chased the buffaloes on horseback, firing from close range. Usually this exciting chase lasted more than an hour. In that time a hunter with an ordinary mount would kill three or four shaggies, while one with an unusually swift and well-trained horse might down ten or twelve. The hunters spent the rest of the day in skinning and butchering the buffaloes and in packing the hides and meat in the carts, which were driven laboriously to Pembina.

That year the hunters from Pembina killed about 3,500 buffaloes. Besides the hides, they took back 375 bags of pemmican and 240 bales of dried meat. In most cases they saved only the tongue and hump, leaving the rest of the carcass to the wolves and vultures. These annual hunts continued until 1847. In that year, settlers along the Red River sold large numbers of robes in St. Paul at $3.50 each. Later the scarcity of buffaloes in the region made such expeditions less profitable.

Another yearly hunt by Canadians was made west from Fort Garry onto the White Horse Plains. This, too, brought a marked thinning of the herds. By 1857, buffaloes had become so scarce around the headwaters of the Qu'Appelle River, 250 miles west of Winnipeg, that the Cree Indians who lived there banned any further hunting by whites or half-bloods. The only outsiders allowed to travel through their country were traders looking for dried meat, pemmican, skins, and robes.

In 1844, Canadians had opened the Red River Trail, over which they hauled their furs and buffalo robes in carts to St. Paul. In 1856 the export of Pembina and Red River pelts through St. Paul included 7,500 robes. In 1858 six hundred carts arrived at St. Paul with about $200,000 worth of goods, two thirds of it furs and buffalo robes and meat. This trade continued until the United States killed it by imposing a twenty-per-cent duty on robes and one of thirty per cent on moccasins.[3]

## III

Another large source of buffalo robes, along with the pelts of beaver and other small animals, was the Southwest. There the lack of navigable streams compelled the fur traders to rely on pack animals and wagon trains to carry their loads to market. A pack mule or horse could carry 200 to 250 pounds and could live on grass the year round. But most of the robes were hauled to Independence in caravans of traders' wagons that crept slowly over the Santa Fe Trail.

Of the many fur traders in the Southwest, the most successful were buckskinned Charles and William Bent and Ceran St. Vrain. Forming the partnership of Bent, St. Vrain and Company, they built in 1833–4 the large, castle-like adobe trading post known as Bent's Fort, on the Arkansas River in southeastern Colorado. The situation of this post on the Santa Fe Trail made it a landmark and rendezvous for hundreds of traders.

A young Army officer who was at Bent's Fort in 1835 noted

---

[3] Alexander Ross: *The Red River Settlement*, pp. 69–72, 241–74; Elliott Coues, editor: *New Light on the Early History of the Greater Northwest: The Manuscript Journals of Alexander Henry and David Thompson, 1799–1814,* I, 160–75.

that fifteen wagons were being loaded for Independence. They carried buffalo robes which the traders "buy for about twenty-five cents' worth of goods and sell at St. Louis for five or six dollars." Among the traders associated with the Bents and St. Vrain was the celebrated Kit Carson.

Indians of several tribes brought robes to Bent's Fort and did trading there. Julia Archibald Holmes, who stopped at the fort in the spring of 1858, wrote in a letter: "The price paid for a buffalo robe at present is ten cups of sugar, about eight pounds. They formerly were bought for from one to four cups of sugar."

Most of the robes, though, were brought in by white traders who had obtained them in the Indian villages. On setting out from the fort, the traders loaded their pack mules or carts with such goods as Navajo blankets, red cloth, beads, iridescent abalone shells, butcher knives, small axes, and hoop iron used for making arrowheads. They took along coffee and sugar largely as good-will gifts to start the trading.

For safety, two or three traders usually traveled together. At each village the principal chief assigned several young braves to help the visitors and protect their goods. Often the traders decked these "soldiers" in gaudy uniforms that might include stovepipe hats and gilt-handled swords. Then they distributed trinkets as presents to the chiefs and prominent warriors and spread an array of trading goods for inspection.

The trading began with slow dickering and often continued for several days. Both men and squaws brought in robes to barter for the goods they wanted most. If interest lagged, the visitors might serve sweetened coffee to lure more of the villagers.

Although the Bent firm discouraged the dispensing of firewater to the Indians, most of the mountain men with whom it dealt carried liquor, especially in the later days of the fur trade. Some, on arriving at a village, would open a keg on the prairie and serve free drinks to all comers. In their barter they often could obtain a fine robe for three three-gill drinks of diluted raw alcohol. The drinks quickly reduced the Indians to debauchery and fighting. Some intoxicated warriors gladly sold their daughters for a night with the visitors. Another outcome was that the tribesmen, to satisfy their craving for strong drink, killed nearly all the buffaloes from certain ranges.

For the Bents and St. Vrain, the trading was highly profitable. In the summer of 1840 they delivered in St. Louis fifteen thousand robes and a large quantity of furs. In the winter of 1841–2 they loaded eleven hundred large bales of buffalo robes, weighing about fifty tons, along with a ton of glossy beaver pelts. On the trips out, the Bent wagons hauled trading goods and government goods to be handed out to the Indians as annuities for ceded land. For transport of the latter, the government paid an average of seven and a half cents a pound, making about four hundred dollars to a wagon.[4]

## IV

Meanwhile, the Missouri River continued to be the chief avenue for furs and robes acquired in trade with the Indians of the Northwest. In 1850, Captain Joseph La Barge, after a quick trip to the Yellowstone River for the American Fur Company, brought the steamer *St. Ange* back down the Missouri to St. Louis with a load. In the following summer the steamers *Alton* and *St. Ange* brought down robes. In 1852 the *St. Ange* and two other steamers reached St. Louis with furs and robes.

By 1853 some of the traders had begun floating robes from the upper forts down the Missouri on rafts or flatboats to Council Bluffs. This made it unnecessary for all of the steamers to risk the shoals, bars, and snags of the upper

[4] David Lavender: *Bent's Fort,* pp. 49–161, 184, 207, 229, 328.

stream, though some continued to do so. Captain La Barge, who had bought the small *Highland Mary* in the fall of 1852, piloted her to Council Bluffs in the following spring. Early in June this steamer and the *El Paso* arrived back in St. Louis with nearly 1,200 bales of robes. In the same month the *Banner State* came in with a load of robes and tongues.

The trade in buffalo robes was still strong in 1857, when an agent of the American Fur Company estimated it at 75,-000 robes. That year Fort Benton shipped 3,600 bales, while Fort Union and Fort Pierre sent down smaller cargoes. By that time, buffaloes were becoming scarce in some parts of the Missouri Valley; but in the fall of 1858, William T. Hamilton, out from Walla Walla, did profitable trading with the Blackfeet and Crows of Montana in robes and dried tongues.

In the latter days of the fur trade the Missouri River steamers and the wagon trains of the Santa Fe Trail shared the hauling of robes with the railroads. Some of the robes had been brought long distances by wagon to the railroad towns. As late as May 4, 1871, the Wichita *Tribune* noted that a northbound wagon train loaded with buffalo robes had passed through that frontier village on the preceding Sunday evening. The freighter was Robert M. Wright, who had taken a load of goods from Junction City to Fort Sill and was returning with robes.

As late as 1874, recalled Hamlin Russell, "one could buy a beautiful fur-robe overcoat, well made and lined with flannel, at the retail clothing stores in St. Paul for ten dollars." [5] By that time, though, the trade in robes had almost ended. It had given way to the much larger dealing in hides. Those Indians and others who had lamented the killing of the buffaloes for their warm robes were witnessing the much more extravagant slaughter of the animals for their hides, which, with the hair removed, would be tanned into leather.

[5] Russell: op. cit., p. 796. Although the robe and hide periods overlapped, the white hide hunters seldom bothered to put aside fine winter hides to be converted into robes.

# 4

# THE ROYAL CHASE

All through the era of trading in robes, sportsmen had found the buffalo a target hard to resist. In an almost continuous procession, men with keen eyes and long rifles had trooped west to see for themselves the fabulous herds and to enjoy the excitement of the chase.

Some of those who hunted for sport were Europeans who had crossed the Atlantic to find a new type of game. Others were men from the more settled Eastern states who wanted to see whether the stories they had heard about the West and its almost endless herds of buffaloes were true. Most of the hunts, made far beyond the fringe of frontier newspapers, went unchronicled; but accounts of a few were set down in diaries and journals.

One of the more noted of those who went out to the buffalo country for pleasure in the early days was Washington Irving. Back from seventeen years in Europe, he made a tour of the Southwest in the fall of 1832, accompanying Henry L. Ellsworth, one of the three Indian Commissioners President Andrew Jackson had appointed to study the country west of

Arkansas, mark the boundaries, and pacify the warring tribes. Included in the party were a Swiss youth, Count de Pourtales, and his English tutor, Charles J. Latrobe, nephew of the famous architect.

The party traveled by steamer from Cincinnati to St. Louis and overland to Independence and Fort Gibson. At the edge of the Indian country Irving bought a better horse, a fine bay; and Ellsworth engaged as a guide and interpreter Pierre Beatte, a Frenchman who had been living with the Osages.

On October 10 the party set out on horseback for the western wilds, escorted as far as the Verdigris River, four miles away, by Sam Houston and several officers of the post. The travelers had planned a swing into the Indian country that would keep them in the open for nearly a month.

In what later became central Oklahoma they found a large herd of buffaloes and spent several days in chasing them. Irving was much impressed. "There is a mixture of the awful and the comic in the look of these huge animals," he wrote. "They heave their great bulk forward with an up-and-down motion of the unwieldy head and shoulders. Their tails cock up like the queue of Pantaloon in pantomime, in the end whisking about in a fierce yet whimsical style; and their eyes glare venomously with an expression of fright and fury."

Irving, although well mounted, had no luck at first. Not only was he without experience, but also the pistols he had borrowed at Fort Gibson proved defective. But on October 29, dashing about in a herd of several hundred between the future sites of Oklahoma City and Norman, he borrowed a double-barreled gun from Latrobe, who had just killed a buffalo. With this he quickly brought down one. Beatte removed the tongue and handed it to Irving, who proudly carried it back to camp.[1]

[1] Washington Irving: *A Tour on the Prairies*, pp. 263–78; Henry Leavitt Ellsworth: *Washington Irving on the Prairie*, pp. 120–4.

The next few decades saw many such hunting parties, several of which included visitors from abroad. Among these was a Scottish baronet, Captain Sir William Drummond Stewart. Sir William, who had hunted big game in Africa and had made earlier trips to America's West, formed a hunting party in St. Louis in 1843. The leader was the lanky Kentucky-born William L. Sublette, a seasoned fur trader.

The Stewart expedition set out in style. Its wagons were loaded with provisions that included flour, sugar, hams, tinned meat, pickles, brandy, and wine. The white jacket and Panama hat worn by Sir William drew snickers from some of the rugged frontiersmen; but when they saw that he could ride and shoot with the best of them, they took a friendlier view.

An account of this hunting trip was set down by one of its younger members, nineteen-year-old William Clark Kennerly of St. Louis. Kennerly was a nephew of General William Clark of the famous Lewis and Clark expedition.

On reaching the broad valley of the Platte River, Kennerly recalled, the party of about eighty men found plenty of game. "We encountered buffaloes in numbers which gladdened the heart of Sir William, who had come four thousand miles to shoot them. The horses fell readily into the excitement of the chase and seemed to enjoy dashing along beside the shaggy monsters until we could reach over and put the muzzles of our guns almost to the buffalo's shoulders. The prairie was strewn for miles with the bodies of the dead bison."

Kennerly admitted that many more buffaloes were killed than were needed to supply the party's larder. But what man, he asked, "could resist the temptation, when the whole earth, it seemed, was a surging, tumbling, waving mass of these animals? In butchering, the hide was cut from the hump back to the tail; and the 'fleece,' extending along either side of the backbone, was taken out. These two pieces, which weigh about eighty pounds, together with the tongue and hump, represented the meat taken from a buffalo weighing from fifteen hundred to two thousand pounds."

One morning, as the men prepared to go out on their daily hunt, they saw approaching a herd that they estimated must contain a million head. "The pounding of their hoofs on the hard ground," said Kennerly, "sounded like the roar of a mighty ocean, surging over the land and sweeping everything before it. Here was more game than we bargained for, and the predicament in which we found ourselves gave cause for alarm. On they came. As we were directly in their path and on the bank of the river, there was great danger of our being swept over. This danger was averted only by our exerting every effort to turn them off in another direction. As it took the herd two entire days to pass, even at a rapid gait, we were kept busy placing guards of shouting, gesticulating men in the day and building huge bonfires at night."

An equally large and even more expensively mounted and much longer hunt for buffaloes and other game was made a dozen years later by a wealthy bachelor from northern Ireland, Sir St. George Gore. This Oxford-educated baronet with straw-colored whiskers outfitted his expedition in St. Louis in the spring of 1854 and headed up the valley of the Missouri River.

Gore spent an estimated half-million dollars on his hunt, which covered at least six thousand miles and lasted nearly three years. He had with him forty servants and several scientific companions. His livestock included three milk cows, eighteen oxen, and 112 carefully chosen horses. Gore's own mount was a Kentucky Thoroughbred called Steel Trap. If the hunter tired of the saddle, he could ride in his large carriage.

For hauling his equipment, the sportsman from Donegal had twenty-one two-horse Red River carts, four six-mule wagons, and two three-yoke ox wagons. One wagon was filled with firearms, including many pistols, a dozen or more shot-guns, seventy-five muzzle-loading rifles, and one of the new Sharps breech-loaders.

On most nights Gore slept comfortably on a brass bed-stead that servants set up in his large tent of striped green and white linen. He had a rug underfoot and kept within reach a supply of imported wines and several of his favorite books, including works by Shakespeare and Scott. If the weather was bad or the ground wet, his bed could be assem-bled in a covered spring wagon.

For chasing game, Gore had between forty and fifty dogs, mostly greyhounds and staghounds. At Westport, which the expedition reached in mid-June, a local correspondent called the hounds "the most magnificent pack of dogs ever seen in this country." Over the rolling terrain of the river valley, the hounds took out after coyotes, timber wolves, and any other animals they could find.

On the prairies beyond Fort Leavenworth, Gore had his first taste of buffalo hunting. But he quickly pushed on to-ward the more exciting wilds to the northwest. At Fort Lara-mie at the end of June, he added several trappers to his reti-nue. Then, with Joseph Chatillon as guide, he went south to hunt in the mountains of what later became Colorado. By the time cold weather set in, he was back at Fort Laramie to sit out the winter. There, among Indians, trappers, and trad-ers at this frontier outpost, he found one of the most rugged of the mountain men. He was a tall, sinewy fellow, buck-skinned Jim Bridger, better known as Old Gabe.

Gore quickly took a liking to this famous fur trapper, who could not read but who knew just about every trail in the Rockies. He engaged the grizzled Bridger to go with him as a guide as soon as the spring thaw allowed in 1855. Bridger led Sir St. George and his party up the North Platte River and over the emigrant road to Casper Creek. Then the hunters crossed northward to the Powder River and followed Dry

Creek down to the future site of Fort Conner, later called Fort
Reno. From there they drifted down the valley of the Powder
to the Yellowstone River, went up the Yellowstone to the
mouth of the Tongue, and then turned up that stream.
All of this country was full of buffaloes and other game, a
paradise for hunters.

After resting during another winter, the party went out
again in the spring of 1856, hunting along the Rosebud, the
Tongue, and the Yellowstone. Before winter, Gore and his
outfit turned up the Little Missouri into the Black Hills. By
the time Gore broke up his outfit and returned down the Missouri by boat in the spring of 1857, he had killed 2,000 buffaloes, 1,600 deer and elk, 105 bears, and many other animals. This slaughter for sport caused resentment among
many of the Indians of the northern plains and led to com-
plaints to officials in Washington.[2]

## I I

Visitors from afar were by no means the only ones who
hunted the buffaloes for sport. Soldiers at the frontier outposts often went out on shooting forays, as did some of the
farmers, stockmen, and pioneer merchants from the fringe
of settlement. In May 1867 officers of the Seventh Cavalry
at Fort Hays, in western Kansas—most of them green at buffalo hunting—held a competitive chase that took them on a
ride of fifteen to twenty miles. On different days, two parties
of eight men each rode out at sunrise to see how many buffalo tongues they could bring back before sunset. The winning party, with twelve tongues to the other's eleven, was
dined by the loser.

As the Union Pacific laid its rails westward across Kansas
and Nebraska that summer and fall, the buffalo country

[2] William Clark Kennerly: *Persimmon Hill*, pp. 147–8; F. George Heldt,
editor: "Narrative of Sir George Gore's Expedition, 1854–1856"; Clark
Spence: "Sir St. George Gore: A Celtic Nimrod in the West," MS.

came within easier reach of sportsmen. Many travelers took pot shots from the open windows of passenger cars, leaving the victims for the wolves and buzzards. On either side of the track, observed Colonel Henry Inman, "the most conspicuous objects were the desiccated carcasses of the noble beasts that had been ruthlessly slaughtered by the thoughtless and excited passengers."

In Hays City the *Railway Advance* reported an exceptional instance in which the meat was used: "On the down train the other day a buffalo was killed by the conductor, rolled upon a flatcar, and taken to Ellsworth to feed the community."

By the summer and fall of 1868, excursion trains were carrying parties of sightseers and hunters into the buffalo ranges. Exhibitions of animals in cities farther east helped to spur the interest of visitors. Joseph G. McCoy, who had established a new market for Texas Longhorn cattle at Abilene, Kansas, included three buffaloes in a Wild West show he staged that year in St. Louis and Chicago to advertise his business.

McCoy had sent Texas and California cowboys farther west in a special train to rope the animals he wanted. After a week of strenuous chases, they captured twenty-four bulls; but some of them died from overheating, fright, or rage. Others were discarded when they lay down and sulked, refusing to eat. Early in the fall, following his circus, McCoy took a group of Illinois cattle feeders on a hunting trip at the end of the Union Pacific rail line as a means of bringing them to Abilene.

James B. (Wild Bill) Hickok had trouble similar to that of McCoy's men when he and several helpers went out on the Nebraska range after live shaggies in the spring of 1870. Wild Bill, who had just quit his job as marshal of Hays City, Kansas, found a large herd on the Republican River. After two weeks of hard efforts, the party captured six buffaloes, which they loaded into a stock car at Ogallala. Hickok used the animals in a Wild West show at Niagara Falls in the summer; but the project soon failed and left him broke.

Meanwhile, excursions from Cincinnati, St. Louis, Chicago, Kansas City, and Leavenworth, in addition to the regular trains, brought visitors to marvel at the buffalo herds and to try their marksmanship. Almost every day they could see an animal circus. On the morning of October 2, 1868, the westbound Union Pacific train ran into a nearly solid herd about thirty miles west of Hays City. Most of the buffaloes were north of the railroad, where they darkened the plain for fifteen miles.

One of the score of passengers, De B. Randolph Keim, recalled the scene in his memoirs. The buffaloes near the track, alarmed by the sound of the locomotive, set off at a lope. They raised so much dust that "for a few minutes it was impossible to see more than a long line of hindquarters and elevated tails." Some of the smaller bunches south of the track began to cross ahead of the train to join the main herd. In trying this, "one specimen found himself lifted into the air and thrown into the ditch, where he lay on his back, his cloven feet flourishing madly."

Passengers shot several animals from the cars, and the engineer stopped the train long enough for them to carve out a few rumps. While this hurried butchering was in progress, wrote Keim, "a party of six or eight of us started down the track to dispatch the buffalo bull, still kicking and bellowing with suspense and rage. After one shot was fired, the old bull, with a desperate effort, regained his feet." Several more shots seemed to have no effect. Then, instead of retreating, the angry beast charged on his tormentors. He came at a full jump, said Keim, "head down, tongue out, bleeding and frothing at the mouth, eyes flashing, and roaring frightfully."

The party scattered quickly. "Losing sight of us, the enraged animal, smarting under the blow he had received from the locomotive and the tickling he had sustained from our rifles, wreaked his anger on the opposite side of the embankment." He tore great furrows in the clay bank, stamped the earth with a terrible sound, and raised a cloud of dust. Finally, after receiving a dozen more bullets, he staggered and fell dead.

Four days later, on the morning of October 6, an excursion train of five coaches, a smoking car, a baggage car, and a freight car left Lawrence for the west. Before it reached the buffalo country, the passengers had time to listen to the Lawrence Cornet Band and to take a straw vote on the presidential race, a poll that strongly favored General Ulysses S. Grant over Horatio Seymour. The train stopped for the night at Ellsworth, since the danger of Indians to the west made night travel unsafe. Before they reached Hays City, the passengers began to see buffaloes, and toward Sheridan the herds became thicker. A party of hunters from the train killed a score in six hours.

A similar excursion from Leavenworth was advertised for the 27th but was delayed a day to await Eastern passengers. The fare was ten dollars for the round trip, and patrons were assured that buffaloes would be near enough to be shot from the cars. That usually was the case. Occasionally a mass of the animals held up a train. After two Santa Fe engines were thrown off the track in one week while trying to run through the herds, engineers learned to stop—for hours if necessary—while a bellowing herd crossed the rails.[3]

Shooting buffaloes for pleasure continued into the period of commercial hide hunting. Invited by an Indian agent, Albert L. Green, a party of Philadelphians, including Clement Biddle, went with the Otos on a tribal hunt in June 1871. Their trip of six hundred miles across southern Nebraska

[3] "The Buffalo Hunt"; *Weekly Journal of Commerce,* Kansas City, January 11, 1868; De B. Randolph Keim: *Sheridan's Troopers on the Border,* pp. 37–40. In 1875 the railroad, then called the Kansas Pacific, banned shooting from its trains.

gave them an insight into the life of the Indians, as well as into the habits of buffaloes.

In the fall of that year General Philip H. Sheridan took more than a dozen of his New York, Philadelphia, and Chicago friends on a hunting trip across the plains. Included in the group was James Gordon Bennett II, publisher of the New York *Herald*. After arriving by palace car at Fort McPherson, Nebraska, on the North Platte, the sportsmen ranged southwest to Fort Hays, Kansas. Their outfit included sixteen wagons—two of them for ice and wine. In addition, there were several horse-drawn ambulances to carry the guns and any hunters who tired of riding horseback.

As a guide the party had young William F. Cody, who made himself useful to the green hunters. Cody, who had become known as Buffalo Bill, wore a new suit of white buckskin and a broad-brimmed hat. He had grown a goatee and had let his hair grow down to his shoulders.[4]

### III

The hunts which attracted the most attention, although they lasted only a few days, were the two staged for the Grand Duke Alexis, one of the younger sons of Russia's Tsar Alexander II. The blue-eyed sailor prince was a tall, handsome bachelor of twenty-two, with light brown hair brushed back from his high forehead. Despite his side whiskers and downy mustache, which made him look older, the ladies found him most attractive and lionized him in every city he visited.

At a dinner in the White House, Alexis met General Phil Sheridan, who invited him to go on a buffalo hunt in the West. The prince, who had done some shooting in Europe, accepted eagerly.

[4] Thomas L. Green, editor: "Notes on a Buffalo Hunt—the Diary of Mordecai Bartram"; [Henry E. Davies]: *Ten Days on the Plains*.

When the grand duke reached Omaha, Lieutenant Colonel George A. Custer boarded the luxurious private train and rode with General Sheridan and the Russians to North Platte, reached early on January 13, 1872. There a cowboys' six-shooter salute greeted the party, and the royal visitor and General Sheridan rode through the Nebraska town in an open carriage drawn by four horses.

At the Platte River, Colonel Innis N. Palmer met the party with a cavalry escort. Saddle horses, five Army ambulances, a carriage for the grand duke, and a light wagon for baggage were ready. The trail led across a bleak prairie to wintry Camp Alexis, which had been set up among the cottonwoods along Red Willow Creek, at the foot of low bluffs.

The ride of fifty to sixty miles from the North Platte to the camp, which took the whole day, may have reminded the visitors of the Russian steppes. It gave them a view of prairie-dog towns, a few skulking coyotes, and—in the distance—several antelope. The only signs of buffaloes were the occasional skeletons whitening in the short-grass uplands. The grand duke and two of his staff stuck to their saddles all morning, but the other Russians soon changed to the more comfortable ambulances. At midday the party stopped along Medicine Creek for a change of horses, a hot lunch, and the warmth of quickly built campfires.

Camp Alexis, reached in the evening, had been formed hastily for the occasion. Besides the tepees of invited Indians, it had two hospital tents for meals and ten wall tents for sleeping. Three of the latter were floored, and that of the grand duke was carpeted. All of them had stoves. In addition, there were smaller tents for the soldiers and servants. The camp was well stocked with food, including buffalo humps, flour, sugar, and coffee. For the Indians, the commissary had a thousand pounds of tobacco. On hand to entertain the prince were Captain James Egan's troopers of the Second Cavalry and the fine Second Cavalry Band.

A touch of Indian life was provided by Chief Spotted Tail and fifty of his Sioux warriors and their families. The braves shouted greetings to the prince, and the band played "Hail to the Chief." But evening entertainment was cut short, as the men were tired from their long ride and wanted to be out early the next morning for the hunt.

At frosty dawn on the 14th, the scouts engaged for the party rode out to look for game while the others ate a steaming breakfast and saddled their horses. The Russians, set off by their long fur coats, were eager for the chase as they warmed themselves by the fires. By the time they were ready, one of the scouts was back with a report. Buffalo Bill Cody had seen a large herd grazing nearly fifteen miles away, on the divide between Red Willow and Medicine creeks.

Quickly they rode off for the hunt. The grand duke, with side whiskers flying in the wind, wore a simple jacket and trousers of heavy gray cloth trimmed with green. The buttons bore the imperial Russian coat of arms. His pants were tucked inside his boots. His hat was an Australian turban with a cloth top. He was armed with a Russian hunting knife and a recently presented Smith and Wesson revolver that bore on its handle the coats of arms of Russia and the United States.

Custer and Cody appeared in their buckskin hunting suits; but Custer, instead of his usual sealskin cap, had only feathers fastened in his flowing hair, giving him the appearance of an Indian. Custer, Cody, and two of the Indians rode with the prince. It was agreed by the whole party that no one else would shoot a buffalo until Alexis had downed one.

The riders crossed broken country, with snow eighteen inches deep in some places. Several wolves greeted them with howls, but were careful to keep out of bullet range. Finally the hunters saw the herd, which they approached against the wind. After stopping in the mouth of a ravine to map their strategy, they charged into the buffaloes.

"Ride as fast as your horse will go," Cody advised the prince, "and don't shoot until you are close."

The young prince was riding Cody's favorite mount, Buckskin Joe. In his excitement he forgot most of the advice that Buffalo Bill had given him. He missed the first buffalo at which he shot. Then, picking out a large bull that seemed about to charge him, he put a couple of pistol shots into the animal at ten feet. As the wounded shaggy started down the ravine, Cody handed Alexis his rifle, Lucretia.

"Now turn old Letty loose," shouted Cody as he brought his quirt across the rump of Buckskin Joe. Alexis, galloping beside the panting bull, soon felled him.

As a cheer rose from other members of the party, the elated grand duke took off his turban and waved it. Then he dismounted and, with his hunting knife, slashed off the tail of the buffalo bull to take back to the camp as a trophy. He sat on the buffalo carcass and shouted in Russian as the other hunters rode up to congratulate him and to toast him with champagne. Alexis recalled that, two years earlier to the day, while hunting with his father, he had killed a Russian bear.

While eating lunch in the open, the prince noticed that all the Indian hunters carried bows and arrows. "Why do they carry those absurd toys?" he asked. When told that they killed buffaloes with them, he refused to believe this. To convince him, Custer sent out two Indians to drive a buffalo into camp. As they ran in a panting cow, one of the Sioux warriors, Two Lance, drew his bow and sent an arrow deep into her shoulder. The cow fell at once, pierced through the heart. This performance so impressed Alexis that he handed Two Lance a twenty-dollar gold piece and later bought his bow and quiver of arrows to take back to Russia as souvenirs.

During the day, four other members of the party, including Count Olsenfieff, each killed a buffalo. At the camp in

the evening, everyone feasted on buffalo meat and champagne. For those who hadn't seen it, Custer described with
humorous frills the grand duke's killing of the bull. During
the evening, Custer and Alexis flirted with the two daughters
of Chief Spotted Tail, with the girls giggling in appreciation.

On the second morning, with the sun out in all its splen-
dor, the party rode out again, the grand duke on a superb
black charger. This time the uneven country in which they
found the buffaloes called for harder riding and more strategy than on the preceding day. But the men killed fifty-six
buffaloes, including two downed by Alexis. The proud prince
had the head of one animal cut off and taken back to camp to
be mounted and sent to Russia. He also drove in a buffalo
calf. As the party approached the camp in the evening,
Alexis started firing his pistol in a salute in which the others
quickly joined. The hunt, ranging over about fifty miles, had
overtaxed some of the horses. That of Colonel Mike Sheridan
failed him before the day ended and had to be led back to
camp. Custer's mount died from exhaustion soon after reaching camp.

To entertain the grand duke and his party that evening,
the Sioux warriors, in paint and feathers, staged a sham battle and a war dance. Later Alexis presented the Indians with
twenty beautiful blankets, a number of hunting knives, and
fifty dollars in fifty-cent pieces. General Sheridan gave Chief
Spotted Tail a dressing gown, an officer's belt, and a scarlet
cap with beads. After the pipe of peace had made its silent
round, General Sheridan made a speech. He was followed by
Chief Spotted Tail, who asked that his tribe be allowed to
hunt south of the Platte River and that it be assigned an additional trader. Then the hilarity was resumed and lasted until nearly midnight.

The visitors broke camp early on the 16th. Turning back
toward the North Platte, the grand duke and General Sheri-

dan rode in a double-seated open carriage drawn by six spir-
ited cavalry horses. They reached the special train about
five o'clock in the evening. After dinner on the train, Alexis
presented Buffalo Bill with a scarf pin and a large, well-filled
purse. Some of the military officers remained on the train
when it pulled out at ten o'clock that night.

After visiting Cheyenne, Denver, Golden, and the mines
in Clear Creek Canyon, the prince decided to hunt buffaloes
again. So, on the morning of the 20th, his train was stopped
at Kit Carson, Colorado, 130 miles east of Denver, near the
Kansas line. There the party had to use Army horses from
Fort Wallace. They were not trained for buffalo hunting,
but Alexis decided to ride out anyway. The early morning
was cold and cloudy, with a threat of snow; but about ten
o'clock the sky cleared and the sun came out brightly. Alexis
was dressed in a gray suit and Custer in buckskins.

When the men found a large herd drifting on a level
prairie about five miles southeast of town, Custer and the
prince rode on ahead. But their horses, frightened by the
buffaloes, raced out of control. They had to be turned and
headed into a dusty alkali flat some distance away before
they could be brought under rein again.

On the second try, Alexis plunged into the midst of the
herd and quickly downed an enormous bull. Alexis and Custer dismounted; and the duke, greatly excited and elated,
clasped his arms around the whiskered American officer and
kissed him.

The prince's kill left the others free to start shooting.
Soon the buffaloes began stampeding and raising a cloud of
dust. They led the hunters through a prairie-dog town in
which some of the horses stumbled. But before the day
ended, Alexis killed five altogether, Custer three, and Sheridan two. About fifty carcasses spotted the plain. One was
that of a calf that had been wounded by a poorly aimed shot.

A young scout, Chalkley M. Beeson, had caught the injured calf and held him by the tail while General Sheridan
used his revolver to put him out of his misery.

Butchers from Kit Carson followed the hunters, cut the
humps from the downed animals, and loaded them in an
Army ambulance drawn by six horses. But as a butcher
walked up to one old bull to slit his throat and remove his
hump, the supposedly dead beast rose to his feet and started
after him. The butcher raced for his horse, which he reached
just before the pursuing buffalo fell for the last time.

When the hunters returned to camp, all were saddle-sore
and covered with dust. Some had lost their caps and had replaced them with bandannas tied over their heads. But, after
packing the commissary car of the royal train with buffalo
humps and feasting on others, washed down with champagne, the men soon were gay again. By the time the last
cork was popped, hunters were strewn about the camp,
seemingly as dead as the buffaloes they had shot.

On the morning of the 22nd the grand duke's train
reached Topeka. Excursionists already had arrived; and the
Kansas legislature had recessed for a big parade, with music
by the Topeka Cornet Band, and a midday banquet at the
Fifth Avenue Hotel. At four in the afternoon the private train
pulled out for St. Louis, carrying from the buffalo country
the grand duke, his staff, his trophies, and his memories of
the chase.[5]

Sportsmen like Prince Alexis had made only slight inroads into the great herds of buffaloes. Yet at the time of his
visit, unnoticed by many even in the West, the commercial
hide hunters had started a slaughter that threatened to wipe
out the buffaloes from the whole of the plains.

[5] *Kansas Daily Commonwealth*, Topeka, January 18, 21, 1872; *Rocky
Mountain News*, Denver, January 21, 1872; James Albert Hadley and Chalkley M. Beeson: "A Royal Buffalo Hunt."

---◄ **5** ►---

# ADVENTURE IN THE

# WEST

**Y**ears before Prince Alexis hunted buffaloes on the grassy plains, the lure of the West had begun to attract youths who were growing up in the states east of the Mississippi. Teenage boys wanted to fight Indians, rope Longhorns, and shoot buffaloes. Some of the more adventurous ones did so, even if they had to run away from home.

All across the West, opportunities for an exciting life were opening up. The Army had uniforms and steady grub for those willing to risk the danger of Indian scalpers. Goverment contractors wanted teamsters to haul supplies to the frontier forts and men to chop firewood. Railroads building across the plains needed brawny construction workers. In the mountains, discoveries of new lodes of gold and silver were attracting prospectors. In Texas, cowmen were branding half-wild cattle and sending them over long trails to Kansas towns. Finally, a growing market for buffalo meat made it possible for some to earn a living by killing buffaloes.

Among the youths who went west in 1867 were two from New York State, George and Matthew F. Clarkson. George had let his hair grow long because he hoped to become an Indian scout. An older brother, Charles, a veteran of the Civil War, had preceded them to Kansas and at the time of their arrival was down at the edge of the Indian country, trapping wolves along the Cimarron River.

Matt and George arrived in the spring at Fort Hays, situated on a knoll overlooking the valley of Big Creek, in the buffalo country. The two obtained jobs as teamsters, hauling supplies to Fort Hays and to Camp Supply, about two hundred miles to the south. They worked at this for two months. Then Charlie came in to sell his load of wolf pelts and to file on a homestead.

That summer the three brothers chopped firewood along Big Creek and sold it to the government. They received ten dollars a cord for elm and fifteen for ash.

Many hostile Indians were on the prowl that summer, stealing horses and scalping isolated settlers and hunters. On June 8, while more than three hundred soldiers looked on, dumfounded, fifty-two Kiowas led by Chief Santana rode into Fort Dodge, a fenced half-circle of dugouts and sod houses on the north bank of the Arkansas River. They stampeded and drove off all the horses and mules.

Farther north, Sioux and others were raiding at will. Indians took the stage stock of the Downer station on July 12 and that of Chalk Bluff on the 16th. They killed and scalped an officer and ten soldiers at Fort Sedgwick at the head of Beaver Creek. The small force that Lieutenant Colonel George A. Custer had in the field, weakened by desertions, seldom caught up with the bronze warriors.

Kansas plainsmen had little faith in the ability of the Army to cope with the raiders. "Talk about regulars hunting Indians!" snorted one. "They go out, and when night comes, they blow the bugle to let the Indians know that they are going to sleep. In the morning they blow the bugle to let the Indians know that they are going to get up. Between their bugle and their great trains, they manage to keep the redskins out of sight."

The Clarksons, though, did their chopping without being molested. With part of the money from the sale of their wood, they outfitted themselves for hunting buffaloes. Soon they were spending two days a week in obtaining meat to sell at Fort Hays and in the wild frontier village of Hays City, which was springing up along the railroad near the post, providing liquor and supplies for bullwhackers, mule skinners, and hunters. In September the brothers quit cutting wood and began giving all their time to hunting and drying buffalo meat.

When the weather became cold enough to ship fresh meat, the Clarksons dispatched some of it to Kansas City. Much of the remainder, especially that from the big carcasses, they dried and salted in Indian style. Soon they had several carloads of dried or jerked beef to ship to Kansas City, Chicago, and Buffalo. In salting, the brothers would dig a hole in the ground and line it with buffalo hide. This would hold enough meat to fill two barrels. They had seventy-five barrels and could salt a hundred carcasses at once. It took only a short time to fill their smokehouse. They saved all the tongues so that they would know how many buffaloes they had killed and butchered.

With George Clarkson busy in the smokehouse, Charlie and Matt did most of the killing. When the hunting was good, they hired two or three men to help with the skinning and hauling. With their three four-mule teams and two two-mule teams, they could haul six to seven tons at a time. The brothers did most of their hunting afoot, preferring the low country and often killing ten to forty animals in one place. Their biggest kill was fifty-four by Charlie in a single stand. From most of the animals they took only the hams and

tongues. In the fall of 1867 they killed several thousand buffaloes along the Smoky Hill River and the Saline. They dried
and sold a few of the hides that looked as if they would make
good robes.

On the Kansas ranges that fall the Clarksons were competing with many other hunters, some of whom used horses
hired in Hays City. One of the better-known hunters was
William Hodges, who went by the name of California Bill.
Early in November he brought into town a large load of meat.
A few days later a party of hunters arrived with twenty-five
hundred pounds, and another outfit brought three thousand
pounds. In Hays City the meat was a drug on the market at
seven cents a pound, compared with twenty-five cents for
bacon; but quantities were being shipped by express to St.
Louis.

With the hunting equally good in 1868, the Clarkson
brothers continued to supply meat to the fort and the town.
They also shipped fresh meat to Kansas City in cold weather
and dried a big supply for later sale. In addition to buffaloes,
the Clarksons killed many antelope.

In August of that year the brothers were camped on the
bank of Spring Creek, south of the Smoky Hill River. One
night when they and their two helpers came in from hunting,
they found their whole camp gone, including grub, ten blankets, and a mule. They discovered too late that a roving band
of Indians had camped about a quarter of a mile below them
the night before. While they were out after buffaloes, the
redskins had taken everything left in the camp and had departed south. The indignant hunters drove all night to the
nearest railroad station. There Charlie took the morning
train to Hays City, where he spent about four hundred dollars to replace the stolen property. The Clarksons never
caught sight of the marauding Indians.

On August 6 a band of Cheyennes led by Chief Black Kettle had been in Hays City. They had with them a white child

who they said was the offspring of an officer at Fort Dodge and one of their squaws. But some Hays City residents thought that the child had no Indian blood. They guessed that it had been stolen from Texas settlers by Kiowas or Comanches and sold to the Cheyennes.[1]

Although the Indians complained that white hunters were destroying the buffaloes on which their living depended, herds continued to come within view of the booming town of Hays City. One of the herds inspired the editor of the Hays City *Railway Advance* to write:

"Yesterday a large herd of buffaloes appeared on the bluffs overlooking Hays City. Like immense shaggy monsters of some forgotten age, they stood in bold relief against the horizon, their great forms towering specter-like between us and the setting sun. Cow and calf, sportive young bull and savage old one, there stood the bison multitude pondering evidently in the language of the buffaloes over the magic change being wrought beneath them.

"Long and silently stood the providers of delicate tongues and snug robes. One huge old patriarch, with a wonderful air of wisdom, advanced before his friends. Slowly his head commenced shaking as if the burden of surprise and sorrow was too great for bearing. Then a few angry stamps of the feet, a quick turn, and away they fled back toward the setting sun." [2]

## II

As long rifles boomed on the buffalo ranges of western Kansas, many hunters besides the Clarksons attained repute

[1] Matthew F. Clarkson, diary, MS.; Junction City *Weekly Union,* July 13, 27, 1867; Hays City *Railway Advance,* November 9, 21, 1867; *Kansas Daily Tribune,* November 17, 1867. Fort Dodge, on a campground of the Santa Fe Trail, had been located by General Grenville M. Dodge in 1864 and occupied the next year.

[2] *Kansas Weekly Tribune,* November 28, 1867, citing the Hays City *Railway Advance.*

as marksmen. One such was William Mathewson, who started a ranch on Cow Creek and who traded among the Comanches and other tribes for robes. Mathewson built a trading post in the Indian Territory and later became one of the first residents in the frontier town of Wichita, on the Arkansas River. In 1860, when drought and clouds of ravenous grasshoppers had left many pioneer Kansas farm families near starvation, Mathewson took some men out to kill buffaloes, sending back whole wagon trains of meat to feed the hungry settlers. In gratitude they called him Buffalo Bill.

This and similar nicknames were bestowed on other hunters. The one who made the most of such a title was wind-bitten William F. Cody. Born in a log cabin on an Iowa farm early in 1846, Will had been taken to Kansas by his parents when he was eight years old. At eleven, after his father died, Will worked for a month as a mounted messenger, carrying dispatches for a freighting firm between Leavenworth and Fort Leavenworth. Then, for two months, he was a horse herder. A few years later he began making trips west as a teamster for wagon trains, and for a short time he was a Pony Express rider.

Cody's mother died in 1863; and on February 19, 1864, Will enlisted in the Union Army. His military papers described him as a five-foot-ten teamster with a fair complexion and brown hair and eyes. In the final year of the war he saw only minor skirmishes in Tennessee, Mississippi, and Missouri. In 1866, at twenty, he married a St. Louis girl who was nearly three years older than he.

After running a hotel in a Kansas village for six months and going broke, Will became a freighter; but, on his first trip, Indians captured his wagon and horses. Then, with a partner, he engaged in land speculation along the route of the new Union Pacific Railroad. For sport and meat, Cody would ride out and shoot buffaloes. Brigham, the horse he had bought from a Ute warrior, was an especially fine mount for the chase. If a buffalo did not fall at the first shot, Cody recalled later, Brigham would stop and allow a second chance. But if the second shot failed, he would go on.

When the land bubble burst, Cody and his former partner went to work at grading five miles of roadbed for the railroad. The fleet Brigham was hitched to a scraper while his master blistered his palms on the handles of a wheelbarrow.

That fall, after the railroad had reached Hays City, Cody found work more to his liking. The firm of Goddard Brothers, which had contracted to feed the railroad construction hands, wanted a hunter to bring in buffalo meat. The twenty-one-year-old Cody obtained the job and went out with Brigham and his breech-loading gun, a .50-caliber Springfield, which he called Lucretia Borgia.

A good shot, he had no trouble in killing enough meat within easy hauling of the railroad camp. Like Bill Mathewson, he had learned to approach a herd afoot and to shoot as many as he could in a single stand instead of chasing them over a wide stretch of prairie.

The railroad built on west, but Cody stayed in Hays City. At the outset of 1868 he was hunting on his own and selling meat in the new town. On Saturday, January 4, he went out with a wagon and Brigham. When he returned on the following Tuesday, he had killed nineteen buffaloes and brought back four thousand pounds of meat. He sold the meat at seven cents a pound. Within a month Cody led nine other Hays citizens on a buffalo hunt that lasted about two weeks.

Cody was proud of Brigham and liked to match him against other horses. Early in March he was trying to find someone who would pit a pony against his in a ninety-mile race to be run in twelve hours. But soon he was using Brigham in other work. In the next few years Cody received occasional assignments as a civilian scout for various military commanders, including Lieutenant Colonel George A.

Custer, General Phil Sheridan, and General Eugene A. Carr.

In the winter of 1868–9, Cody was a scout for General Carr, who was looking for Indians in No Man's Land, later the Oklahoma Panhandle. As the troops had lost their beef herd in a blizzard and had been without fresh meat for more than a month, the General had Cody take twenty wagons and drivers and go out after buffaloes. With the ground broken and covered with snow, this was not an easy chore. But on the fifth day out, the party found a small herd. As Cody came up behind them, the animals took fright and plunged into a deep arroyo filled with snow. Cody shot all fifty-five of them with his Springfield, and the men used mules and ropes to drag them out of the snowdrift. A few wagons were sent back to the camp with this meat. Before many days the party had enough meat from other buffaloes to fill the rest of the wagons.[3]

The big moment for Cody came in the late summer of 1869, when he was twenty-three. Out of a job, he was loafing at Fort McPherson, in Nebraska. He and several other men were lying under a wagon, trying to escape the flies and the heat. But he came to life quickly when a stranger called him out and began questioning him about recent Indian fighting on the frontier. The visitor was a New York author of dime novels, E. Z. C. Judson, who did most of his writing and editing under the pen name Ned Buntline.

Buntline, on his way home from San Francisco, had stopped off to see Major Frank North, who recently had outsmarted and killed a renegade Cheyenne, Chief Tall Bull. North refused to talk, but referred Buntline to Cody, who, although he had missed that scrap, was familiar with its details. Buntline quickly found in Cody the type of frontier hero he needed for his stories. He dubbed him Buffalo Bill, attributed to him the deeds of others and those concocted by his

[3] Leavenworth *Daily Conservative*, January 11, March 5, 1868; Luke Cahill: "An Indian Campaign and Hunting with Buffalo Bill"; Richard J. Walsh: *The Making of Buffalo Bill*, pp. 20–176.

3   SHEDDING SEASON

4   INDIAN CHASE

active imagination, and made his name a household word.

The publicity given him by Buntline and other fiction writers was not lost on Cody. With his new goatee, long hair, and fringed buckskins, he looked the part that the hack writers had given him. He cashed in on his new reputation by hiring out as a guide to sportsmen. After such experiences, Cody was easily wooed from the plains. Soon after helping with the hunting party of the Grand Duke Alexis of Russia, he left the West for the more promising life of depicting it on the vaudeville stage and later in the circus ring.[4]

## III

More effective than either the Clarksons or Cody in clearing the plains of buffaloes was a hardy New England youth who, with a companion, stepped off the westbound train at Hays City in the early fall of 1870. He was a blue-eyed blond, Josiah Wright Mooar, who had turned nineteen in August. Nearly six feet tall, he was a native of Vermont. His father and one of his uncles had been in the sawmill and lumber business there and in Michigan. Wright worked in a Vermont woolen mill for several summers, between terms of school.

In the winter of 1868–9, Wright attended school in Michigan, living at the home of an uncle. From there he went to Chicago, where, for a short time, he was a conductor on a Madison Avenue streetcar. Back in Vermont, he worked at weaving for most of the winter. Then he decided to seek his fortune in the West. In March 1870 he went by train to Chicago, and from there to Rochelle, Illinois, where an old friend of his father lived.

This friend was Jim Ladd, a carpenter. Wright stayed in Rochelle for three months, working for Ladd. Working with

[4] Jay Monaghan: *The Great Rascal*, pp. 1–14.

him was another youth, a little older than he—John Lindley, from Massachusetts, a nephew of the carpenter. When the wheat harvest started in midsummer, the two youths found more lucrative work in the fields. Following the reapers, they bound the sheaves of wheat by hand, with straw. When the season ended, each had two hundred dollars in his pocket. That was enough to take them to the real West.

After three days in Kansas City, Mooar and Lindley went on to some of the towns on the Kansas Pacific—a name given a year earlier to what had been the eastern division of the Union Pacific. They visited Lawrence, Topeka, Junction City, Ellsworth, and finally Hays City. This still was a wild frontier town, even though James B. (Wild Bill) Hickok had spent a term there as marshal. Its saloons and gambling rooms served a roistering crowd of soldiers, railroad workers, and buffalo hunters. Along with them were rugged bullwhackers and mule skinners, some of whom had come over the long trail from Santa Fe.

Since Wright Mooar didn't drink or gamble, he wasn't as interested in the entertainment at Hays City as in the opportunities it offered. Soon he and John Lindley found jobs chopping firewood for a contractor who supplied wood to Fort Hays. Most of the cutting was done along Walnut Creek, thirty miles south of the fort. For protection against Indians, each chopper had a rifle, which he leaned against a near-by tree while working. From their camp the woodmen often could see buffaloes on the prairie, and sometimes they could hear the boom of hunters' rifles.

In the woodmen's camp each chopper received two dollars a cord for his work, and usually he could cut two cords a day. On Sunday the men rested from their saws and axes and went out to kill a buffalo or two to keep the camp well supplied with meat. Near their camp on Walnut Creek was one kept by Charles Rath, whose wagons, each drawn by a six-

mule team, traveled from Fort Hays south to Fort Dodge and Camp Supply. On his way back north, Rath often would kill a few buffaloes near Walnut Creek and take the frozen saddles into Hays City to sell or ship them. Rath, who had lived among the Indians and spoke both Cheyenne and Arapaho, was a veteran frontiersman and one of the best of the hunters.

Wright Mooar could cut firewood as readily as the next fellow, but he hadn't come west for that kind of work. He would swing an ax only long enough to save money for putting together a small hunting outfit.

The market for buffalo meat was growing. More Easterners were acquiring a liking for the tongues and hams that could be shipped fresh in winter or in cured form at any time of year. Flesh and robes helped to save the lives of the passengers on four Kansas Pacific trains stalled in a blizzard in late December. Snowdrifts, some of them fifteen feet deep, blocked the tracks for two weeks from the cuts west of Box Elder, Colorado, to Wilson, Kansas. Two eastbound trains were held at Kit Carson and two westbound ones at Wallace. With the mercury below zero and the wind at times reaching fifty miles an hour, the passengers celebrated Christmas on the trains and feasted on buffalo meat.

After five months in the woodmen's camp, Mooar was ready for the buffalo range. He had assembled an outfit of three wagons—two drawn by horses and the other by a team of four oxen. For skinning and other work, he hired four helpers, including John Lindley. Mooar started his hunting along Pawnee Creek and the Smoky Hill River, but he ranged as far south as Fort Dodge, on the Arkansas River. He and others sold part of their meat in Hays City and shipped some to Kansas City, St. Louis, and the Illinois town of Quincy.

Like Charles Rath, who still hunted along Walnut Creek,

Mooar had the Fort Hays sutler Bill Wilson ship the meat that he couldn't sell locally. Wilson did not buy the meat, but merely handled it for the hunters. When he received the money from the buyers, he passed it on to the men who had brought in the meat.

On the buffalo range Mooar often crossed the paths of other hunters, and he became acquainted with many of them. Among those he knew, besides Charles Rath, was A. C. (Charlie) Myers, who did most of his hunting along Pawnee Creek. Another was rugged Jim White, who was in his late thirties. Jim had been a bullwhacker on the Sante Fe and Chihuahua trails and had known the excitement and danger of an attack by Indians. Later he had served as a wagon boss and a grain buyer in the Civil War. A native of Illinois, he had dropped his original name in the summer of 1868 when New Mexico officers took his trail. He had committed no crime, he told Mooar. But he had been present at a Mexican dance near Fort Union, a fandango that had ended in a brawl in which one Mexican was killed and several others were wounded.

In Kansas in that winter of 1870–1, most of those who hunted buffaloes for meat either discarded the hides or left parts of them attached to the quarters and other parts that they loaded in their wagons. "We would kill a buffalo," Mooar recalled, "and cut it in two, right down the middle. We would leave the hide and hair on. We shipped the hindquarters and the saddles."

Mooar and the other hunters sold much of their fresh meat at Hays City and other towns along the railroad, where the price had gone down to three cents a pound. By that time, buffalo steak was a regular item on the menus of Western hotels and eating houses. In winter the fresh meat shipped to Eastern cities was bought as a novelty or, in many cases, was passed off as beef. It could compete at least with the flesh of the tough Texas Longhorns being brought up the Chisholm Trail and shipped to Illinois feed lots.

With more patience than some of the other hunters, a few like the Clarksons cured part of their meat so that they could ship it at any time of the year. Charlie Myers built a smokehouse on Pawnee Creek, where he prepared buffalo hams for Eastern markets, shipping some as far as Buffalo. He divided each quarter into three chunks, sugar-cured and smoked them, and sewed them into canvas. His extra effort brought him a good price for his meat.

To the southeast, where the Little Arkansas flowed into the Arkansas River, buffalo meat was a major food item in the village of Wichita. The animals ranged to within five miles of the town and could be seen by the thousands. On a winter morning Wichita men would start out to the prairie in pairs, each pair with a wagon, and would return in the evening, the wagons loaded with meat.

There still was a market for buffalo robes, which brought eight to sixteen dollars each in New York, depending on the quality. Most of the robes continued to come through trade with the Indians, although Eastern tanneries were processing a few. But there was almost no market for the dried or flint hides. Unlike those to be converted into robes, which had to be taken in winter when the hair was thick and long, the ordinary hides could be taken at any time of the year. Tanned buffalo leather was being put to a few uses, such as machinery belting, but it was too soft and spongy for most purposes. Unless the tanneries could find a way to make this leather more serviceable, most of the hides would continue to be wasted.

As they sat about a campfire of blazing wood or glowing buffalo chips in the evening, Wright Mooar and Jim White often remarked on the waste of hides that attended the butchering of the buffaloes for their meat. If the hides could be converted into useful leather, hunting on the plains would become much more profitable and could be pursued all through the year.[5]

[5] Don H. Biggers: "Buffalo Butchery in Texas Was a National Calamity"; interviews with J. Wright Mooar, MS. transcripts in Panhandle-Plains Historical Museum, Canyon, Texas, and University of Texas library, Austin; J. Wright Mooar, as told to James Winford Hunt: "Buffalo Days," *Holland's*, January 1933, p. 13. In transcripts of interviews with Mooar, the last name of the companion with whom he came to Kansas is spelled variously as Lindley, Linley, Lindsay, and Linsey.

# DOLLARS FOR HIDES

**O**thers besides Wright Mooar and Jim White were aware that fortunes might stem from properly treated buffalo hides. Several tanneries in this country and even a few in Europe were trying to find ways to convert the skins into more useful leather and thus broaden the market. If buffalo hides could serve most of the purposes of cowhides, the buffalo's thick skin might be worth more than his flesh.

In 1870, J. N. DuBois, a Kansas City dealer in hides, furs, and wool, shipped several bales of buffalo hides to Germany, where tanners had developed a process for making them into good leather. Other orders followed, and soon some American tanners either learned of this process or developed a similar one of their own.

In the spring of 1871, DuBois sent hundreds of circulars out to the buffalo ranges, offering to buy at an attractive price all hides taken at any time of year. DuBois also encouraged the hunters by telling them how to peg the hides, flesh side up, for drying. In addition, he sold them a poison, imported from South America, to kill the bugs that infested and damaged many of the hides. Soon other enterprising dealers, including W. C. Lobenstein of Leavenworth, were finding markets for hides and buying them from hunters.

Among the men hunting buffaloes in western Kansas in the winter of 1870–1 was George W. Brown, a Missouri-born youth of twenty-three who had served with Illinois cavalry in the Civil War. In the spring of 1868, George had gone to Kansas, where, in turn, he worked on a farm, hauled wood, helped trail a herd of cattle, and served as a scout for frontier troops. In 1870, forty miles south of Denver, he helped cut ties for the Kansas Pacific Railroad.

Then, in the fall of that year, Brown and five others began hunting buffaloes in western Kansas. They worked mainly along Turkey Creek, which ran into the Smoky Hill River from the north. They lived during the winter in the ruin of an abandoned stagecoach station, which they roofed with canvas. This was eight miles from Fort Wallace. From fear of an Indian attack, the men slept in their clothes every night. They shipped their meat to Denver, where it sold readily.

In March 1871, Brown and John Burdett bought out the other partners and continued to hunt. Two months later, after spring rain and sun had sprouted the grass and burst the leaf buds, they were talking with other hunters at Fort Wallace. Brown remarked that the weather was becoming so warm that it was almost impossible to bring the meat to market before it spoiled. One of the other hunters asked: "Why don't you skin the buffaloes and take the hides and let the meat lie?"

"What the devil would I do with the hides?" asked Brown.

"Ship them to Leavenworth and sell them to W. C. Lobenstein," he said. "Lobenstein will buy your hides and send you a check for the money."

Brown knew that Lobenstein, with headquarters at Cherokee and Third in Leavenworth, was one of the West's biggest dealers in pelts, hides, and leather. So he decided to follow this advice. Soon he and John Burdett went out on the new venture. Green at skinning, they took about an hour to pull the hide off of the first buffalo they killed. But they finally hauled in about forty hides and shipped them to Lobenstein. In five days they received their checks—$1.75 for the hide of each buffalo bull and $1.25 for that of each cow. Lobenstein paid the freight. This was better than selling meat.

In the fall of that year, Brown made his headquarters in a dugout near Coyote Station, the second station west of Ellis on the Kansas Pacific. With Burdett gone, he hired as a helper a youth who had been working as a railroad section hand. Several miles away, Brown had a temporary dugout camp on a spring-fed creek that flowed into the Saline River from the south. To dry the hides, he recalled, "we made pins out of small willow sticks. Then we stretched our hides on the ground and put ten to fifteen pins in each. That would leave our hides in good condition to load on the wagon."

On the night of November 15 a howling norther struck the camp, pushing the mercury down to twenty below zero. The blizzard froze one of the horses to death and kept Brown and his helper in the dugout for four days. In another camp, on the trail six miles south of Hays City, eight woodchoppers on their way to town were caught in this storm. If they had gone on, the men might have made it into town, but they chose to camp overnight in a ravine that had plenty of wood. They built a fire, but the wind and snow put it out. Only one of the men reached the town. The others froze to death in what later was called Freeze-Out Hollow.[1]

Despite the hazards of hunting, the new market for hides quickly attracted more frontiersmen to the buffalo ranges in

[1] George W. Brown: "Life and Adventures of George W. Brown," edited by William E. Connelley, pp. 98–118.

1871. One was Dick Bussell, who had been working as a guard for railroad construction workmen at five dollars a day. He and several others made a hunt about twenty-five miles north and west of Newton. Although armed only with Long Tom needle guns and Spencer carbines, they made a good killing. They hauled their hides to Newton, which had acquired a railroad July 17, and sold them there.

One of the most successful hunters that summer was tall, black-bearded Bill James, who had been a railroad construction contractor west of Omaha. With a big outfit that included another hunter, a dozen skinners, and the necessary cooks, hide peggers, and teamsters, he took ten thousand hides along the Platte. After selling the hides for twenty-five thousand dollars, he paid his men's wages and his debts and left money at a store for provisions for his outfit and supplies for a fall hunt. Then, with the remaining twenty thousand dollars he went to St. Louis and put up at the Planters' Hotel. In sprees and gambling he lost all his money and, two months later, had to borrow enough to get back to Nebraska.

Active in the Kansas hunting in 1871 was Billy Dixon, a wind-bitten youth of West Virginia birth who had gone to Kansas late in 1864, when he was only fourteen. He had worked as a mule skinner for a big freighting outfit and later had trapped beaver, otter, and wolves along the Republican River. For a while he sold provisions and drinks at a picket-house road ranch at a spring ten or eleven miles south of Hays City, near where the trail from Fort Hays to Fort Dodge crossed the Smoky Hill River. There he sold whisky, tobacco, and groceries to the teamsters. Sometimes he left the road ranch in charge of Billy Reynolds or an Irishman named Finn while he freighted with his four-mule team.

After Reynolds skipped out with his money, Dixon turned to buffalo hunting. With hides coming into demand, he easily could make a new start. Sometimes as the only hunter and sometimes with a partner, he would go out on the range with a single wagon and two skinners, each hired at fifty dollars a month.

Dixon hunted over a wide area in northern Kansas, often going as far west as Fort Wallace. Later he drifted farther south. In the winter of 1871–2 he and Jack Callahan followed the herds back and forth along the Smoky Hill River, Hackberry Creek, the Pawnee Fork, and Walnut Creek. One of their skinners, off and on, was a redheaded Irishman, Mike McCabe. A hard worker, Mike could skin fifty buffaloes in a day; but he couldn't hang on to his earnings. When he went into town, he quickly lost his money in the gambling rooms.[2]

## I I

Meanwhile, Wright Mooar continued to kill buffaloes for their meat. In 1871 he began to do more of his hunting in southwestern Kansas, along the Arkansas River above Fort Dodge. He had four other men with him and used a Springfield Army rifle of .50 caliber. Its load was seventy grains of powder and a swedge ring ball.

Presumably to finance his wider range of hunting, which took him farther from the market towns, Mooar wrote that fall to his older brother, John Wesley Mooar, in New York, asking him to send the remaining $103 he had in a bank there.

Wright Mooar and those others who shifted to the Arkansas Valley for their hunting found this region ideal for their purpose. Along with bands of elk and antelope, the valley had an abundance of buffaloes. The river had a broad, shallow channel and low banks, which made it easy to cross except in floods. The country was one of open prairies, but it had plenty of trees along the streams to supply wood for campfires. The trees, which were of a wide vari-

[2] Olive K. Dixon: *Life of Billy Dixon*, pp. 7–76; Dick Bussell to J. Evetts Haley, Canadian, Texas, July 19, 1926, MS. transcript in Panhandle-Plains Historical Museum, Canyon, Texas.

ety, included post oak, blackjack, elm, ash, box elder, hackberry, cottonwood, persimmon, and occasionally Osage
orange or *bois d'arc*. Some of the more exposed trees were
stunted and scrubby from repeated singeing by prairie fires.

Any hunter who tired of buffalo meat could feast on wild
turkey, prairie plover, quail, or—in the spring or fall—wild
ducks and geese. The men in their camps could fall asleep to
the howling of distant wolves and awaken to the cheery call
of the meadowlark and the whistle of the bobwhite. They
could be sure they would not have to ride far to find all the
buffaloes they could skin in a day.

Yet the hunters were kept aware of the risks they took.
Blizzards could sweep down across the plains with sudden
ferocity. In their camps the men heard of the fate of the
woodchoppers who lost their lives in Freeze-Out Hollow.

Equally disheartening to the timid were the stories of Indian raids and scalpings. Details of one of the worst raids
had been seeping north from Texas to the hunters' camps.
On the flats of Salt Creek on May 17 a band of Kiowas and
Comanches had attacked a wagon train of Captain Henry
Warren, a government contractor. The Indians stole forty-
one mules and killed the wagonmaster and six of the eleven
teamsters. One man, after being scalped, was tied to a wagon
wheel and roasted to a crisp. Other victims were left stripped,
scalped, and otherwise mutilated, with surplus arrows stuck
in their bodies. Some had their heads chopped off and their
brains scooped out. Others had fingers, toes, and private
parts cut off and stuffed in their mouths. Some had their
abdomens slashed open and live coals placed inside.

To the more hardened hunters, though, the rewards
were worth the risk. And now the new demand for hides
promised greater returns from the hunting. In the winter of
1871–2, W. C. Lobenstein, the Leavenworth dealer, received
from an English tannery an order for five hundred buffalo
hides for experimental use in making leather. Lobenstein

passed his order on to Charles Rath, asking him to obtain the hides and ship them to him, at $2.25 each. As this number was too large for Rath alone to provide, he parceled the order out among his hunter friends, including Wright Mooar.

It didn't take Mooar and the other hunters long to remove and dry the hides that Lobenstein needed to fill his order from England. But after he had delivered his quota, Mooar had fifty-seven hides left. He wondered what he could do with them, since there was no local demand for hides and since Lobenstein apparently had all he could dispose of at that time. Mooar thought that there should be a better American market for such hides. So he decided to ship the fifty-seven to his older brother, John Wesley, who worked for a business firm in New York City, and see whether he could find a buyer.

Soon after learning that the fifty-seven hides were on the way, John Mooar went to the office of an old dealer in pelts and hides, J. J. Bates and Company. The elder Bates said he never had seen a dry or flint buffalo hide and that none had appeared on the New York market. He added, though, that he would like to see one. Mooar said he would have the hides stored at 91 Pine Street, where anyone could inspect them.

When the hides arrived in New York, they were hauled down Broadway in an open wagon and attracted much attention. One of the men who saw them was a Pennsylvania tanner who happened to be in the city. He followed the wagon to Pine Street, and later in the day he and another tanner from Pennsylvania called on Mooar. After examining the hides, they offered to buy them at $3.50 each to see what kind of leather could be made from them; and Mooar readily accepted the offer.

A few weeks later, Mooar heard from the Pennsylvania tanners. They were pleased with the outcome of their tests and wanted him to send them two thousand additional hides. Realizing the significance of this order, John Mooar decided to quit his New York job in the fall and go into the business of buffalo hunting with his brother Wright. With his business training and New York connections, John could handle the marketing end of the enterprise.[3]

Out in Leavenworth, W. C. Lobenstein again was soliciting hides, but he was paying less and was becoming more choosy as to quality. On June 19 he wrote to Bob Cator: "I want a large lot of buffalo hides. If you have any to sell, ship them to me and I will allow you all they are worth. They are lower than they have been during the last two months, but I always have led the market and pay more than anybody else, either here, in Kansas City, or in St. Louis. Motheaten and tainted hides are not worth as much as good ones by 50¢ to $1. I always remit promptly on arrival of the hides at Leavenworth." [4]

### III

Meanwhile, in the summer of 1872, Wright Mooar continued to hunt and skin buffaloes along the upper Arkansas River, where they were plentiful.

By this time Mooar had replaced his Springfield rifle with a new .50-caliber Sharps, made especially for buffalo hunters. This was the long-range rifle that the Indians said "shoots today and kills tomorrow." With some models weighing as much as sixteen pounds, the new Sharps was too heavy for convenient use in the saddle, but it was ideal for those who hunted afoot. As Mooar soon learned, it would kill a tough buffalo bull at six hundred yards.

Developed from earlier models of Christian Sharps and made in Hartford, Connecticut, this was rapidly becoming the favorite weapon of the hide hunters. R. W. Snyder, from

[3] John W. Mooar to J. Wright Mooar, New York, October 10, 1871, MS. in John W. Mooar Papers; J. Wright Mooar, as told to James Winford Hunt: "Buffalo Days," *Holland's*, January 1933, pp. 13, 24; J. Marvin Hunter: "John W. Mooar, Successful Pioneer."

[4] MS. in John W. Mooar Papers.

the Kansas town of Buffalo, called it the pet of the plains. Snyder had a Sharps .44 with which he killed three thousand buffaloes, once downing ninety-three in a single day. After he bought a Sharps Big Fifty, he sold his old gun to another hunter, who afterward used it to kill one hundred and nineteen in a single day. On the third day he had his Big Fifty, Snyder killed twelve buffaloes with thirteen shots.[5]

Wright Mooar, as he went up the Arkansas Valley, realized that he was edging into wilder country. Even with his long-range Sharps, he would have to watch out for Indian scalpers. Before long he learned that white renegades, too, might imperil a hunter's life. On this trip he had taken along two other men. One was a middle-aged ruffian who had drifted west from Michigan. The other was a newcomer from Maine, a little younger than Mooar. The New England youth kept the camp while Mooar and the older man, each with a wagon, hunted, skinned, and prepared meat to sell to the Santa Fe railroad graders who were working up the valley past Fort Dodge.

About a hundred miles up the river from Fort Dodge, the three made camp in an abandoned rock and sod house that had been the Aubrey Spring station of a stagecoach line. There they cut and stacked a supply of prairie hay for their horses.

One evening, as a crescent moon appeared, Mooar and his older partner put a load of meat on one of the wagons and made ready to leave the next morning. They would drive north, sell their meat at Fort Wallace, and bring back provisions. The boy would take care of the camp while they were

[5] Sharps Rifle Company catalogue, 1875. Christian Sharps, whose carbines had gained an enviable reputation for accuracy in the Civil War, died March 12, 1874. Early in 1876 the company moved into its new plant at Bridgeport, to which city it had gone from Hartford after an invitation in the preceding year by Mayor P. T. Barnum, the noted showman. In the mid-1870's the Sharps .45 proved even more satisfactory than the .44 and the .50 in buffalo hunting and virtually displaced the earlier models.

gone. But in the night Mooar awoke and heard a whispering outside his window. The older man was telling the youth that he planned to kill Mooar and take his wagon and team. It would be easy to lead friends to believe that Indians had made off with him.

Mooar slipped back into his blankets and pretended to be asleep. But sleep refused to come. At breakfast he said he was ill and would have to go back to Fort Dodge. So, taking his wagon and his share of the provisions, he drove off alone, keeping a sharp eye on the treacherous pair. When he came to a deep place in the river, he dumped all his food, fearing it might have been poisoned. Stopping only long enough to kill and butcher one buffalo, he drove on until evening, when he reached the camp of an outfit trailing north a great herd of Longhorn cattle.

After a night in the cowmen's camp, Mooar began killing and skinning buffaloes, camping alone in the woods along the river. When he had forty-two hides and eight hams in his wagon, he drove off to sell his load and to buy groceries.

On the way, he found new hunters heading west. All over the buffalo ranges, excitement was mounting. Other tanneries besides those in Pennsylvania were discovering the value of buffalo hides and were ordering them in large quantities. On July 21 the Leavenworth *Daily Times* reported that W. C. Lobenstein was doing a large business in robes and hides, shipping about three carloads a day to Eastern markets.

Out on the range, August 10 was a day that Wright Mooar would remember as long as he lived. Not because it was his twenty-first birthday, but because it brought the most impressive sight his eyes had seen. When he and his fellow hunters arose in their camps on the north side of the Arkansas River, they saw, on the south bank and beyond, the greatest mass of buffaloes they ever had seen. This enormous herd had come from the south, crossing in the night the ridge separating the valley of the Cimarron from that of the Arkansas.

West, south, and east—as far as the eye could make out —were millions of buffaloes, nearly all of them in prime condition. In relays they were drinking from the swollen stream, then seven hundred yards wide. When the flood subsided, they began crossing the river in large groups, stampeding horses in some of the camps and causing several traders to flee from their path.

The great herd took six or seven weeks to cross the Arkansas. It attracted from near-by ranges hunters who wanted to get in on the easy killing. George Causey deserted the camp of the railroad graders and became one of the most successful hunters. Another arrival on the Arkansas was the impetuous Irishman, Mike McCabe, who had worked for Billy Dixon farther north. Mooar hired McCabe as a skinner. Thousands of the mighty shaggies went down as the long rifles boomed across the prairies.

This was an ideal season for Mooar and the other hunters in southwestern Kansas. Game was as plentiful as anyone could ask, and the new and growing demand for hides made a ready market. Too, the hunters had the convenience of new rail points from which they could ship hides and meat. The Kansas Pacific, which until 1869 had been called the eastern division of the Union Pacific, was having competition from the new Atchison, Topeka and Santa Fe line paralleling it on the south. The Santa Fe, after reaching Newton in 1871, had opened service to Wichita in May 1872, and in the late summer to Hutchinson, Great Bend, and Larned. Building up the valley of the Arkansas River, it began serving the new village of Dodge City on September 19.

Dodge City, whose smallness belied its name, was a crude collection of dugouts, tents, and shacks—with a boxcar as a temporary railroad station. The chief engineer of the Santa Fe, Albert A. Robinson, had laid out the town on July 18, and settlers had begun arriving in August. The first business was a saloon opened in a wall tent about nine feet square. There two half-brothers from Toronto, George M. Hoover and J. G. (Jack) McDonald, had a large patronage. Other enterprises soon followed. But the shaggies still grazed so close to the town that sometimes Robert M. Wright, freighter and post trader, shot them from the walls of his corral for his hogs to feed upon.

When first laid out, the new town had been called Buffalo City. But, since Kansas already had towns named Buffalo and Buffalo Station, the Postmaster General in Washington vetoed the name. Then the frontier village on the Arkansas was renamed Dodge City, for the fort five miles away.

Dodge City was well situated to become the principal outfitting point and hide market for the Kansas hunters, since it was in the heart of the buffalo country. The first train to reach the new town had been held up for two hours while a herd about three miles wide and ten miles long crossed the wobbly track. The herd looked as if it contained millions of animals. Men from the train took pot shots at the nearest buffaloes. So many of the wounded were trampled to death that, after the herd had cleared the track, about five hundred carcasses were left on the prairie.

News that money from the sale of hides was burning the pockets of hunters and skinners in Dodge City quickly brought in whisky peddlers, gamblers, and sporting women. Soon visitors were calling Dodge "Hell on the Plains" and "the wickedest town in America." [6]

[6] J. Wright Mooar to J. Evetts Haley, Snyder, Texas, January 4, 1928, MS. transcript in Panhandle-Plains Historical Museum, Canyon, Texas; Robert M. Wright: "Personal Reminiscences of Frontier Life in Southwest Kansas," p. 78. Wright, born in Maryland, September 10, 1840, had gone west at sixteen. He became a freighter on the plains and in 1867 was made post trader at Fort Dodge.

## IV

While the railroad was being built from Hutchinson to Dodge City, a subcontract for supplying the construction workmen with buffalo meat was held by George Rust and Bill Tilghman. Rust had a dugout on a claim south of Ellsworth. Tilghman, only eighteen, had been reared on the frontier and was a crack shot. He was a tall, lithe, slender fellow with curly black hair that tumbled down to his neck. The pair killed forty to fifty buffalo cows a week along Sawlog Creek, about twenty miles northeast of the fort, and sent in by wagon three to four thousand pounds of meat. After their contract expired, they began hunting for hides.

Sleeping in a lodge of poles and buffalo skins, Indian fashion, Rust and Tilghman traveled up the Arkansas and on to Denver. There, with other hunters, they made their headquarters in the big warehouse of a hide buyer, Mark Bedell. With fourteen men to help with his work, Bedell was shipping a quarter-million hides that winter. He allowed hunters to spread their blankets and sleep on his piles of hides without charge, and fed them in his eating hall at fifty cents a meal.

Many of the buffaloes that Wright Mooar had seen crossing the Arkansas River in August 1872 drifted on north, making good hunting that fall as far north as the Platte. In September, when Charlie Clarkson saw the animals thick along the Smoky Hill River, he hurried out to a camp where his brothers were putting up hay on a government contract. He said Matt had better take the two teams and two men and head for the herd. Charlie and George could finish the haying.

Matt, joined later by his brothers, killed 1,300 buffaloes in three weeks and hauled the hides to Wallace, where they brought $3.50 each. The men saved only the hams of the big animals and the hindquarters of the fat cows to ship to

Topeka and Kansas City. Farther north they killed 2,400 in about forty days. Then they went northwest, crossing the Republican River and camping at a big spring. In a month they downed 800 more, hauling the hides to Kit Carson. Then, moving on to the Platte and back to the Solomon and the Smoky Hill, they killed about 7,000 buffaloes that fall, sometimes skinning 150 to 200 in a day.

By mid-October, Ellsworth, on the Kansas Pacific, was shipping five hundred hides a day, and points on the new Santa Fe line were doing a lively business. Many of the hunters had moved their headquarters to Dodge City. Not only was the new town convenient to the herds, but also it offered outfits, provisions, and liquor, as well as a cash market for hides.

Two of the leading hunters, Charlie Myers and Charles Rath, quit the ranges to start stores in Dodge City. They not only sold provisions to the hunters, but also bought and shipped buffalo hides. Their places in the camps were taken by a throng of newcomers. Among them, Jack Callahan and twenty-two-year-old Billy Dixon came down from the valleys of the Solomon and the Saline, where they had hunted during the summer. Another addition to the hunters' ranks was a hardy youth of nineteen, Illinois-born William Barclay Masterson, better known as Bat. One of the most successful hunters was sturdy, dark-haired Tom Nixon, a former Nevada miner and Kansas freighter. From his sod house just outside the military reservation, he had sold shelled corn for the horses used in laying the railroad line through Dodge. Between hunting trips, Nixon found time to operate a blacksmith and repair shop at the edge of the new town. Soon he acquired a fine race horse which he entered in matches, with cattle as stakes.

All the new towns along the Santa Fe were booming with the hide business. In Wichita the *Eagle* reported on November 7: "Thousands upon thousands of hides are being brought here by the hunters. In places, whole acres of ground are covered with these hides spread out to dry. It is estimated that there are, south of the Arkansas and west of Wichita, from one to two thousand men shooting buffaloes for their hides alone." [7]

V

In November 1872, the month in which voters elected General Ulysses S. Grant to a second term in the White House, John Wesley Mooar stepped off the Santa Fe train at the box-like station beneath the water tank at Dodge City. This was a world strangely different from the one he had left in New York City. The new town, although larger than when Wright had first seen it a few months earlier, still smelled of horse droppings and dried buffalo hides. One could hear the crack of long whips and the cussing of mule skinners. Often the muddy streets were crowded with wagons bringing in hides and carrying provisions back to the hunters' camps.

John Mooar, twenty-six, was a tall, handsome fellow of fair complexion, violet-blue eyes, and brown hair, almost black. He was dressed in city clothes and a derby hat. From the station he went to the store of Charles Rath, of whom he had heard. Finding the proprietor, he asked: "Do you know a fellow by the name of J. Wright Mooar?"

"Yes, I know him," replied Rath. "He was in here this morning and sold us some hams. He's out a few miles at his camp, but he'll be in again in about three days with a load of hides and meat."

"Well, I'm his brother."

"All right. Glad to meet you. Hang around."

John Mooar had plenty of time to look over the town, which was adding to its crude buildings. The only place to

[7] Ellsworth *Reporter*, October 17, 1872; Olive K. Dixon: op. cit., pp. 76–7; Zoe A. Tilghman: *Marshal of the Last Frontier*, pp. 22–81.

stay was the primitive two-story Cox House, whose bedrooms were unheated. There one could obtain a meal of pork and beans, with pepper sauce, bread, and black coffee, for seventy-five cents. Zimmerman's hardware store offered many types of guns and ammunition, while medicines were available at the McCary and Fringer drugstore. The stores of Rath and Myers were well stocked with clothing and provisions.

The most common and best-patronized places of business were the saloons. Besides the original one opened by George Hoover and Jack McDonald, three others had sprung up. They were the Beeson and Harris, the Murray and Waters, and that of Kelly and Beaty. Especially popular as a bartender was James Kelly, who had been a scout for Custer. Usually he was called Dog Kelly, because he kept a pack of hounds. The saloons were open most of the night and had back rooms for gambling. The games ranged from five-cent chuck-a-luck to a thousand-dollar poker pot.

The bars, gaming tables, and dance halls had no attraction for John Mooar; but in his wanderings while waiting for his brother to return, he had a taste of life on the frontier. The typical man in the street wore a pair of Colt revolvers in his belt and had his pants stuffed into his boots.

At a cabin beyond the edge of town, the newcomer found two men busy applying black paint to a white horse. Surprised, he asked what they were doing.

Ordinarily the men might have resented such a prying question; but, recognizing Mooar as a harmless tenderfoot, one of them answered: "We stole this horse down on Rattlesnake Creek last night. We're going to paint him black and sell him back to the owner." Later the new arrival heard they had done just that.

After John had been in town for three days, his younger brother drove in with a load of buffalo meat—about thirty-six hundred pounds. He sold the meat at three cents a pound. When he went into Rath's, a clerk yelled: "Hey,

Wright, here's a New York policeman after you. He's going to take you back to New York." Then Wright looked across the store and saw his brother.

After having dinner at the hotel, Wright took John out to his temporary camp on the prairie about a mile from town. There Wright spread a tarpaulin and blankets on the dry grass and made a bed that kept the two men snug and warm through the chilly night. In the morning they awoke to find two inches of snow on the ground.

That day the brothers drove to Wright's buffalo camp on Three Mile Ridge, twelve miles west of Dodge. John stayed there, doing his own cooking, while Wright drove into town with the next load of meat and hides. In Dodge, Wright Mooar met his cousin Charles Wright, who had just arrived. Since both his brother and his cousin wanted to hunt buffaloes, he hired them and Mike McCabe at fifty dollars a month.

Soon afterward the four men headed southeast, crossing the Arkansas River at Fort Dodge and going on to Kiowa Creek, forty-five miles southeast of Dodge and west of Medicine Lodge. There they camped for a month of hunting. Their take amounted to 305 hides and twenty thousand pounds of short-shank hams. Wright Mooar had Archie Dunne and other freighters haul the meat to market, giving them half of the two and a half cents a pound that it brought. He himself hauled the hides to Dodge and sold them to Eugene Le Compte, an agent for W. C. Lobenstein of Leavenworth, at $3.05 each.

Wright liked to sell to Le Compte, who usually stood out in Front Street, ready to pay cash for all hides offered him. His overcoat pockets bulged with thousands of dollars in greenbacks, those of each denomination in a separate roll.

One afternoon when he didn't find Le Compte in his usual place, Mooar began looking around for him and found him in a saloon across the railroad tracks. He was sitting at a poker table with four other men, whose looks Mooar didn't like. At Le Compte's elbow were a stack of chips and one of greenbacks. Sensing that the hide buyer might be in trouble, Mooar pretended to be impatient. Slapping Le Compte on the back, he said: "If you want those hides of mine, come out and count them. I want to get my money and go home."

"Can't you wait until I play this hand out?" asked Le Compte.

"No," replied the hunter, "I can't wait. There's another buyer on Front Street who wants my hides."

At that, Le Compte asked the other players to excuse him and walked out with Mooar, leaving his cards, chips, and money on the table. "You saved my life," he said. He knew the gamblers had framed him, but he didn't dare quit the game until the hide hunter came in and gave him an excuse.[8]

## VI

By the fall of 1872, many of the white hunters were violating the informal ban against hunting buffaloes south of the Arkansas River. A few outfits had even penetrated the Texas Panhandle, to which Dodge was the nearest railroad town. In the spring, after a winter of hunting along the Arkansas, the Cator brothers, Bob and Jim, had headed for Texas. The two young Englishmen, who had crossed the Atlantic in 1871, made a dugout at the headwaters of Palo Duro Creek and built a corral of cottonwood poles. Soon their camp was a popular stopping place for hunters and traders. Another outfit that left Dodge for Texas in 1872 was that of George W. Reighard. With him as helpers were Zeke Ford, Tom Rooney, and Jim Whalen. Reighard took along two .50-caliber Sharps rifles with telescopic sights. They used shells two and a half inches long, with 110 grains of powder.

[8] J. Wright Mooar, as told to James Winford Hunt: "Buffalo Days," *Holland's*, February 1933, p. 10; J. Wright Mooar to J. Evetts Haley, Snyder, Texas, March 2–4, 1939, MS. transcript in University of Texas library, Austin.

The business brought by the Kansas and Texas hunters gave a quick boom to the new town of Dodge City. In its first three months the Santa Fe carried out of Dodge alone 43,029 buffalo hides and 1,436,290 pounds of meat.

In Kansas the winter of 1872–3 was one of deep snows and biting blizzards, one that brought hardship to all the buffalo hunters and tragedy to some. An arctic wind swept over the plains on the night of December 18, bringing stinging snow. For eight days the hunters stayed close to their camp-fires, venturing away only to gather more fuel or to shake the snow from hides they had piled in stacks.

The storm caught a mule train of twenty wagons that had just left Fort Dodge to haul corn to Camp Supply, in the Indian Territory. This outfit, in charge of Robert M. Wright, had crossed the river at Fort Dodge and camped in Five Mile Hollow, five miles from the fort. The night blizzard took the men by surprise. By daybreak the draw in which they had camped was full of snow, and the thick flakes that continued to fall kept them from seeing from one wagon to another.

The shivering teamsters had brought only firewood enough to cook breakfast. After that was gone, they started burning corn; then they burned three of the wagons. On the second day P. G. Cook and another volunteer said they would ride back to the fort for help. Heavily bundled, they mounted sturdy mules and set out through the storm. After several hours they became lost in the blinding snow and decided to leave their course to the mules. Eight hours from the time they left the camp, they reached the fort. They were so numb from cold that they had to be thawed out of their saddles. The quartermaster, Major E. B. Kirk, sent out a relief party with a supply of wood, and the outfit came back to the fort. But Cook's companion was so badly frostbitten that he lost a leg.

By the time this December blizzard came, the Mooar outfit was back near Dodge City, in a camp close to that of Tom Nixon, which had the protection of a dugout. On the 23rd, Wright Mooar came near being shot by accident when two of Nixon's young hunters were out looking for grouse. On Christmas Day he took a tumble in the snow while on his way to Nixon's camp. But he was able to go there the next day to borrow some yeast. Some of the hunters celebrated the holidays with a stag dance in Nixon's dugout. Fiddle music was provided by one of Nixon's men, young H. H. Raymond, an Illinoian who had landed in Dodge only a little more than a month earlier.

On the 26th the Wichita *Eagle* reported bad news from the buffalo ranges to the west. Several hunters had arrived back in town with frozen hands or feet. One man had frozen fingers on each hand and one leg frozen below the knee. On the last day of the year, hunters brought into Wichita the frozen body of a man who had gone out on the range from his home near Eldorado, in Butler County. That evening, in their wintry camp to the west, Wright Mooar and Jim Barber skinned three gray wolves.

In January another blizzard struck the hunters. The Mooar brothers, each driving a wagon team, had taken loads of meat from Kiowa Creek to Mulberry Creek, in company with five of Tom Nixon's men. At Mulberry Creek this wagon train reached the old government trail leading north from Camp Supply. As the teams went on toward Dodge City on January 21, a winter blast swept down from the north, freezing ice on the eyebrows, eyelashes, and beards of the seven drivers. They hardly could see the mules in front of them. Levi Richardson was driving the lead team. Behind him were wagons driven by Pat Baker, Bat Masterson, two other Nixon men, and John and Wright Mooar.

The drivers decided to try to reach John Hunt's ranch, a trail point that had a store, a saloon, and cabins that could provide shelter from the storm. But after two hours of heading into the gale, the team of Richardson stopped, and he told the other men that one of his lead mules appeared to have frozen to death. Richardson himself was blinded by ice on his face until John Mooar, cupping his hands, blew enough warm breath to melt it.

Pat Baker said he would go ahead and drive the lead team, confident that he could make the stubborn mules move. But when he cracked his whip over their backs, they still refused to budge. Then he walked ahead and took hold of the bit of one of the lead animals, trying to tug it forward. As he struggled in the snow, working to pull the team out of its tracks, he staggered against a snow-covered wall. The animals had reached the Hunt ranch and were standing with their heads against the door of a building that the snow had buried and hidden.

Not all who were out in the storm were as fortunate as this party. Major Richard Irving Dodge, in command at Fort Dodge, cited an estimate that more than a hundred buffalo hunters were frozen to death along the Arkansas River in 1872 and 1873. The post surgeon at Fort Dodge performed seventy amputations on frostbitten hunters and railroadmen. One victim lost both hands and both feet. But more hunters kept pouring into the grass-carpeted ranges. They were willing to risk their lives for buffalo hides.

As for the Mooar outfit, Mike McCabe celebrated the return to Dodge by making the rounds of the saloons and going on such a long spree that the others went off and left him. Before beginning another hunt, Wright Mooar formed a partnership with his brother John and his cousin Charles. He lent each $250 to allow each to have a one-third interest in the firm. It was agreed that Wright would continue to do most of the shooting, while the others hauled and marketed the hides and looked after the camp. With that, the partners hired three new skinners and set out for Kiowa Creek. The supply of buffaloes still seemed endless, although the big increase in the number of hunters made it necessary for some to range farther from Dodge.[9]

[9] H. H. Raymond, diary, MS.; J. Wright Mooar, as told to James Winford Hunt: "Buffalo Days," *Holland's,* February 1933, pp. 10, 44; Wright: op. cit., pp. 80–1.

## 7

# ALONG THE CIMARRON

On the Kansas and Nebraska plains, buffalo hunting was becoming a rage. Despite the biting blizzards of the winter of 1872–3, the slaughter went on with little pause. Dodge City was crowded with hide wagons drawn by oxen and mules. Its saloons, gambling rooms, and dance halls overflowed with hunters and skinners between trips to the range. But soon most of the men were broke again and on their way out to the camps on the prairie.

Hide shipments from Dodge mounted to a new peak. At one time enterprising Charles Rath had forty thousand hides stacked in his yard. Robert M. Wright, who had quit freighting to join Rath in his business, reported that during the winter this firm shipped more than two hundred thousand hides. He estimated that together the other buyers shipped at least an equal number. Meat shipments included two hundred carloads of hindquarters and two carloads of tongues.

The most talked-of hide brought in during the winter was that of a white buffalo killed by Dave Morrow—Prairie Dog Dave. Wright paid Dave a thousand dollars for it, had it mounted, and shipped it to Kansas City. This was the only white specimen found in the whole Arkansas Valley.

As a result of the intensive hunting during the winter, the herds about Dodge were noticeably thinner by early spring. Some blizzard-bitten hunters and skinners left for other occupations. Many outfits still were on the ranges; but, to find good stands, they had to travel farther from the railroad. Some of the hide men, ignoring the oral agreement at Medicine Lodge and the danger of losing their scalps, crossed the Arkansas River and traveled south to the Cimarron or beyond, into the Indian Teritory. One of them, Sumner Beach of Ellsworth, gained the nickname of Cimarron Beach.

The hunters who went down into the Cimarron country that spring and summer were sure of finding all the hides they could handle. To them this river was much more attractive than it had been to early travelers on the Santa Fe Trail. To the pioneer traders, the Cimarron, which some called the Red Fork of the Arkansas, was a dreary and dreaded stream that suggested drought and Indian attack. The river had a shallow channel and such low banks that one almost stumbled into it before seeing it.

Often crossing the Cimarron brought encounters with treacherous quicksands. In flood, the stream might be a mile wide, holding up caravans for a week. At other times it was a mere trickle that disappeared into the porous sand, forcing travelers to dig for water for themselves and their horses and mules. For much of the course of the river, its water was too salty for drinking. Travelers unable to find springs near by had to scrape holes in the sand.

To the west, the upper Cimarron was almost without trees, although clumps of willows or cottonwoods grew in some of the bends. Except for a few dwarf cedars in the sand hills, the upper valley showed little other vegetation taller than sagebrush or prickly pear. Yet it grew enough grass to support several million buffaloes.

Tom Nixon and his outfit, which included Jim White and H. H. Raymond, left Dodge City for the Cimarron on March 6 and camped that night on Crooked Creek. The hunters reached the river the second day, and on the third they drove upstream about fifteen miles to the springs and began killing. Along with buffaloes, they found many antelope and deer. This was fine game country, abounding in wild turkeys, quail, grouse, and plover.

The Mooar brothers also went to the Cimarron, but were delayed in starting. While in camp on Kiowa Creek in the early spring, John was stricken with pneumonia. Wright brought him as quickly as possible to the military hospital at Fort Dodge. After a long struggle he overcame the disease, but his illness kept the outfit in town for six weeks. As soon as John was well enough to travel, the Mooar wagons rumbled south to the Cimarron, where the outfit hunted all summer.

Another outfit departing for the Cimarron in late spring was Billy Dixon's. During the late winter Dixon and Jack Callahan, rehiring the broke and sobered Mike McCabe as a skinner, had hunted along the Arkansas and Crooked Creek. After selling their hides in Dodge at $2.50 to $4.00 each, bringing a total check of $2,000, they went up the Arkansas again, thence to the South Pawnee, the North Pawnee, Walnut Creek, and Silver Lake. In the spring Callahan departed to go into the saloon business at Granada, Colorado; but Dixon decided to keep on hunting.

After going back to his old camp on the Pawnee Fork, Dixon forded the Arkansas in May and went up to Aubrey Crossing, on the old Santa Fe Trail. As he didn't find many buffaloes there, he worked south toward the forbidden Cimarron country. He and his outfit struck the Cimarron at Wagonbed Springs, southwest of Dodge. Finding buffaloes plentiful, Dixon and his men ranged between the Cimarron and the

5    REMOVING A HIDE

6    INDIANS HUNTING ON SNOWSHOES

Arkansas, working as far west as Bear Creek and hauling their hides to Granada, Colorado.

Still another outfit heading south in the spring of 1873 was that of young Bill Tilghman and Charlie Roudebush. Tilghman's former partner, George Rust, had died of pneumonia. His new one, who had been working for a feed dealer at Great Bend, readily quit his job to go with Bill. The two bought a team and outfit and hired Ed Robertson as a helper. Driving twenty miles south to Big Lake, they found all the buffaloes they could kill; and soon they had a load of hides for Charlie to haul to Great Bend.

Next they crossed Medicine Lodge Creek and made a new camp, where they killed and skinned about thirty-five animals a day. Everything seemed to be going well, but a few weeks later they ran into hard luck. To their chagrin, they discovered that the fourteen hundred hides stacked around their camp had been ruined by moths. Like many of the other hunters, they learned the hard way to carry a barrel of arsenic water on their wagon and sprinkle it on each hide.

All through the spring, wagons piled high with dried or flint hides kept coming in to the railroad towns. Soon their freight was stacked high on the platforms along the tracks. "The shipment of buffalo hides from this point is astonishing," said the Wichita *Eagle* on March 20. "An average of two carloads per day, or about a thousand hides per day, for the last two months has been forwarded from Wichita. Some of the hides have been consigned to Liverpool and will be manufactured into leather. The destruction of these animals for the last winter has been fearful. Whole carloads of buffalo tongues have been shipped."

From the Cimarron to the Platte, the slaughter continued. West from Dodge City a Santa Fe construction train was held up for three hours while a herd crossed the tracks. But the hunters were doing their best to clear the ranges. East of

Dodge, the small town of Great Bend shipped 4,852 hides in August. Some said that along the banks of the Arkansas a man could jump from carcass to carcass without touching the ground. Major Richard Irving Dodge, the commanding officer at Fort Dodge, wrote: "I have counted 112 carcasses of buffaloes inside a semicircle of two hundred yards radius, all of which were killed by one man from the same spot in less than three quarters of an hour." [1]

## II

By this time the more successful buffalo hunters were following, with variations, a pattern designed to bring them a large number of hides with the least possible expense of effort and time. As a rule, the lone hunter had given way to the outfit, which might vary from three men with one wagon to a dozen or more with two or three wagons. The group gave a measure of protection against attack by Indians and allowed division of work among hunters, skinners, and freighters. One unusually large outfit of sixteen men included two hunters, a cook, one man who reloaded the guns, one who pegged out the hides, and two who hauled them. The other nine were skinners.

The wagon carried water kegs, cooking utensils, sleeping rolls, and other equipment, sometimes including a small grindstone for sharpening knives. A few outfits carried tents. Others might make dugouts for winter camps, or crude huts of pickets and hides. In summer, most of the men slept on the open prairie, with only the protection of blankets or buffalo robes.

The wagon was designed for utility rather than for looks

[1] H. H. Raymond, diary, MS.; Robert M. Wright: "Personal Reminiscences of Frontier Life in Southwest Kansas," p. 78; Olive K. Dixon: *Life of Billy Dixon*, pp. 82–94; Zoe A. Tilghman: *Marshal of the Last Frontier*, pp. 85–6.

or comfort. "We threw away our spring seats whenever we were on the range," Wright Mooar recalled, "and sat down in the bed of the wagon. This was to offer as little target to the Indians as possible. We always kept one gray horse in our outfit and always worked him in the lead so that, when off killing the buffaloes, I could see him. This kept me from riding up to a bunch of Indians or some other outfit by mistake." [2]

In traveling to new camp sites and in going out on the range toward the herds, the hunters rode saddle horses; but they did nearly all their shooting on foot. By making the final approach afoot, the hunters usually could come close to a herd without starting the animals off on a run. Sometimes one marksman could kill a score to a hundred or more before the others became frightened enough to flee.

The hide hunters had abandoned shooting from horseback because it tired the mounts and wasted time and ammunition. Also, by keeping the buffaloes on the run, it left the bodies of the dead too scattered for efficient skinning and hauling. Traveling to and from the carcasses took valuable time needed for the skinning. Skelton Glenn observed that the best shot wasn't always the best hunter. The one who got ahead was "the man who piled his buffaloes in a heap to be convenient for the skinner to get at and not to have to run all over the country."

Each outfit would keep shifting its camp as the herd moved, sometimes staying a week in one place. George W. Reighard, who had a wagon and three helpers for skinning, drying, and stretching the hides and cooking the meals, used methods that were typical. Each morning, he recalled, "I went to the top of some rise to spy out the herd. I would creep and crawl, taking advantage of gullies and ridges, to

---

[2] J. Wright Mooar to J. Evetts Haley, February 11, 1928, MS. transcript in Panhandle-Plains Historical Museum, Canyon, Texas.

sneak up within range. About 200 to 350 yards was all right, the closer the better."

Reighard would choose a spot behind some natural screen —a soapweed, cactus, or bit of sagebrush. "I would lie flat on my stomach, get my guns ready, spread a lot of cartridges out on the ground, adjust the gun sights, and be ready to shoot. Usually I carried a gun rest made from a tree crotch. I would stick this in the ground and rest my gun barrel on it." [3]

The weight of the big buffalo guns made the forked stick almost a necessity. The hunter with two guns had an advantage in that he could use one while the other cooled. After repeated firing, a gun barrel would become hot and begin to expand. This would cause the bullets to wobble. Continued use might even cause the gun to explode. Hunters remembered that Hugh Henry, who had come north with a herd of Texas Longhorns and turned buffalo hunter, had had a hand ruined by an exploding rifle.[4] Some of the hide men carried a bottle of water to cool the gun barrel. Wright Mooar, if without water, would urinate on the barrel.

Only a seasoned hunter could hold a bunch of buffaloes in a stand while he downed one after another without causing the others to rush off in a stampede. George Reighard tried to find a group that was grazing slowly and seemed without suspicion of danger. Usually he tried first to pick out and shoot the leader, often an old cow. He aimed to pierce her lungs.

The victim would make a startled movement, leap forward a bit, and look around, with blood gushing from her nostrils. On hearing the report of the gun, said Reighard, the animals near the victim "would look at her, probably with an idea of running if she would lead the way, but without initiative to start a stampede. They would see her standing still and

[3] Kansas City *Star*, November 30, 1930.
[4] Indian-Pioneer Papers, MS. XLI, 204–28. Later the Oklahoma town of Henryetta was named for Hugh Henry.

would resume their grazing. The wounded cow would wobble, then stagger forward and fall."

Meanwhile, Reighard would have jammed another shell into the breech. "Watching the herd carefully, I would note any movement on the part of any buffalo to take fright and start off. That would be my next victim. It would begin bleeding, lurching unsteadily, and would fall. Several would walk up and sniff at the two on the ground. They would throw up their heads and bawl, and one or two might start off. Then I must drop them. Sometimes a whole bunch would start. Then I must shoot quickly, dropping the leaders. That would turn the others back. The idea was to keep the buffaloes milling around in a restricted spot, shooting those on the outskirts that tried to move away."

The only strange thing the buffaloes could see, he explained, "was a little puff of white smoke now and then from a distant bush or rock. Usually that was not alarming. They generally would stay—milling, bawling, bewildered—until most of them were shot."

Reighard made his biggest kill as he lay on a slight ridge behind a tuft of weeds, a hundred yards from a bunch of about a thousand buffaloes that had come a long distance to a creek. After drinking their fill, they had started to lie down. Reighard killed about twenty-five of them, then changed guns. By the time he was ready to change back, the air was so thick with smoke, with no wind to carry it away, that he no longer could see the buffaloes. So, carrying his guns, he had to crawl to another position on the ridge. From there he killed fifty-four more.

From his two positions, in an hour and a half, Reighard fired ninety-one shots and killed seventy-nine buffaloes. By that time his right hand and arm were so sore that he was not sorry to see the rest of the herd start off at a brisk run that soon carried them out of range.[5]

[5] Kansas City *Star*, November 30, 1930.

### III

The Mooar brothers followed a routine similar to that of Reighard. Wright Mooar would leave the camp on horseback at nine in the morning, followed by his wagons and skinners. He did most of his killing between ten o'clock and noon. That gave the skinners time to get the hides off and back to camp before dark. It wasn't safe to leave the skinning until the next day, since wolves likely would get at the carcasses and tear the hides. Also, day-old carcasses were harder to skin.

One reason why Mooar didn't start shooting earlier in the day was that he wanted the buffaloes to complete their morning grazing. Then they would be less restless and easier to handle. As he approached the herd, he would stake his horse and go closer afoot. Finally he would get down on his hands and knees, wearing pads to protect his knees, and crawl still closer. To avoid startling the animals, he usually wore a hat as near the color of grass as he could find.

Wright Mooar regarded a shot in the lungs as even better than one in the heart. "When you'd shoot a buffalo in the lights," he said, "he'd throw blood out of his nose. Then he'd step backward a step or two, flop over, and die. If you shot him through the heart, he'd run about four hundred yards before he'd fall, and he'd take the herd with him."

There was much science to killing a buffalo, Mooar explained. "You had to shoot at the vital spot. Usually you were quite a distance from the buffalo. Your bullet described an arc, and you must judge the distance and tell how much above the vital spot to shoot to hit it. As the slightest wind, at a considerable distance, will deflect the bullet, you must judge the wind."

One would think, he said, "that ordinary air wouldn't drift the bullet away. I've killed hundreds of buffaloes when the air was drifting sideways. I'd draw my bead on the horn and would hit the right place. The greater the distance, the more the wind would drift the bullet."

When slipping up on a herd, Mooar, like most of the other hunters, tried to pick the leader. Not always, he noted, would the leader be the largest buffalo. Nor would he always be at the head of the bunch. "Sometimes he would be behind. There was something about him that told me he was the one. Sometimes there would be two or three leaders to the bunch. Sometimes I failed to pick the leader; but as soon as I shot, I always knew. The moment they broke after a shot, I could tell whether I had picked the right one. If I had not, I quickly threw another cartridge into my gun and killed the leader as soon as I could, to get a stand. As soon as I killed him, the others would stop running. They would mill around, bellow, paw the ground, and smell the blood."

Then Mooar would move up to a new position. "The best bunch you'd get a stand on," he said, "was one of two or three hundred. We'd try to get within one hundred yards, but I've killed more buffaloes at two hundred yards than at one hundred. I never used a rest stick. I shot off my knee or sat down and rested both elbows on my knees. Sometimes I lay flat on my stomach, with elbows spraddled."

After making his day's kill, Mooar would sit on a knoll and watch his men scattered about the prairie as they did their work of skinning and loading. His main concern was to see that no Indians bothered them. At various times the Mooar brothers used one to six skinners, but usually they had three wagons and four skinners.

"The men in the wagons would stay at a distance and watch the shooting," said Wright. "When I got through and gave them the signal, they'd go to the first buffalo and skin him and throw the hide in the wagon. When we were saving meat, they could skin and cut more meat than a team could pull. I used to have four skinners go out with me with two wagons, and a fellow would come along with three or four yokes of steers and two wagons and follow the skinners."

The skinners would leave the hide and meat where they worked, and the freighter would come along and load them in his bull wagon. "When he had it loaded, he'd tell the skinners that was all he could take, and they'd load the rest in their wagons."

Usually the Mooars saved only the hams and tongues to sell and the humps to eat in camp. If buffaloes were scarce, they used also the clod pieces cut out of the shoulder. They cut each ham into four or five pieces, separating them in the seams.

In camp the Mooar outfit varied the diet of hump with tongues. After being boiled until tender, the tongues were fried in marrow from the big bone of the buffalo hip. "We pushed the marrow out with a stick," said Wright Mooar. "We poured it into a barrel. It wasn't hard like tallow but was soft like lard. We used it to season biscuits. Sometimes we stuck bones in the fire and roasted them, then used the marrow as butter."

In curing meat to be sold, the Mooars would dig a square hole and line it with a fresh green hide, pegging the edges to the ground at the rim of the hole. This would hold about a thousand pounds of meat. The men would salt the meat and leave it in the hole seven or eight days, then take it out and wash it. Next they hung it in a smokehouse made of poles and hides and built a slow fire under it. The fire was made in a small hole in the ground. Green wood was used, as it smoked more than dry wood and gave the meat a better flavor.

The hide hunters used a great variety of weapons, from old Kentucky muzzle-loaders to condemned Spencer military rifles. The Henry, the Remington, and the Winchester had their partisans. Other hunters agreed with Bill Cody in preferring the .50-caliber, single-shot, breech-loading Springfield, which some called the Long Tom. But most of the professional hide men who could afford one chose the Sharps Big Forty-five or Big Fifty, whose long range made them especially effective in killing buffaloes.

Bill Tilghman and Billy Dixon preferred a Sharps when they had a choice, and Wright Mooar used two of them for most of his killing. With its strong action and breech, the Sharps could handle unusually heavy bullets and powder charges. It suited those hunters who wanted to place a big piece of lead accurately at a long range.

The term *needle gun,* which crops up in some accounts of buffalo hunting, was used loosely. Originally it appears to have been applied to the Dryse rifle, which a German, J. N. von Dryse, developed in 1836. This was a single-shot, breech-loading rifle, with a bolt breech closure. It fired a conical bullet encased in a paper cartridge, together with a powder charge. The Prussian Army used it against Austria in 1866 and against France in 1870. But on the buffalo ranges, as one of the hunters, John R. Cook, pointed out, any trap-door breech-block might be called a needle gun.

Sometimes a hunter would have a gunsmith make a change in his rifle to adapt it to his special needs. Charlie Justin had the metal sights taken off his guns and bone ones put on to avoid the reflected glare of the sun.

Of his Sharps rifles, Mooar preferred the smaller one. "I killed 6,500 buffaloes with my fourteen-pound gun," he estimated, "and 14,000 with the eleven-pounder. The barrel was octagonal half way up from the breech, then it was round." The brass shells, some of them bottlenecked, were three inches long. Many hunters, including Mooar, preferred to load their own shells with black gunpowder.

Wright Mooar, who bought bullets by the thousands and powder in twenty-five-pound kegs, used to wrap a piece of paper around each bullet before he put it in the shell. Wrapping the bullets instead of greasing them, he explained, kept the interior of the rifle barrel from becoming coated with lead. "The bullets were made with a concave butt. When the barrels of our guns became so hot that they began swelling, the bullets with the concave butt would be expanded when shot by the charge of powder, thus filling the barrel and making it true."

When he loaded the shells, Mooar said, "I would fill the shell with powder within half an inch of the top. When I got the powder in, we set the shell down and put the rimmer in and hit it a lick with the hammer, putting a wad on top and then a little powder on top of the wad and the bullet on top of the powder. As time went on, we went a little stronger on powder until we loaded a 90-grain cartridge with 100 to 110 grains."

Since every type of rifle made a different boom, the hunters soon learned to tell one from another. "I knew the sound of every one of my guns," said Wright Mooar. The white men on the range felt safe as long as they heard only the big guns of the hide hunters. But the sharp crack of a smaller rifle alerted them to a possible attack by Indians.[6]

## IV

The skinners who followed the marksmen had hard work that quickly smeared them with grime, blood, and vermin. Most of the skinners were paid thirty to fifty dollars a month, but some worked at piece rates, commonly twenty-five cents a hide, or for a share in the proceeds. Usually they worked in pairs, and the most expert ones did their tasks with amazing speed.

To prop the carcass in a position for convenient skinning, the men used a prod stick, sometimes called a pritchell stick. This was about three feet long, with one end sharp-

[6] J. Wright Mooar to J. Evetts Haley, Snyder, Texas, November 25, 1927, MS. transcript in Panhandle-Plains Historical Museum, Canyon, Texas; Stanley Vestal: *Queen of the Cowtowns: Dodge City*, pp. 40–1.

ened and with ,a nail driven through the other. The men
stuck the nail into the flesh of the carcass and the sharp
end of the stick into the ground. This kept the dead buffalo
on his back and threw his legs out of the way.

The skinners used various methods. Ordinarily, with a
pointed ripping knife, sharp as a razor, one man slit the
hide from beneath the lower jaw, along the neck, and down
the belly to the tail. Then he ripped the hide down the inside of each leg. Next, the skinners, with a crescent-
shaped but less pointed skinning knife, cut around the neck,
taking the ears but leaving the skin of the head, and loos-
ened the hide from the carcass. Finally, with a rope
noosed around the skin of the buffalo's neck and ears, a
horse pulled off the hide. If no horse was at hand, the skinners kicked the hide under and flopped the carcass over and
off the hide.

A variant method was described by John R. Cook: "We
fastened a forked stick to the center of the hind axletree of
a wagon, letting the end drag on the ground on an incline of
twenty degrees, and fastened a chain or rope to the same
axle. Then we drove up quartering to the carcass and hooked
the loose end of the chain over the front leg. After skinning
the upper side down, we started the team and pulled the
dead animal up a little and stopped. The stick prevented
the wagon from backing. Then we skinned the belly down
mid-sides, started the team again, and pulled the carcass
over, having rolled the first side of the hide close to the
backbone. Next we skinned down to the backbone, and the
hide was separated from the carcass. Then we threw the
hide in the wagon and proceeded as before until all the hides
were skinned." [7]

To keep their knives sharp, the skinners carried butch-

[7] John R. Cook: *The Border and the Buffalo*, pp. 116–17. Cook, a hunter
from Ohio, knew many of the other hunters in Texas.

er's steels in their belts. To supplement the frequent whet-ting, some occasionally used a small grindstone that they might have in their camp or find in that of a near-by outfit.

Loading the hides was no easy task. A green bull hide might weigh eighty to a hundred pounds. The skinners rolled each hide and lifted it into the wagon to be hauled back to camp. There it was spread out on the grass, hair side down, to cure in the sun. Arsenic or another poison was sprinkled on each side of the hide to kill insects. To hold it taut, the men drove sharpened pegs, six or seven inches long, through slits cut near the edges. A big hide might have as many as two dozen pegs.

After three to five days of sun, the skin was dry and stiff. Then it was turned over to dry on the other side. Of-ten a camp had hides drying in several rows two hundred or more yards long.

Usually the hides, when fully dried, were crimped or folded once down the middle, with the hair inside, and piled in stacks to await loading and hauling. Some freighters, though, loaded them flat, without folding. The cured or flint hides had lost about half their green weight. They ranged from twenty pounds for a small cow to fifty for a large bull. The average was about thirty pounds for a cow hide and about forty for a bull hide.

A sturdy wagon could haul five hundred flint hides. While most of the hunters hauled their hides into town, some sold to buyers who, with their wagons, made the rounds of the larger camps. In the early years of hide hunt-ing, oxen drew most of the wagons. Later many of the oxen were replaced with mules, which made better time.

Some of the hunters were beginning to set records that would be hard for their grandchildren to believe. One Kansas marksman, Zack Light, while out in the winter of 1873–4, crouched in a wallow with his Sharps Big Fifty. From that single position he downed 74 head. He killed 2,300 buffaloes that season. Thomas Linton of Troy, Kansas, who also used a Sharps, had killed more than 3,000 in 1872.

Those marks did not stand long. Wright Mooar once shot 96 from a single bunch. Kirk Jordan, who had three four-horse teams and twenty men in his outfit and sold hides in towns along the Santa Fe Railroad, was said to have killed 100 in his best stand. Charles Rath left his business in Dodge City long enough to show that he had not lost his prowess as a hunter. Down on the Canadian River in 1873, he shot 107 buffaloes in a single stand. In Montana, Vic Smith would tie that figure in the winter of 1881–2, taking about 5,000 hides during the season. Another hunter in the North, Doc Zahl, was said to have killed 120 in one stand. In the Texas Panhandle, Frank Collinson, using a fifteen-pound Sharps .45, downed 121. His record probably was exceeded only by that of Tom Nixon, who killed 204 in one stand.

Even more impressive to his fellow hunters was the mowing down of 120 head by Nixon in forty minutes. He did this on September 15, on the headwaters of Bluff Creek, in Meade County, Kansas. After picketing his horse in a ravine, he crept toward a small herd. The first crack of his heavy rifle caused the buffaloes to move about uneasily, but soon they began nibbling again at the grass. When the victim, shot in the lungs, fell a few minutes later with a bellow of rage, the other buffaloes smelled the blood and began to bawl. Their pawing and bellowing kept them from hearing Nixon's later shots.

At this stand Nixon used two rifles. When one became too hot, he threw the breech block down, ran a wet cloth through it, and let it cool while he used the other weapon. From that day on through October 20, Nixon killed 2,173 buffaloes.

In a later year Orlando A. (Brick) Bond killed 300 in a single day. From mid-October to mid-December 1876, Bond slaughtered 5,855 animals, or an average of about 97 a day. Using a Sharps Big Fifty rifle with an octagonal barrel and a tripod, he kept five skinners busy. Finally he was deafened by the sound of his own gun. In Texas, Joe McCombs downed 4,900 in the winter of 1877–8.

Jim Cator, who hunted in Kansas and later in the Texas Panhandle, was said to have killed more than 16,000 buffaloes in three years, 1872–5. Wright Mooar estimated that he downed 20,500 in his nearly nine years of hunting. William Frank (Doc) Carver, who later became a showman, claimed that he killed 160 buffaloes from horseback in one day in Nebraska in the winter of 1873. He said that he killed 5,700 in 1875 and estimated that he shot at least 30,000 during his hunting career. But the inaccuracy of the memory of Carver on other points casts doubt on the uncorroborated figures he gave out in his declining years.[8]

## V

For many Kansans, 1873 was a trying year. Grasshoppers ravaged the crops of so many farmers that the Army sent several companies of soldiers to the Republican River to obtain buffalo meat to keep the families from starving. But the troopers found that nearly all the buffaloes already had been slaughtered by the hide hunters.

Even down on the Cimarron the supply was beginning to lessen. Late in the summer, after hearing of large herds in the Panhandle of northwestern Texas, Wright Mooar and John Webb rode south to see for themselves. Each took along his Big Fifty, two or three hundred rounds of ammunition, and a pocketful of salt. They could sleep on their saddle blankets and live on wild game.

[8] Dodge City *Times*, August 18, 1877; Harry Young: *Hard Knocks*, pp. 56–7; Vestal: op. cit., pp. 43–4; Raymond W. Thorp: *Spirit Gun of the West*, pp. 67–75. Kirk Jordan had lost his family in an Indian raid in northwestern Kansas. The savages burned the home and drove off all the livestock.

The pair crossed the north prong of the Canadian River, known as Beaver Creek, at a point about twenty miles east of the future site of Beaver City. Riding on into Texas, they crossed Wolf Creek and turned west on the divide between the North Canadian and the South Canadian. They rode until they came in sight of Tucumcari Peak.

Before they reached the breaks of the South Canadian, they found buffaloes in an almost solid mass as far as they could see. There were hundreds of thousands of them, fattening on the upland grass. "All day," said Mooar, "They opened up before us and came together behind us." Pushing on west through the lanes they made in the great herd, the two saw all the shaggies that a hide hunter could desire. After camping that night in the midst of the herd, they turned back north. They reached the Cimarron at Wagonbed Springs, then turned down the valley to their home camp.

When they returned to Dodge City, the Mooars and others who had been hunting along the Cimarron found the valley of the Arkansas almost as populous with hunters as with buffaloes. Construction on the Santa Fe Railroad had halted at Granada, Colorado, on July 17; and many of the workers laid off there had turned to buffalo hunting. Then, in September, came a severe financial panic, making it unlikely that the railroad building would be resumed soon. The panic also caused cattle prices to fall, thus throwing some cowboys out of work and leading them to turn to the buffalo ranges.

Overproduction already had caused a sharp decline in the prices of buffalo hides. Those hauled into Dodge City on September 6 brought only 80 cents to $1.50 each. With too many hunters and too few buffaloes on the Arkansas River ranges, and with prices down, hide hunting had become much less profitable there.

Signs of butchery were apparent all along the river. William Blackmore, a sportsman from London who traveled thirty to forty miles along the north bank of the Arkansas east of Fort Dodge in the fall of 1873, was shocked by what he saw. "There was a continual line of putrescent carcasses," he wrote, "so that the air was rendered pestilential and offensive to the last degree. The hunters had formed a line of camps along the banks of the river and had shot down the buffaloes, night and morning, as they came to drink. I counted sixty-seven carcasses on one spot covering four acres."

With more newcomers at work along the Arkansas, the slaughter had become more wasteful than ever. So many hides were lost to wolves, insects, and improper skinning and drying that every hide sold represented two to twelve buffaloes killed. For the professionals who demanded an abundant supply, the Kansas hunting had about played out.

The scarcity of live buffaloes along the Arkansas made the hunters in Dodge City listen closely to the story that Wright Mooar and John Webb brought back from the Texas Panhandle. Many wanted to hunt in Texas, but they weren't sure that such a venture would be worth the risk of their scalps. Too, some wondered if, by going so far south of the established line of the Arkansas, they would incur penalties imposed by the government.

Finally they decided to ask the view of the commanding officer at Fort Dodge, Major Richard Irving Dodge. As delegates, they chose Wright Mooar and another young hunter, Steel Frazier. The two, after donning new clothes, rode six miles to the fort and obtained an audience. After introducing themselves, they explained the hunting situation and asked the major what his policy would be if they and other hunters crossed the Neutral Strip to hunt buffaloes in Texas.

Major Dodge, himself a hunter for sport, seemed glad to see the hide men and asked Mooar many questions about his trip south and about the habits of the buffaloes. But, before they left, Mooar pinned down the commander for an answer to his question: "Major, if we cross into Texas, what will be the government's attitude toward us?"

"Boys," he replied, "if I were a buffalo hunter, I would hunt where the buffaloes are." [9]

[9] J. Wright Mooar: "The First Buffalo Hunting in the Panhandle"; J. Wright Mooar, as told to James Winford Hunt: "Buffalo Days," *Holland's*, February 1933, pp. 10, 44.

---- ⑧ ----

# SOUTH INTO TEXAS

**T**o the restless hide men, the Texas Panhandle had become a loadstone. Now that the Army no longer barred the way, the flat plains to the south, teeming with buffaloes, loomed more attractive than ever. In the Dodge City saloons and around the campfires, Texas was on almost every tongue in that fall of 1873. Some of the hardier hunters and skinners were ready to start.

The stubble-faced men knew that the danger of Indian attack would be greater than in Kansas. Although Texas had moved nearly all of its bronze warriors to the Indian Territory, bands of Comanches and Kiowas often slipped away from their reservations. They rode old trails into Texas to hunt buffaloes, to steal horses, to burn the cabins of settlers, to scalp, and to take captives for ransom.

The Indians resented the hide hunters more than any of the other intruders. They were alarmed by the slaughter and waste of the animals they had depended on for much of their living. They would kill the whites at almost every opportunity. The high plains of the Texas Panhandle would not be safe for lone hunters; the men would have to band together in fairly large groups to have any assurance of being able to repel an attack.

At this point Charlie Wright, cousin of the Mooars, decided that he'd had enough of the buffalo hunting and withdrew from the partnership. John Webb, just back from the Texas Panhandle, also concluded that the risk of hunting there was too great, although he might do some freighting.

"Wright, I've had all I want of it," he said.

But John and Wright Mooar chose to hunt in Texas in spite of all the redskins. In September they made ready for an expedition that would keep them on the wind-swept Texas ranges all winter. On the 13th, Wright took one of his wagons to Tom Nixon's shop and had H. H. Raymond repair it. The next day he was there again to have the hammer on one of his guns fixed.

Finally the outfit was ready. The two Mooars, with four teams and ten men for skinning and hauling, set out for the wilds of the Lone Star State. Crossing the Arkansas River, they drove south through familiar hunting grounds to the Cimarron. Beyond, they went on through the eastern part of the almost barren Neutral Strip or No Man's Land, later Beaver County in the Oklahoma Panhandle. After reaching the high, flat plains of Texas, carpeted with lush grass, they hunted awhile in the breaks of the South Canadian. There they had several set-tos with New Mexican outfits—Comancheros—engaged in contraband trade with the Indians. One of the parties attacked the Mooar camp, but failed to inflict any casualties.

Then, in November, the Mooar outfit turned back and pitched camp near the dugout of Jim Cator, who had come down from Kansas in the preceding year. This was on Palo Duro Creek, in what later became Hansford County. There they found the hunting good and took many hides.

This country still was beyond the fringe of settlement. The Indians and the buffalo herds made it too risky for either farmers or cattle raisers. The fenceless land belonged to the state, which had retained the public domain of the former Republic of Texas when it joined the Union twenty-eight years earlier. This broad expanse of plains was not policed, except for an occasional troop movement in mainly futile pursuit of Indian raiders.

Several other groups of white hunters followed the tracks of the Mooar wagons south from Dodge. One was led by George Causey and Sam Carr. Another was headed by two men known only as Lane and Wheeler, who had ten helpers. This outfit camped under a bluff, six or seven miles west of the Mooars, and soon had stacks of hides.

Each outfit, Wright Mooar recalled, "would take a wagon, a keg of water, a roll of bedding, and a little grub and, with a four-mule team, would drive out on the divide that separates the North Palo Duro from the Canadian. There we would intercept the buffalo herds that were crossing, east to west, from the headwaters of Wolf Creek to the Blue and the Coldwater. We stayed there on the divide until we loaded our wagon with hides and meat. We could haul 10,000 pounds with four mules when the ground was frozen. We could load, come back to camp, unload, and go back again. We could keep track of Wheeler's outfit, and his of ours, by the sound of the guns. If either of us got into trouble, the other would know it because the sound of the buffalo guns would be interrupted with the reports of lighter guns."

In February the Lane and Wheeler outfit did run into trouble, not out on the range but in its own camp. One morning, while the men were eating breakfast, eight or ten Indians rode into the camp. They got off their horses to look around, and one of them picked up something. Wheeler, who had a quick temper, reached for a blacksnake whip and struck the Indian with it. At that, the visitors grunted, got back on their ponies, and rode down the river. But, unknown to the hunters, they circled back and approached the camp by crawling through the grass on the near-by bluff. From this ambush, one of them shot Wheeler, the bullet penetrating just below his collarbone. The bullet could be felt in the flesh of his back.

A brother of Wheeler brought him to the Mooar camp, but the men there were unable to help him. So the wounded man was taken by wagon over the long trail back to Dodge City. By the time he reached there, he was feverish and unable to eat. He was taken by train to Wichita, where soon afterward he died.

Several other hunting outfits were roaming about the Texas Panhandle that winter. One, with Billy Dixon as a hunter, crossed the South Canadian and went on to Palo Duro Canyon. But it did more prospecting than hunting. Dixon returned to Dodge City in February to prepare for a bigger hunt in Texas in the spring.

That winter the prices of hides slumped further. The excess of the supply over the demand hit the hunters a hard blow. So did the business depression brought on by the financial panic of September. Dealers who had been paying three dollars for almost any hide delivered at a railroad town began checking hides for size and quality. Most of them offered only a dollar for a bull hide, sixty cents for a cow hide, and forty cents for a calf hide. Yet, if he hunted where buffaloes were plentiful, an expert marksman could get along, even at those low prices. Many were ready to try their luck in Texas.[1]

[1] Olive K. Dixon: *Life of Billy Dixon*, pp. 94–110; J. Wright Mooar to J. Evetts Haley, Snyder, Texas, November 25, 1927, MS. transcript in Panhandle-Plains Historical Museum, Canyon, Texas; J. Wright Mooar, as told to James Winford Hunt: "Buffalo Days," *Holland's*, February 1933, p. 44. Dodge City was closer to the Texas Panhandle than was the nearest Texas railroad point.

## II

In March 1874 so many of the hunters in and about Dodge City were preparing to move down into the Texas Panhandle that A. C. (Charlie) Myers decided to go with them. Myers, a former hunter, had been successful as a merchant and hide shipper in Dodge. He was known afar for the sugar-cured, boneless hindquarters of buffalo meat from his smokehouse on the Pawnee Fork. Now that the hunting around Dodge had almost played out, Myers wanted to move his business to a more favorable location.

With only two wagons and teams of his own, Myers had to find a way to transport the rest of his fifty-thousand-dollar stock of goods for the store he planned to open in the Panhandle. For part of this hauling, he engaged a former hunter who claimed that once he had killed 106 buffaloes before breakfast. He was E. C. (Ed) Jones, about twenty-three and better known as Dirty Face Jones. He had turned freighter after the buffaloes became scarce in Kansas. Since the hunting outfits would be going to Texas with almost empty wagons, he engaged several of them to help haul the stock. When the caravan finally was ready to pull out, it included about fifty men and thirty heavily loaded wagons. Each man had a saddle horse and was well armed—as ready for redskins as for buffaloes.

Some of the men on the expedition were old enough to be veterans of the Civil War. Others were adventurous youths like Billy Dixon, twenty-three, and Bat Masterson, twenty. Yet nearly all were seasoned to the rigors of frontier life. One of them, James Hanrahan, in addition to taking along his hunting outfit with seven skinners, brought a stock of liquor so that he could open a small saloon at whatever place Myers decided on for his store.

On leaving Dodge, the long caravan splashed across the Arkansas River and headed south, over a trail that many of the hunters had followed. The first night camp was made on Crooked Creek. The fresh March air had whetted appetites for the dinner served around the campfires. After the meal, several men unpacked fiddles and harmonicas, while others pegged down a dry buffalo hide for jig dancing. It was late before the camp entertainment gave way to the howls of wolves and coyotes on the distant hills.

The second day's drive brought the party to the Cimarron, beyond which lurked greater danger of Indian raiders. Putting the heavily loaded wagons across the sandy bottom of the river was an arduous job, but it was completed without accident. On the south bank, the travelers gathered to decide what they should do if they met a band of Indians. They agreed that if the Indians showed signs of being friendly, the whites would do likewise. But they needed to guard against a surprise attack.

Crossing No Man's Land often brought heavy pulling through sand and rough country, but on the fourth day out from Dodge the party reached the Beaver, the main prong of the North Canadian. Heading on south, the caravan reached the mouth of Palo Duro Creek and began to pass the camps of buffalo hunters who had gone earlier to the Panhandle. One of the camps was that of Bob and Jim Cator and Fred Singer. The hunters were glad to see the newcomers, since added numbers assured better protection against hostile Indians.

Looking for the best buffalo country, the party from Dodge moved on south to the source of Moore's Creek, a narrow, swift-flowing stream with steep banks. Disappointed by the sparsity of the grass there, the hunters followed this creek down to the South Canadian, which flowed through a broad bed of reddish sand.

While camped on the South Canadian, the men decided to play a trick on one of their number. The victim was a tenderfoot who had joined the party shortly before it left Dodge and who seemed overeager to shoot Indians. Since hundreds of wild turkeys had been roosting each night in a grove of cottonwoods above the camp, the hunters invited the greenhorn to go out with some of them at night and shoot a few.

In advance, Bat Masterson and two others went secretly to the woods and built a small fire, one that would look like an Indian campfire. Then he and Charlie Myers and the tenderfoot went out after dark, all well armed. When they came near the fire, Bat said he was sure it had been built by Comanches. Then half a dozen shots whizzed through the branches. Bat and Charlie, as they fired a few shots into the woods, yelled for the greenhorn to run for his life.

Out of wind, the victim reached the camp with just enough breath left to yell that the woods were full of Indians and that Masterson and Myers had been killed. One of the men—all of whom were in on the joke—ripped the victim's shirt down the back, and another poured on his bare skin the contents of the coffeepot, which made him fear that he'd been wounded. He was ready to head back to Dodge at once and was furious when he learned later that night that he'd been duped.

While looking about for a site for a permanent camp, the hunters spent a night on the north side of the South Canadian. They were near the ruins of an old fortified trading post a mile above the mouth of a clear, swift stream later called Bent Creek. This place, called Adobe Fort or Adobe Walls, had been built by William Bent about 1843. Soon afterward his trading company abandoned it as a post because the Comanches and Kiowas in the region remained hostile. Late in 1864 troops led by Colonel Kit Carson made use of the crumbled walls in a battle against marauding Indians. When the buffalo hunters arrived, nearly a decade later, remnants of the walls still stood four or five feet high.

The hunters liked this part of the plains, which appeared to be fine buffalo country. It had a good stand of bluestem grass, along with some bear grass, pokeweed, and sagebrush. Beside the creeks were thin strips of woods, mainly cotton-wood, hackberry, and willow, with occasional plum trees, chinaberries, and skunk brush. The men decided to look no farther for a camp site.[2]

## III

The spot chosen was a mile or so northeast of the ruin, on the west side of a little stream which the hunters called Adobe Creek. The men unloaded the wagons near the center of a meadow that gave a view of the silvery South Canadian on the south and an irregular string of hills on the east, north, and west. Before they began hunting, some of them lent Charlie Myers a hand in building a crude picket store, about thirty by sixty feet. Dirty Face Jones and others, with four-mule teams, hauled small logs from the Canadian. The logs were set upright in trenches to form the walls. Near by, to the south, Jim Hanrahan put up a sod house, twenty-five by sixty feet, for use as a saloon. Between the two, Thomas O'Keefe drove pickets into the ground to build a blacksmith shop fifteen feet square. All three buildings faced the east. All had sod roofs on a framework of poles.

While this construction was under way, Billy Dixon and three others rode southeast as far as the future site of Clarendon to look over the country. They found some buffaloes, along with many deer and wild turkeys. When they arrived back, fifteen days later, the three buildings were almost completed. In addition, Charles Rath had come down from Dodge City with a big wagon loaded with twenty-thousand-dollars' worth of goods for a branch store to compete with

[2] Dixon: op. cit., pp. 110–34.

that of Charlie Myers. Rath was building a sod house just south of the saloon. A little smaller than the Myers store, it had doors in the east and west ends and two windows on the south side. Rath had brought along a carpenter, Andy Johnson, to make the windows and doors. Johnson, aged twenty-eight, was of Swedish birth. He had hunted buffaloes for Rath and had worked in his hide yard at Dodge. Rath left this branch of his Dodge store in charge of James Langton. All four places were open for business by the first of May.

To provide more safety for the horses of those who would use the new trading post, Myers built a stockade corral about two hundred feet square, with his store forming the northeast corner. He hired any men he could to cut cottonwood logs along Reynolds Creek, about six miles away, haul them across the Canadian, and set them in the ground. In the southwest corner of the corral the men built a storehouse of logs, with a lookout on the top. Later this building served also as a mess house.

Quickly this cluster of picket and sod buildings became the headquarters of the Panhandle buffalo hunters. Despite its use of different materials, the men called it by the name of the near-by ruin, Adobe Walls. The two stores, the saloon, and the blacksmith shop did a big business from the start. Soon the merchants had to send back to Dodge City, 150 miles to the north, for new stock.

Before long, wagon trains were on the road north with loads of buffalo hides. In one, John Mooar went with a man named Warren, who had a family in Dodge and wanted to stay there, and the freighter Dirty Face Jones. Each drove a six-mule team that pulled two wagons. On the return trip Mooar and Jones brought new stocks for the Adobe Walls stores.[3]

3 Ibid., pp. 134–7; J. Wright Mooar, as told to James Winford Hunt: loc. cit.

## IV

By this time the hunting outfits were scattered over much of the Panhandle and were finding all the buffaloes they could kill and skin. One of the smaller outfits was that of Billy Dixon, who went out for hides two days after returning from his first excursion. With him were two skinners— Charlie Armitage, who had come over from England, and a Frenchman known only as Frenchy. The latter did most of the cooking and was an expert at broiling buffalo steaks.

After going up the South Canadian as far west as Hell's Creek, the Dixon outfit crossed the river and followed the Fort Bascom Trail to Antelope Creek. From there the men crossed over to the Arroyo Benito, which Dixon called "one of the prettiest streams in the Panhandle, with a good flow of water and lots of timber." Then they recrossed the Canadian and rode north to Grapevine Creek, where they camped a few days.

At intervals, Dixon found small bunches of buffaloes, which he killed; but he still was looking for a big herd. So he moved on down the river and camped between Big Creek and what later was named Bugbee Canyon. There he found a patch of lamb's quarter and picked enough for a pot of greens. The May weather was invigorating, but buffaloes still were scarce. Back at Adobe Walls, old hunters explained that the late spring had delayed the great herd, which could be expected soon from the south. Meanwhile the men amused themselves with card games, horse races, and target practice.

About the last of May, Dixon and his skinners pulled out again. Crossing the South Canadian at the mouth of White Deer Creek, they followed the latter to its source, then rode to Dixon Creek. There they made camp in a spot that offered plenty of water, grass, and wood. After a few days Dixon heard early one morning a deep rumble like that of a distant railroad train crossing a bridge. That was the sound for which he had been listening for weeks.

After a hurried breakfast Dixon saddled his horse and rode south for about five miles. Then he began seeing small bunches of buffalo bulls, all moving north. Riding on, he saw a herd that extended as far as the horizon—a mass of millions of animals slowly grazing in his direction. Some of the bulls were letting out loud bellows, as they would in the breeding season a little later.

Back in camp, Dixon and the skinners quickly went to work. Without leaving the camp, Dixon could shoot enough to keep ten skinners busy. As soon as he had a load of dry hides, he drove to Adobe Walls. He found the trading post almost deserted, since the arrival of the great herd had kept the other hunters as busy as he had been. He did find one man who was willing to work for him as a skinner for a week or ten days, until his partner returned with a load of hides. Dixon hired him at twenty-five cents a hide, and the two started off on the trail to the camp.

When the time came to take his temporary skinner back to Adobe Walls, Dixon hitched his two mules, Joe and Tobe, to his light wagon and drove north. When they reached the South Canadian, the river was in flood, too deep and too swift to cross. So they drove on to the mouth of White Deer Creek, hoping to find a shallower place that would allow them to ford the stream safely.

Dixon waded out into the swollen river in search of a solid footing. He decided to leave the wagon on the south side and try to swim the mules across. But as he waded back to the camp, two hunters arrived with alarming news. On Chicken Creek, twenty-five miles down the river, Indians had killed two hide men a few days earlier. The victims, Tom Wallace and long-haired Dave Dudley, had been hunting with Joe Plummer, camped on the west side of the creek. Plummer had gone to Adobe Walls for supplies.

On his return, Plummer had found a horrible sight. On the ground were the bodies of his two companions, both scalped and shockingly mutilated. The killers had slashed off Dudley's ears and had driven a stake through his abdomen, pinning his body to the ground. Then they had cut off his testicles, fastened them in his hand, and tied his hand to a stake. Finally they had propped his head so that whenever he opened his eyes he would have a bloody view.

Plummer, who thought he saw Indians in the distance, hurriedly cut the harness from one of the horses, mounted, and galloped back to the trading post with the tragic news. Two hunters there, joined by a surveying party of fifteen men encamped on John's Creek, went back to the camp with him to bury the dead.

When he heard this news, Dixon decided against leaving his wagon on the south side of the river, three miles from Adobe Walls. So he picked what looked like the best place and drove in. As the mules were swimming, a swift current caught them, plunging them under the surface and whirling and overturning the wagon. Dixon sprang into the swirling water to try to calm the frightened mules and guide them to safety.

Finally he had to cut the harness and free the mules from the overturned wagon, which drifted a short distance downstream and lodged against the bank. When, after long exertion, he dragged the mules to the north bank, Joe lay down on the sand and died. Tobe seemed all right, but both men had lost their guns. When the two of them, bedraggled and unarmed and leading their waterlogged mule, arrived at Adobe Walls, the men there feared they had been attacked by Indians.

Unable to obtain another mule, Dixon bought a horse to team with his mule and retrieved his wagon. To replace his lost rifle, he bought a round-barrel Sharps. He was able to hire Orlando A. (Brick) Bond as a skinner in place of the temporary hand he had brought back to the trading post. But on the night before he and Bond left for the camp, they heard another report of Indian trouble. Anderson Moore arrived from his camp on a tributary of the Salt Fork of the Red River, north of the future site of Clarendon. Two days earlier, he said, Indians had destroyed his camp, run off all the stock, and killed two of his companions. The dead were a young Englishman, John Holmes, who went by the name Antelope Jack, and a German known as Blue Billy.

With this news, Dixon and his skinner hurried back to the camp on Dixon Creek, fearing the worst. There, after Dixon's absence of only three days, they found Armitage and Frenchy safe and unaware that the Indians had been raiding some of the other camps. But Dixon thought that staying on would be too risky. So the four men loaded part of the hides and drove in to Adobe Walls, where they found many of the other hunters gathering for safety.

After a few days, in which Jim Hanrahan's saloon did a big business, the Indian scare began to subside. Buffaloes were plentiful on the range, and most of the hunters were willing to risk their scalps for hides. So they began going out again, some of them for shorter distances than before. Most of the hunting was done north and west of the trading post, since the Indians were believed to be to the south, on the headwaters of the Washita and the Sweetwater. But Dixon and his three skinners went back to his old camp to load the hides they had left there. After those were hauled in to Adobe Walls, Dixon began buying supplies for a possible stay of two months near the head of Moore's Creek.

While Dixon was laying in supplies, Jim Hanrahan questioned him one evening. "Billy, where are you going?"

"Northwest," he answered.

The saloonkeeper then asked the young hunter if he would like to throw in with him as a partner. Hanrahan still had his big hunting outfit, but was giving his personal attention to the saloon. He'd been unable to hire a hunter who could keep his skinners busy. He thought Dixon was the man he needed and offered to give him half the profits of the combined hunting venture. So the outfits were joined and the wagons loaded with supplies. On the evening of June 26, they were ready to pull out the next morning. Dixon's wagon was in front of Tom O'Keefe's shop, where it had just been repaired.[4]

## V

During this period the Mooar brothers had been among the busiest of the hunters. Early in May, before John was back from his freighting trip to Dodge, Wright went down on the South Canadian with his hide outfit. With him were five skinners. Two of them, six-foot Mark Gallaway and dark-haired Philip Sisk, had come from North Carolina. The others were big Dave Campbell, slim John Hughes, and blond Lem Wilson, tall son of a pioneer Kansas farmer.

The men took three teams and three saddle horses. After reaching the mouth of Red Deer Creek, they crossed the river and followed that creek upstream, south, and on to the head of the Washita River. From there they moved to the Middle Washita at the mouth of Gageby Creek, then went up the creek a few miles and camped on a flat prairie.

On their first morning in this camp, as a dim light appeared in the east, the men were awakened by the hoofbeats and yells of an Indian attack. The redskins charged into the camp from the south, lying on the far side of their mounts and shooting under the horses' necks. As they sped through the camp, they peppered the beds with bullets.

John Hughes, who was sleeping with Wright Mooar on the east side of the wagons, was the first to leap into action. He grabbed his gun, which had been left leaning against the

[4] Dixon: op. cit., pp. 137–54.

7    INDIANS HUNTING IN THE MISSOURI RIVER

8   HUNTERS AT WORK

wagon, and fired at the leading horse. His charge tore through the Indian mount. From the opposite side it dropped the rider, who appeared to be dead.

The other savages circled to the west and took cover in a thicket. They continued to shoot into the camp, but were too far away to do much damage. Although it was not yet fully light, the whites, with their rifles of longer range, soon smoked the Indians out of their hiding place. But before the redskins left, two of them made a second run past the camp and picked up and carried off their fallen companion.

The next day the Mooar party crossed the North Fork of the Red River and camped on the Salt Fork of that stream. There they found the buffaloes coming up from the south in vast numbers. Staying there ten days, they worked steadily and took 666 hides. Wright Mooar had Philip Sisk ride in to Adobe Walls to ask John—by this time back from Dodge—to drive out to the camp and help haul in the hides.

While Sisk and John Mooar were preparing to leave Adobe Walls for the hide camp, six strangers arrived at the trading post about June 18. They were five soldiers and a half-blood Cheyenne scout named Amos Chapman, in Army employ. All were from Camp Supply, an outpost in northwestern Indian Territory, about a hundred miles from Adobe Walls.

When a curious buffalo hunter asked why the soldiers had come to the new post, one of them replied that they were looking for horse thieves. This statement was resented by some of the men whose past would not bear much scrutiny, particularly by Red Loomis and members of his outfit. They began muttering that Chapman must be a spy for either the government or the Indians. In either case, they said, he ought to be hanged.

While the soldiers went up the river, presumably to look for trails, the suspected Chapman held a secret meeting with some of the permanent residents of Adobe Walls—the two traders, Charlie Myers and Charles Rath, and Jim Hanrahan, the saloonkeeper. To them he told the real purpose of his visit.

At Camp Supply the post traders, Lee and Reynolds, had heard that a large force of Indians was planning to attack Adobe Walls about June 27 and kill all the traders and hunters found there. The Indians were determined to stop the inroads being made on the buffalo herds in Texas. Lee and Reynolds wanted to warn the whites at Adobe Walls of the impending attack. Especially so, since they were friends of Robert M. Wright, who had been the sutler at Fort Dodge and had become the partner of Charles Rath. So they sent Chapman with a warning and asked the commander at Camp Supply to give him a military escort.

Hanrahan, Myers, and Rath decided not to pass this warning on to the hunters, skinners, and freighters who happened to be at Adobe Walls. They feared that the men would either scatter to distant camps or take a bee line to Dodge City, leaving the trading post almost defenseless. To protect Amos Chapman from possible hanging, Hanrahan suggested that he sleep with John Mooar in the latter's wagon, which was back of the Rath store.

So, after dark, Amos went into the saloon and bought a drink. When he had downed it, he said he was going over to the Myers store, but would be back to sleep.

"All right," said Hanrahan. "Come back."

As the scout left, Hanrahan diverted attention from him by calling everyone present to the bar for a drink on the house. Later, when they looked for the half-blood Cheyenne, they failed to find him. He had gone to the wagon, where he disclosed his mission to John Mooar.

The next morning Mooar and Philip Sisk left for the camp on the Salt Fork of the Red River. They took three teams besides John's, and two extra men. Because of the warning of an Indian attack, they made forced drives.

When they reached the camp, John told his brother of the danger, and all the men began loading the wagons with dry hides. John also mentioned to Wright that the buffaloes had gone as far north as the Canadian and thus could be killed nearer to whatever protection Adobe Walls might offer.

On the way back to the trading post the loaded wagons moved slowly, especially on the second day, when rain began to fall and soften the trail. That day the outfit made its noon camp on a flat between two small lakes near the head of Red Deer Creek. Many buffaloes were in sight, but the men dared not take time to kill and skin them. The horses and mules were nibbling at the grass and drinking from the pools.

Before the men were ready to bring in and hitch the teams, they saw a large band of Indians about a mile away, following their trail. The Indians were riding in order, as the white cavalrymen did. One of those in the right column carried a bugle, which he started blowing for an attack.

The men in the Mooar camp ran to bring in their livestock. Philip Sisk and Lem Wilson sped toward the stock on the left, and close behind them was Wright Mooar. Unfortunately, both Sisk and Wilson had left their rifles uncleaned since the last killing of buffaloes and were unarmed. But Wright Mooar had his faithful Sharps Big Fifty in his arm.

Wilson, as he ran toward the horses and mules, looked back and yelled: "Is your gun ready, Mooar?"

"Yes," he replied, "and I have forty rounds of ammunition."

"Well, hold 'em back," shouted Wilson, "and Sisk and I will get the stock."

Dropping on one knee, Wright Mooar took careful aim and sent a ball whistling across the front of the charging Indians. This caused them to jerk back their horses in confusion. Before they could reform their lines, Mooar sent another bullet a bit closer. The attackers didn't like its sound any better and fell back a little. Mooar's third shot brought down one of the warriors' horses, sprawling the rider on the prairie.

The bugler rallied the redskins, and they started another charge; but again Mooar's Big Fifty caused them to break ranks and fall back. Some of the Indians fired their guns, but their shots fell short. Mooar kept on shooting until the other men in the outfit had brought in the teams and hitched them to the wagons. Then the party drove on as fast as the heavily loaded wagons would allow. After a mile, the men reached Red Deer Creek, which they crossed near its head at Upper Cottonwood Tree.

As the party forded this creek, a frightful bolt of lightning split the cloud above them. The crash of thunder that followed, Wright Mooar recalled, "seemed to jar the world. Hardly had we gained the opposite bank when a cloudburst sent a wall of water roaring down the channel and out into the valley. It flooded the crossing twenty feet deep, completely cutting the Indians off from immediate pursuit."

The outfit hurried on toward Adobe Walls by the most direct route and reached the South Canadian River about midafternoon of the third day. The men found this stream flooded from melting snow in the Rockies. While the others waited on the south bank, John Mooar and Philip Sisk swam the river and went to Adobe Walls to engage the ox teams of Charlie Myers to come and help pull the loaded wagons across the river. After they had gone, the pursuing Indians charged into the camp. They rode between the wagons, leaped the campfires, and knocked pots and pans in all directions. But there were no casualties.

The next morning John Mooar and Philip Sisk returned with John Webb, an expert wagonmaster. He brought two large, heavy wagons with frames like those of hay wagons. Each was drawn by twenty-four yokes of oxen. The oxen, swimming when necessary, pulled the big wagons across the

swollen river. On the south side, the men reloaded the hides on the big wagons, lashing them down with strips of rawhide to keep them from floating away. The empty wagons were tied on behind. With horsemen prodding and guiding them, the oxen pulled their heavy loads safely across the river and on to Adobe Walls. Then the horses and mules were swum across. The whole operation took most of the day.

While John Webb went off to the stockade with his loads, the Mooar outfit, tired and wet, camped on the north side of the river. There, as they were preparing supper, they suffered another attack from the Indians, who shot right and left as they dodged through. But the hunters returned their fire with bigger rifles and saw several of the redskins carried off. No one of the campers was hit.

On the following morning the whole Mooar party arrived at Adobe Walls. There they were just in time to hear the reports of Joe Plummer and Anderson Moore of the attacks by Indians on two hunters' camps, with two men killed in each.

The next day Charlie Myers began loading his big wagons with hides for John Webb and others to haul north over the long trail to Dodge City. The Mooar brothers reloaded their hides on their own wagons and prepared to go along. They lent their spare rifles to the drivers of the Myers wagons, so that each would be armed. Wright Mooar asked Rath and Myers if they planned to stay on at Adobe Walls. They replied that they did; but, in view of the warning of an Indian attack, Mooar did not believe them.

The wagon train left the next morning. Eight miles out, the freighters met Dirty Face Jones, who was driving south alone with a wagon drawn by six mules. He had a load of guns, powder, and lead. Told to hurry, he had driven ninety miles without stopping to sleep or even to unharness the mules. Jones drove on to Adobe Walls, took off his load, slept five hours, put on half a load of hides, and started back north. He was relieved to catch up with the Myers-Mooar caravan at Palo Duro Creek. To Wright Mooar, who was driving the rear team of the train, he said: "Now I can drive more slowly again."

The next day, at Rifle Pits on the Palo Duro, the wagon train passed another freighter headed for Texas. He was Ike Shadler, with four six-yoke ox teams, one of them driven by his brother, Shorty. John Webb, in charge of the Myers wagons, called to him: "Ike, you hurry back or the Indians will get your scalp."

On Beaver Creek the next morning Charles Rath and Charlie Myers, on good saddle horses, caught up with the caravan. They stayed with the wagons one day, then made a night ride on to Dodge. Rath had left James Langton in charge of his store, while Myers had put Fred Leonard in charge of his.

At Sharp's Creek the freighters found a hunting outfit of five men, headed south. One of the men, Billy Tyler, said they had had a fight with Indians on the Cimarron on the preceding day. The northbound caravan plodded on to Dodge City. When it arrived there on June 29, the men learned that Warren, the freighter who had refused to go back to Texas from fear of Indians, had been killed and scalped by redskins on the outskirts of Dodge. The ire of the Indians against the buffalo hunters had risen to such a pitch that no white man on the plains could be sure of safety.[5]

---

[5] Interviews with J. Wright Mooar, MS. transcripts in the University of Texas library, Austin; J. Wright Mooar, as told to James Winford Hunt: "Buffalo Days," *Holland's*, March 1933, pp. 8, 24; Amarillo *Globe-News*, August 14, 1938.

# ━━● 9 ●━━

# COMANCHE WRATH

As buffalo hunters from Dodge City invaded the Texas Panhandle in large numbers in the spring of 1874, they received more notice than most of them realized. From the crest of many a knoll, dark eyes peered at the wagon trains and at the camps along the creeks. Scouts of the roving plains Indians reported to the tribal chiefs the goings and comings of the hunting outfits. The slaughter had incensed the red men to a point at which they were ready to join forces in a war against the intruders.

The warriors mistakenly viewed this butchery far south of the Arkansas River as a violation of the treaties of Medicine Lodge, which they and the white leaders had agreed to in 1867. In any case, the Indians would have opposed the taking over of the best hunting grounds that remained to them after the virtual clearing of the Kansas ranges. True, the tribes had agreed to stay on their reservations in the Indian Territory, where they received occasional handouts of beef and blankets. But they had not given up the hunting of buffaloes on the plains. They did not intend to do so.

Especially alarmed at this invasion by the white hide hunters were the Comanches, the Kiowas, and the Cheyennes—tribes that had refused to settle in fixed places and to till the soil. The fierce Comanches, related to the Shoshones of the Northwest, were the most expert horsemen on the plains. They also were adept at horse thieving, and made a long journey into northern Mexico each fall to steal from the ranches. In battle they gave no quarter and asked none. Equally brave and defiant were the Kiowas, who had spread into the plains from the Rocky Mountains. The proud Cheyennes, closely associated with the Arapahoes of the Northwest, had, in earlier generations, done some farming and pottery making; but they had given up settled life to become nomadic buffalo hunters.

In opposing the invasion of the southern plains by the white hunters, the tribes had a common cause. "The buffalo is our money," declared Chief Kicking Bird of the Kiowas. "It is our only resource with which to buy what we need and do not receive from the government. The robes we can prepare and trade. We love them just as the white man does his money. Just as it makes a white man's heart feel to have his money carried away, so it makes us feel to see others killing and stealing our buffaloes, which are our cattle given to us by the Great Father above to provide us meat to eat and means to get things to wear."

At the time when white hunters and traders built the new Adobe Walls, the Indians on the southern plains already were irritated and chafing for action. The spring of 1874 had been hard on the Comanches. Torrential rains had held up the freighting of supplies to their agency. As a result, the Quaker agent, James M. Haworth, was forced to issue only half-rations. This was not the first time that had happened. To keep from going hungry, some of the Comanches had to butcher horses and mules.

The Cheyennes in the Territory also were becoming

restive. They complained that white thieves had come down from Kansas and run off many of their horses. A son of Little Robe, with several other Cheyennes, followed the outlaws to Dodge City, but failed to recover the mounts. After they started back, the disappointed and angry Cheyennes drove off some horses belonging to white men. When pursued, they became engaged in a fight in which one Cheyenne was wounded.

Soon afterward a party of disgruntled Cheyennes rode down into the Comanche country. They invited the Comanches and Kiowas to join them in a raid into Texas. All three tribes were well armed with new pistols and rifles. These weapons, along with large supplies of ammunition and whisky, had been sold to them by white and Mexican traders in violation of federal law.

The Kiowas and Comanches, who had been making sporadic raids into Texas all along, were receptive to the suggestion of joint action in an invasion of larger size. All were near fever pitch over the invasion of their hunting grounds by the white outfits from Kansas. In addition, the Comanches were being whipped into hostile action by one of their medicine men.

This was a young and untried brave, Ishatai, or Little Wolf, who had become a prophet and conjurer. The new messiah claimed to have unusual powers, and many of the Comanches believed him. They said he could turn away bullets and that he had brought dead persons back to life. They believed that he had ascended above the clouds and communed with the Great Spirit. A year earlier, Little Wolf had predicted that a comet in the sky would disappear in five days and that a summer-long drought would follow. When those forecasts proved true, his reputation was assured. Several Comanches said they had seen Little Wolf belch forth a wagonload of cartridges, one at a time, then swallow them again.

Little Wolf told the Comanches that the Great Spirit had given him a message for them. The Great Spirit did not want them to follow the white man's way as had the Caddoes and the Wichitas, who were becoming more miserable every day. If they wanted to become prosperous and powerful again, he said, the Comanches would have to make war on the whites and kill every paleface.

To prepare the Comanches for this conflict, Little Wolf called the tribe together for a ritual Sun Dance. This was late in May, when new grass carpeted the prairies and the ponies had shed their winter coats and again were fat. The great gathering was held near the Red River, close to the border of the reservation. Every band was present, which was unusual for the Comanches. Mexican traders were on hand with whisky that added to the excitement and confusion. The war party was dominant and tried to keep any peaceably disposed Comanches from leaving the gathering, even threatening to kill their horses. But a few did slip away and return to the agency early in June. They reported that the war makers showed the effects of firewater. They had "a great many hearts—would make up their minds at night for one thing and get up in the morning entirely changed."

The Comanches Sun Dance on the bank of the Red River was an invocation of the Great Spirit. The ceremony was a simplified version of more elaborate rituals used by the Cheyennes, Arapahoes, and Kiowas. While the campers laughed at clowns whose bodies were smeared with mud and willow leaves, chosen warriors took four days to build a special lodge for the dance. Atop the center pole they mounted a freshly killed and stuffed buffalo.

While the preparations were under way, Little Wolf exhorted the braves with inflammatory talk. If they would turn to the warpath and wipe out the white interlopers, he said, the buffaloes would come back to the plains in vast numbers.

They need have no fear of failure, he told them, because he would share with them his power to ward off the bullets of the white enemies.

Before the dance lodge was completed, some of the warriors built near a creek a group of structures to represent a fortified enemy camp. Ordinarily that would have been a cluster of tepees, but this was a stockaded post that looked like the new Adobe Walls. When the work was done, a scout brought word that an enemy camp had been discovered. Then the braves, with loud war whoops, charged into the mock camp. A few minutes later they rode back, singing the victory song and carrying what they pretended were enemy scalps.

The Sun Dance, which lasted four days, kept time to the thumping of a big drum by half a dozen men with sticks and rattles. Each dancer, adorned with gaudy paint, kept his gaze fixed on the center pole as he made little jumping movements. With each jump, he gave a short blast on an eagle-bone whistle held between his teeth. As the dancing went on in relays through the day and into the night, the people brought gifts and hung them on the center pole. The Comanches expected the dance to revive the power of their tribe and to assure its success on the buffalo range and on the warpath.

When the Comanches opened their big gathering on the Red River, the war party planned to attack the Tonkawas in Texas as the first step in regaining command of the plains. They regarded that tribe as traitors because its men had acted as scouts and guides for the white soldiers in many battles in which Comanche blood had been shed. But the Tonkawas were camped dangerously close to Fort Griffin, on the Clear Fork of the Brazos River. Too, Little Wolf and his councilors may have learned that their plan of attack on the Tonkawas had been disclosed to the commander at Fort Griffin. At any rate, they finally decided to start their new campaign of terror with a surprise attack on the white buffalo hunters and traders at Adobe Walls.

On the day after the completion of their Sun Dance, the Comanches sent out messengers to gather recruits from other tribes for their war of extermination. Envoys carried the peace pipe to the Kiowas, the Cheyennes, and the Arapahoes. The Cheyennes occupied a spreading camp at the head of the Washita River not far away, where Crazy Mule had been making medicine. They had been the first to propose this joint attack. They still were in a mood to throw in with the Comanches, although at times the latter had been their enemies.[1]

## II

The Comanches gave a big feast for the Cheyennes and other allies and formally asked their help against the buffalo hunters. They held this war council at the mouth of Elk Creek, on the North Fork of the Red River. More than two hundred tepees were set up as the chiefs and warriors answered the calls of the tom-toms and camp criers and gathered at the council lodge.

Present at the council, along with the Comanches, were many Cheyennes, led by Stone Calf, and a large band of Kiowas, led by Lone Wolf. Absent was another band of Kiowas which followed the lead of Kicking Bird, who counseled peace. Chief Quanah Parker of the Comanches, whose mother was a captive white woman, presided at the council. After sending a puff of smoke to the sun, the earth, and the four winds, he passed the peace pipe about the circle.

For the Cheyennes, Stone Calf recited many of the Indian grievances against the palefaces. He told of the mas-

[1] George Bird Grinnell: *The Fighting Cheyennes*, pp. 310–12; Rupert Norval Richardson: *The Comanche Barrier to South Plains Settlement*, pp. 371–6; Ernest Wallace and E. Adamson Hoebel: *The Comanches: Lords of the South Plains*, pp. 318–25. Wallace and Hoebel translate the name of Ishatai as Coyote Droppings.

sacre of Indian women and children by Colonel J. M. Chivington's troopers at Sand Creek, in Colorado, nearly a decade earlier. He recalled Lieutenant Colonel George A. Custer's unprovoked attack on a peaceable camp on the Washita in 1868. He reminded his hearers that the red men had been crowded from their favorite hunting grounds along the Arkansas and confined to reservations that they disliked. He mentioned the poor rations, the advance of white settlement, and the increase in travel across the western plains. "The white agents give rations and some goods," he said bitterly, "but we do not like bacon and flour. Our women do not want to make bread. We are hunters and like to eat buffalo meat."

For the Kiowas, still smarting under the recent imprisonment of Chief Santana for the Salt Creek massacre, Lone Wolf told of broken promises of the whites. They had continued to arrest Kiowas and to build iron roads. They had refused the guns that the Indians needed to kill buffaloes and to make war better. He spurned the plea of Kicking Bird to live at peace with the whites and till the soil as did the Caddoes and the Wichitas. "I am a warrior," he declared. "I am not going to sit down and do women's work to get food. I want to drive the white man from our hunting grounds. I want to go on a war trail this summer and kill so many that they will stay away."

Another Kiowa, White Horse, asserted that his people would not be satisfied until they got back all their old hunting grounds, from the Missouri to the Rio Grande. "The white men are afraid," he said. "Last year they released our chiefs they had imprisoned. When I talk big to the agent, he does not answer back. The soldiers are all the time asking for peace. They give us gifts to make peace. It is good to have gifts, but it is better to kill all the white men and let only a few traders bring us goods that we want."

For the Comanches, Quanah Parker complained that two years earlier his tribe had had to give up white captives to get back Comanche women and children taken by the white soldiers. He spoke confidently of help from the Great Spirit and referred to young Little Wolf as a powerful medicine man.

Little Wolf made the final speech. Instead of the usual medicine man's paraphernalia, he wore only a breechcloth and moccasins, with a sash of red cloth about his waist. His only decorations were a red-tipped hawk feather upright in his hair, a snake rattle hanging from each ear, wide bracelets of German silver on his forearms, and a little medicine bag of wolfskin hanging from his neck. In one hand he carried a small fan of eagle feathers.

Fanning the council fire, Little Wolf let the purifying smoke curl up about his head and shoulders. Then he chanted an appeal to the Great Spirit for guidance and strength. Standing in the light of the fire, he told the chiefs of a message that the Great Spirit had given him. He warned against making peace with the whites and digging the ground for crops as the Caddoes and Wichitas had done. "Only the warriors will be strong and increase," he said. "They will hold all the land, going where they please. The buffaloes will come back everywhere, so there will be feasting and plenty in the lodges."

Little Wolf said the Great Spirit had told him how to make paint that would turn away bullets. He advised that the first attack be made against Adobe Walls and assured the warriors that they would kill the white men there while they lay asleep. "Those men shall not fire a shot," he promised. "We shall kill them all." After he passed out medicine arrows sent by the Great Spirit and ended his speech with a quavering wolf howl, the Cheyennes and Kiowas accepted the pipe of peace and promised to ride into battle with the Comanches.

At the close of the feast and powwow, a large band of Comanche and Kiowa warriors, with a few Arapahoes and

Apaches, made a friendly charge into the camp of the Cheyennes. Led by Little Wolf and four war chiefs, they circled the camp and rode through it, chanting their war songs. Next the Cheyenne braves made a similar charge on the Comanche camp. In the evening the men of all the tribes danced around the campfire. Everyone tingled with excitement over the coming battle.

On the next morning the great war party of the combined tribes assembled and set out. Riding in the lead were the chiefs and the medicine men. Little Wolf had fastened scalps to his bridle and had covered his pony with magic paint to protect against the white men's bullets. The warriors pointed their horses west, in the direction of Adobe Walls.

Along the way, other warriors kept overtaking the party and finally swelled its ranks to several hundred. On the third evening the Indians camped five or six miles east of Adobe Walls. Each man spent the evening painting himself and his pony for the coming battle and preparing his shield and his war medicine.

Long before daybreak the line of horsemen was formed, ready for the attack. Chiefs Quanah and Big Bow were at the head of the two bands of Comanches, while Lone Wolf and Woman's Heart led the Kiowas. Stone Calf and White Shield were in charge of the Cheyennes. Quietly the bronze horsemen rode up from the river and formed a new line at the edge of the timber along Adobe Creek. Now they were ready to strike, and all were elated at the prospect of killing the invading white hunters and carrying back fresh scalps. On a hill to the right of the line, the young medicine man Little Wolf sat on his painted horse. Spurning the protection of a shield, he was naked except for a coat of yellow paint and a cap made of sage stems.[2]

[2] Grinnell: op. cit., p. 312; Zoe A. Tilghman: *Quanah: The Eagle of the Comanches*, pp. 78–87.

## III

Sleeping in its hill-ringed pocket of the high plains, Adobe Walls showed no sign of alarm. The little trading post made only a slight interruption on the primitive landscape of the Texas Panhandle. Its sod-and-picket structures gave a thin shell of protection to the occupants. They offered cover from wind and snow, but they could promise little against an attack by savages whom traders had armed with the white man's guns and ammunition. A well-planned surprise attack might wipe out every man there.

Yet the grizzled hunters at the post had given little heed to their peril. They knew that Indians had raided several isolated camps, but they were used to danger as part of their everyday existence. Buffaloes were plentiful, and the money brought from selling their hides would buy strong whisky at Jim Hanrahan's bar. At the post there were no redskins in sight. The hide men were confident that, if an attack came, their markmanship and their long-range rifles would serve well in their defense.

At Adobe Walls, hunters and freighters continued to come and go in spite of the Indian scare. Even though savages had destroyed two camps and killed four men in the last four weeks, other frontiersmen kept on shooting and skinning buffaloes. But some were staying closer to the post, now that shaggies again were plentiful there.

One June arrival at the trading post was its only woman, Mrs. William Olds. She had come down from Dodge City with her husband to open a little eating place in the rear of Rath's store. Soon after her arrival, one of the hunters brought her a tiny mustang colt that had become separated from its mother. As the colt was too young to eat grass, Mrs. Olds fed it and, to protect it from mosquitoes, made it a coat from flour sacks. Soon it was a pet around the Walls.

Four of the five men who were aware of the warning

brought by Amos Chapman had started north on the trail to
Dodge City. The Mooar brothers were jolting along on their
loads of hides, moving farther each hour from Adobe Walls.
Charles Rath and Charlie Myers, leaving later on horseback,
had passed them. Of the warned men, only the Irish hunter
and saloonkeeper, Jim Hanrahan, remained. He had decided to stick to his job, come what might.

On Saturday, June 26, the wagon train of Ike and Shorty
Shadler pulled into Adobe Walls. This caravan, which John
Webb and the Mooar brothers had passed at Rifle Pits on
Palo Duro Creek, comprised four wagons, each drawn by a
six-yoke team. The men quickly unloaded their freight and
reloaded the wagons with dry buffalo hides and tied them
down. They also put on provisions for the return trip. They
would be ready to pull out for Dodge in the morning.

The two Shadler brothers decided to sleep in one of their
wagons, just outside the stockade. With them was their big
Newfoundland dog, which liked to sleep at their feet.

Also loaded and ready for early-morning departure was
the hunting wagon of Billy Dixon, who had just merged his
small outfit with that of Jim Hanrahan. In the evening Billy
went to Rath's store and bought from Jim Langton for eighty
dollars a round-barrel Sharps .44 rifle, which he considered
next best to a .50. He also bought a case of ammunition, but
left it in the store while he took his new rifle into the saloon
to show it to his recently acquired partner, Jim Hanrahan.

At his bar, Jim was busy serving drinks to hunters and
skinners and freighters who wanted to celebrate on the eve
of their departure. As the June evening air was warm and
sultry, the doors of all the buildings were left open. Most of
the men stayed up late to talk, drink, and play card games.
For those who expected to hit one trail or another in the
morning, this was the last chance to make merry.

But gradually the men spread their blankets and turned
in to sleep. Some of them unrolled their bedding inside the

buildings. Most of them, in view of the mild weather, bedded down outside. Young Billy Dixon placed his blankets on the ground near his wagon, just outside the blacksmith shop. Between the blankets he laid his new Sharps .44, where it would be within easy reach and would be protected from dew or rain.

Just before turning in, Dixon went down to the creek and caught his saddle horse. He tied him with a strong picket rope to a stake pin near his wagon. Early the next morning he would bring up the other horses and the mules. He wanted his outfit to make an early start for the hunting grounds at the head of Moore's Creek. As they took to their blankets, Dixon and the others could hear from the strip of timber along Adobe Creek the hoots of owls and the barks of coyotes; but they paid them no attention.

Only Jim Hanrahan was uneasy. Tomorrow would be June 27, the day for the savages to attack the trading post if the warning brought by Amos Chapman was well founded. If they came, they might arrive ahead of the sun. The sand hills looked peaceful enough in the starlight, but appearances could be deceptive. It might be well to have some of the men awake before daybreak.[3]

[3] Olive K. Dixon: *Life of Billy Dixon*, pp. 153–5; J. Wright Mooar, as told to James Winford Hunt: "Buffalo Days," *Holland's*, March 1933, p. 24.

# 10

# ATTACK BEFORE
# DAWN

**N**ight had spread its blanket of silence over Adobe Walls. In the small hours of the morning the little trading post was as quiet as if its twenty-eight men and one woman were underground with the prairie dogs. Down by the creek a horse or a mule or an ox occasionally would rouse enough to munch a tuft of grass. But not a sound came from the low buildings.

Then, about two o'clock on that morning of Sunday, June 27, 1874, the crack of a pistol shot rang through the night air. It woke some of the men. Oscar Sheppard and Mike Welsh, who were sleeping in the saloon, sprang from their pallets of buffalo robes. They heard Jim Hanrahan shout: "Clear out! The ridgepole is breaking!"

Soon the commotion aroused others. Before long, about fifteen men were milling about, trying to bolster the heavy ridgepole that held up the sod roof. Although they could see no crack in the ridgepole, they found on the woodpile a forked prop that was an exact fit and put it in place. Not until years later did some of them learn what had happened. Hanrahan, fearful that the warning of Amos Chapman might be well founded, had fired his six-shooter to trick them into an early rising.

When Hanrahan invited the hunters to have a free drink at the bar, some stayed long enough to take several. Later, as most of the men crawled back into their bedrolls for a nap before breakfast, those who looked out could see a bit of pre-dawn light in the east—coming early, as it always did in late June. From the grasslands the cool air carried the first calls of the meadowlarks.

With morning so near, Hanrahan asked his new partner if he didn't think that he and his men might as well stay up for an early start on the trail. When Billy Dixon agreed, Hanrahan sent Billy Ogg down to the creek to bring up the horses from their night grazing, about a quarter-mile south-east of the post. With Ogg off on this chore, Dixon quickly rolled his bedding and lifted it into the front of his wagon. Then, as he stooped to pick up his new Sharps rifle, he saw something that almost froze his blood.

Beyond the horses and near a bit of timber he made out a large number of objects bobbing on the dim horizon. They were coming closer. As they fanned out into a big half-circle, Dixon realized that they were Indian horsemen. They were heading toward the stock of the hunters and freighters—and toward Adobe Walls itself. Dixon stood for a moment as if thunderstruck.

Then from the approaching hundreds of warriors came a terrifying war whoop that split the early-morning air. By this time Dixon and some of the others who were awake could hear the thunder of the horses' hoofs and the yells of Indian braves as they urged their mounts to greater speed.

Dixon, who still thought the Indians were trying only to run off the horses from the post, raced to bring in his saddle horse, which he had staked out near his wagon. The fright-

ened horse was plunging and seemed about to pull out the
stake. But Billy succeeded in grabbing the rope and tying the
horse to the wagon.

Next Dixon dashed for his rifle, hoping to get in a few
shots before the savages reached the livestock. Now he saw
that they were riding straight toward the buildings. They
were not after horses, but were after scalps.

The attackers made a barbaric sight. In the front ranks,
on their finest horses and decked in gaudy war paint and
feathered bonnets, were the chiefs and the leading braves.
They carried rifles and lances and shields of hardened buffalo hide. Some of the ponies had scalps fastened to their
bridles, and feathers in their manes and tails. In the dim
early light the men at Adobe Walls were unable to recognize
the chiefs, but they could see that this was a major raid and
one that had been carefully planned.

The Indians, quirting their mounts and yelling at the top
of their lungs, were swooping in so fast that Billy Dixon had
time for only one shot. Without waiting to try to see the outcome, he ran to the nearest building, which happened to be
the saloon. He found the door closed. With bullets whistling
and thudding about him, he pounded and shouted for what
seemed a long time until it was opened.

As Dixon sprang inside, another figure appeared in the
doorway. It was Billy Ogg, who had sprinted back from the
creek when he saw and heard the attackers. Entering the
little sod saloon with Dixon, Ogg was so exhausted and
breathless from his quarter-mile run that he fell to the
floor.

Other men were rushing to get inside one store or the
other. At the Rath store, Andy Johnson, who had charge of
Rath's stock and hide yard, had decided it was too early to
picket the horses that had been tied to the wagons for the
night. So he had closed the door and gone back to bed. Mean-

while the blacksmith, Tom O'Keefe, had gone to the saloon to look at the supposedly cracked ridgepole. When he heard the alarm, he rushed back to Rath's and began kicking the door and shouting: "The Indians are coming!"

Even a man as strong as O'Keefe couldn't kick in that door. It was made double, with two-inch planks, and was fastened with a crossbar on the inside. But Andy Johnson quickly opened the door and let in O'Keefe, along with Sam Smith, who had been sleeping outside. By the time the door was closed again, the Indians were within rifle range. Jim Langton, whom Rath had left in charge of the store, and George Eddy, the bookkeeper, were still in their underclothes. But each had a rifle in his hand and a belt of ammunition strapped around him.

By this time all the occupants of Adobe Walls except the Shadler brothers were awake and in one or another of the buildings. Some of the men had just awakened. Several in each building were barefoot and had on only the underwear in which they had slept. But windowpanes were popping, and everyone was rushing to barricade the windows and doors. Against these openings they piled sacks of flour and grain and whatever else was handy.

The Shadler brothers, sleeping in one of their wagons, had failed to hear the approaching attackers. Early in the fight, the Indians killed the two men and their big dog. They scalped the dog, along with the freighters, and ransacked the wagon, which was stocked with provisions. Some rode right up to the occupied buildings—the saloon and the two stores—banging the butts of their rifles against the doors and trying to poke their lances through the windows.

Since the buildings lacked portholes for defense, the men inside were at a disadvantage in firing at their attackers. But soon some of them began to find small openings through which they could see and fire. Most of the defenders were young fellows still in their twenties. Andy Johnson was twenty-eight, Billy Dixon twenty-three, and Bat Masterson only twenty. Yet everyone gave a good account of himself. In the first half-hour the whites took such a heavy toll that the Indians began to fall back. Some of the attackers hid behind the stable, while others sought safety behind piles of buffalo hides.

In their early charges on the trading post the Indians followed the calls of a dark-skinned bugler, who was careful to stay out of range of the white men's buffalo guns. As several of the whites had served in the Army, they recognized the bugle calls and thus knew what move the Indians planned next. At first some thought the bugler must be a Negro deserter from the Tenth Cavalry. Others guessed that he was the half-blood Mexican whom the Kiowas had captured as a boy on the Rio Grande in the sixties.

After the initial attack, one Comanche and two Cheyennes lay dead. The latter were a son of Chief Stone Calf and a brave named Horse Chief. Repeatedly the warriors risked the fire of the buffalo hunters to try to rescue their dead and wounded. Chief Quanah Parker himself raced his mount in front of Rath's store, through a rain of bullets, to pick up a wounded Comanche. Leaning from his horse, he lifted the warrior and, with almost unbelievable strength, carried him back to safety.

From their peepholes, the besieged men saw one of the Indians speed on a white horse to a fellow who had fallen in the tall grass. The wounded man climbed on the horse behind his rescuer. As they started back, a bullet from a buffalo gun struck the horse. But, with blood gushing down one leg, the overloaded pony was able to stagger far enough to carry the men out of range.[1]

---

[1] Leavenworth *Times*, November 17, 1877; Topeka *Capital*, July 1, 1923; Olive K. Dixon: *Life of Billy Dixon*, pp. 155–64; J. W. McKinley, narrative, MS. in Panhandle-Plains Historical Museum, Canyon, Texas; John L. McCarty: *Adobe Walls Bride*, pp. 44–50.

## II

Almost as disturbing to the besieged men as their own danger was the fate of their horses. All of the oxen of the Shadler brothers, along with their horses, lay dead. The mounts were easy marks for the Indians. Billy Dixon's prized horse, tied to the wagon, was one of the first to be shot. Another was the saddle horse that Charles Rath had ridden for eighteen years. Mrs. Olds's affectionate little mustang colt, still in its coat made of flour sacks, was dying with a feathered arrow sticking from its back. Wounded horses from the creek, as well as those from the stockade, came near the buildings as if asking for help; but the men inside could do little for them except put them out of their pain.

Early in the battle Fred Leonard and Billy Tyler ran out from the Myers store to look after the horses in the stockade. But, with the Indians firing at them through the openings between the cottonwood pickets, they had to retreat. As Tyler paused in the doorway for a final shot, an Indian's bullet struck him, passing into his lungs.

Friends quickly dragged the wounded man inside. They could see that his wound was serious and likely to prove fatal. In a lull in the fighting Bat Masterson ran from the saloon to the Myers store and climbed in through a window. Gently raising the head of his dying friend, he tried to comfort him and to ease his pain. Tyler called for water, but there wasn't a drop in the building. The nearest water was in the well out in the stockade. To reach it would mean going through a fusillade of Indian bullets. The chance for anyone to get back alive with water was slim.

Disturbing to some of the defenders, as young Tyler lay stricken, were the calls of a young pet crow that, through the fighting, kept flying from one building to another and in through one of the openings. Between the explosion of the guns, the men could hear the calls "Caw! Caw! Caw!" until they chased out the bird that some considered an omen of death.

As the fighting went on, the weakening Tyler continued to moan and to call feebly for water. Then one of the men spoke up. "Gi' me a bucket," he said.

The volunteer was elderly but rugged Billy Keeler, who had been hired as a cook at the Myers store. The others knew him only as Old Man Keeler. Taking the bucket, he climbed out through the window by which Bat Masterson had entered a few minutes earlier. As he started toward the well, his dog followed him.

The moment the Indians saw Keeler, they began firing. By the time he reached the well near the mess house, he was in a rain of bullets. As he started working the rusty pump, which had seen its best days in Dodge City, the men in the store could hear every rasping squeak. The Indians heard it, too, and more of them began pointing their rifles at Keeler from the west end of the stockade, sixty yards away.

The Indians fired volley after volley at the old man. The blazing of their rifles was so fierce that Fred Leonard said it seemed as if the whole west end of the stockade was on fire. The dog died with twenty bullets in his body, but Old Man Keeler seemed to have some invisible protection. He pumped until the bucket was full of water, then started back. The men inside feared he never would reach the window, but he handed in the bucket and then climbed through—still untouched. Glancing back, he said bitterly: "I'd like to get the devilish Indians that shot my dog."

Bat Masterson took some of the water and, after giving Billy Tyler a drink, washed his fevered face. Then, as the guns roared outside, the head of the wounded man fell over to one side. Half an hour after he was struck, Billy Tyler was dead—the third white casualty of the battle.[2]

[2] Dixon: op. cit., pp. 164–8; Edward Campbell Little: "The Battle of Adobe Walls."

By ten o'clock the attacks on the buildings were becoming less frequent. The Indians had learned that they could not gain an entrance and were spending most of their time out of range of the buffalo guns. But they kept up their firing, and occasionally they made a charge. A few tried to make sneak approaches. Once the men in the saloon saw an Indian pony, with red calico plaited in his mane, standing behind a big stack of buffalo hides back of the Rath store. Guessing that a warrior was holding the pony, they shot the animal, leaving the Indian with less cover. A few more shots made him dance back and forth behind the pile. Then Billy Dixon took careful aim with his rifle and fired. With a howl of pain, the Indian leaped into the air and ran off, zigzagging until he could hide in the tall grass.

By noon the mounted Indians had quit charging the buildings; but they still were on hand, stationed in groups around the trading post. Now and then they would fire an especially severe volley. As the men in the saloon were running short of ammunition, Billy Dixon and Jim Hanrahan decided to make a run for Rath's store, which had thousands of rounds that Dirty Face Jones had brought from Dodge City. Dixon especially wanted more ammunition for the new Sharps he had bought Saturday evening but had been unable to use much because he had left most of his ammunition in the store. Most of the morning he had been using Hanrahan's rifle.

After looking about, the two men cautiously crawled out through a window and hit the ground running. Before they had gone far, Indian bullets were falling like hail around them. But they ran on and reached the door of Rath's store without either being hit. They found everyone in the store unscratched. Because Billy Dixon was an unusually good shot, the men at Rath's asked him to stay in the store, and he agreed. Hanrahan ran back to the saloon with a sack of ammunition and arrived there safely.

## III

Despite having the fresh scalps of the Shadler brothers, the Indians were disappointed at being unable to destroy Adobe Walls and its inhabitants with the ease promised by the Comanche medicine man. They were concerned, too, over their own mounting casualties. Even Chief Quanah was not immune to the bullets of the heavy buffalo guns. While at some distance from the buildings, his horse was shot from under him. The sudden fall of his mount pitched Quanah to the ground and caused him to drop his gun.

When the chief saw that his horse was dead, he recovered his rifle and took refuge behind the carcass of a buffalo upon which wood rats had piled grass and weeds. While making use of this shelter, he was stunned by a terrific blow from behind, one that struck between his neck and his shoulder blade. Yet he had only a slight cut in his skin. At first he thought someone near by had hit him with a stone. Then he realized that he must have been hit by a bullet that glanced from one of the boulders behind him.

Despite his injury, Quanah managed to regain his feet and to run and hide in a plum thicket farther back. Then one of the warriors put the chief behind him on his horse and carried him from the field of battle. With his right shoulder and arm useless for hours, Quanah was unable to take part in the fighting during the rest of the day.

As the battle turned more and more against them, the Indians began to scowl at the medicine man Little Wolf, who continued to sit on his pony on a rise beyond the range of the buffalo guns. Some of the warriors began to murmur against the man who had promised them a quick and easy victory. A Cheyenne who had lost a son in the battle taunted Little Wolf. "If the white man's bullets cannot hurt you," he said, "go down and bring back my son's body."

The only explanation by Little Wolf was his assertion

that, just before the attack, one of the Cheyennes had killed a skunk and that this act had broken the effect of the medicine. This excuse did not satisfy the Indians. A bold Cheyenne took hold of the bridle of Little Wolf's horse and was about to quirt the yellow-painted medicine man, but other Cheyennes pulled him back.

"Let him go," they said. For the rest of his life Little Wolf would be a disgraced man.

As the day wore on, the shooting from each side became less frequent. By two o'clock the Indians were staying back near the foot of the hills east and west of the buildings. After several were shot while going from one group to the other, they began riding in a wider circle. The men in the buildings watched for possible further attacks.

During the afternoon several Indians, including the dark-skinned bugler, crept up to the Shadlers' wagon to ransack it further. They carried off bacon, soap, baking powder, and other provisions. But as the bugler was leaving, with a can of sugar under one arm and a can of ground coffee under the other, Harry Armitage shot him through the back with a Sharps Big Fifty, killing him. By that time twelve warriors were dead or dying—seven Cheyennes and five Comanches—and many others had been wounded. The Indians did not want to risk any more frontal attacks.

About four o'clock, with everything quiet, Bermuda Carlisle left the saloon to pick up an Indian trinket that the men could see from a window. No one shot at him, so others began to venture out. As those from the various buildings compared notes, the occupants of the saloon and Rath's store learned the sad news of Billy Tyler's death.

South of the saloon, Billy Dixon found the body of an Indian warrior and that of his gray pony. Fastened to the horse's silver-mounted bridle was the scalp of a white woman, lined with cloth and edged with beads. Elsewhere one of the men found a war shield with a scalp attached.

Behind the little sod house west of Rath's store, the hunters found the body of a painted and feathered warrior. He was sitting upright, with his legs crossed, but his neck was broken. Dixon took as a souvenir this Indian's lance, which was decorated with black feathers. A search in the tall grass revealed the body of a third Indian, naked except for a white breechcloth and a belt that contained a six-shooter. On the ground near by were his shot pouch with about fifteen Army cartridges, powder horn, bow, quiver, and .50 caliber rifle, an Army Springfield.

Near the buildings were the twenty-eight dead oxen that had belonged to the Shadler brothers and fifty-six dead horses. The bodies of twelve horses lay in one pile between Rath's store and the saloon. Arrows were still sticking from the bodies of some; others had succumbed to the bullets of Indian rifles. Additional horses had been killed farther away or had been driven off by the Indians. Several of the dogs, including Dixon's setter, Fannie, had escaped to the woods.

Before sundown the hunters and traders wrapped the bodies of Billy Tyler and the Shadler brothers in blankets and lowered them into a single grave they had dug near the north side of the corral. Without a horse among them and with Indians still lurking in the hills, the white survivors of the battle had no choice except to stay at Adobe Walls that night. There was only fitful sleep as lookouts kept watch through the hours of darkness, but no new attack broke the silence of the June night.

On the day after the battle, the men at Adobe Walls had to do something about the sickening stench from the dead horses. For those piled near the buildings, they dug a big pit and rolled them into it. The others they rolled on buffalo hides and pulled away with ropes. The bodies of these horses, along with those of the three Indians, were left to the elements and the wolves.

That afternoon Jim and Bob Cator came in to the Walls

from their camp to the north. Other arrivals were the men in the outfit of George Bellfield, a hunter of German origin who had served in the Civil War. They brought in two teams and reported that they had seen no Indians.

Yet the alerted men at the trading post could see Indians watching them from the surrounding hills. Once, in the afternoon, when some of the redskins on the bluff to the east seemed within range of the buffalo guns, the hunters fired a volley at them. The Indians fired back, but disappeared. Later the hunters learned that one of their bullets had killed the horse of Little Wolf, deepening the disgrace of the medicine man.[3]

## I V

The beleaguered band at Adobe Walls knew they would have to send someone to Dodge City for help. While two men went out to warn the hunters in near-by camps, Henry Lease, a hunter who had been in the Myers store during the fight, volunteered to ride the 150 miles to Dodge on a horse provided by George Bellfield. He had two pistols and a large supply of ammunition in his belt, and he carried a Big Fifty. He left alone after dark, on the evening of the day following the battle. Few thought he could get through alive, but he was ready to sell his scalp dearly.

On the next day about fifteen mounted Indians appeared on the bluff east of Adobe Creek. Despite the distance, Billy Dixon took a shot at them with his Big Fifty and succeeded in knocking one warrior from his horse. More hunters came in that day and later, and some of them went to work fortifying the buildings against a possible repeat attack. Among

[3] George Bird Grinnell: *The Fighting Cheyennes*, pp. 312–13; Dixon: op. cit., pp. 169–80; Zoe A. Tilghman: *Quanah: The Eagle of the Comanches*, pp. 90–2; Ernest Wallace and E. Adamson Hoebel: *The Comanches: Lords of the South Plains*, pp. 325–6.

9  "A SWELL SPORT ON A BUFFALO HUNT"

Col W.F. Cody "Buffalo Bill"

10   BUFFALO BILL

other improvements, they made sod lookouts on the roofs of the two stores. For reaching the lookouts they built crude ladders.

On the fifth day the sentinel on the Myers store saw a band of twenty-five to thirty Indians to the north, traveling east. He shouted an alarm, at which those men who were outside reached for their guns and ran for the shelter of the buildings. William Olds, who had been watching from the roof of the Rath store, started to come down the ladder, carrying his rifle. Before he reached the bottom, his gun accidentally went off, blowing off the top of his head. His wife, entering from an adjoining room, saw his body fall to the floor at her feet, with blood gushing from his wound. Olds, who died instantly, was buried that evening, about sixty feet southeast of Rath's store.

By the sixth day after the battle, Adobe Walls was crowded with about a hundred men, but no Indians were in sight. Later the hunters learned that after the battle of June 27 the disappointed warriors had separated into tribal bands and had gone on raids over a wide area that included parts of Texas, New Mexico, Colorado, and the southern border of Kansas. Altogether they killed about 190 whites, thirty of them in Texas.

While the Indians were riding off on new raids, Henry Lease was able to push through to Dodge City with news of the Adobe Walls fight. Immediately the news was telegraphed to Fort Leavenworth, and in Dodge the veteran buffalo hunter Tom Nixon organized a relief party of about forty men, many of them rough hunters. As soon as they could get their equipment together, they started south.

But the men at Adobe Walls did not know that relief was on the way and were becoming restive. About a week after the fight, some of them formed a party and started up the trail to Dodge. Jim Hanrahan had charge of the group of about twenty-five, which included Billy Dixon. The first night they camped at the head of Palo Duro Creek and the second on San Francisco Creek. There the travelers found the mutilated body of Charlie Sharp, who had been a hunting partner of Henry Lease. He had been killed by the Indians a week earlier. After burying the body, they rode on to the Cimarron, Crooked Creek, and Dodge City, missing the southbound Nixon party.

Some of the returning hunters, having had enough of the Indian-infested ranges, bought railroad tickets to their former homes in the East or the Midwest. Even Billy Dixon never hunted again for buffalo hides. Early in August he and Bat Masterson obtained jobs as scouts for troops under General Nelson A. Miles. Soon afterward they were back at Adobe Walls with Lieutenant Frank D. Baldwin, six Delaware trailers, and a troop of cavalry. The rescue party headed by Tom Nixon had taken Mrs. Olds and most of the men back to Dodge City. But some of the hunters had remained at Adobe Walls, where one of them had stuck an Indian skull on each post of the corral gate.

Yet the danger from Indians was not far away. Even while the cavalrymen were encamped on near-by Bent Creek, Tobe Robinson and George Huffman, two civilians hunting wild plums along the Canadian River, were attacked by a band of about fifteen Indians, who killed Huffman with a lance. Thus, the Walls had another body for burial.

But Adobe Walls no longer was a trading post, and soon afterward it ceased to be even a camping place for the few buffalo hunters who dared to stay on in the Texas Panhandle. In the fall the Indians burned the abandoned buildings, glad to be rid of a disagreeable symbol. When Billy Dixon was there next with troops, he saw only broken walls. But he was glad to find his setter, Fannie, which had run off during the battle in June. She not only wagged her pleasure at the reunion but brought in, one at a time, four fat pups.⁴

⁴ Dixon: op. cit., pp. 180–98; Rupert Norval Richardson: *The Comanche Barrier to South Plains Settlement*, pp. 381–6. At Dodge City, three years later, Bat Masterson became celebrated as the trigger-fingered sheriff of Ford County. Tom Nixon, the buffalo hunter who led the relief party, was assist-ant marshal of Dodge City when he was killed in a street there a decade later, on the evening of July 21, 1884. His assassin was Mysterious Dave Mather, a deputy sheriff and former marshal, who, with a partner, had operated a dance hall in the opera house.

# 11

# MORE BUTCHERS AT

# WORK

Although the attack on Adobe Walls did not become the massacre that the Indians had planned, it did give temporary fulfillment to one of the aims of the tribesmen. For about a year it cleared the Texas Panhandle of most of the commercial hide hunters. With the Adobe Walls trading post abandoned, white hunters shied from the trail that led directly down from Dodge City. Most of those who hunted buffaloes in western Texas in the fall of 1874 and in 1875 entered the ranges from one or another of the Texas frontier towns rather than from Kansas.

With Indian war whoops still ringing in their ears, those hunters who survived the fight at Adobe Walls were in no hurry to return to the Texas ranges. Some, like Billy Dixon, gave up hunting for other occupations in the growing frontier towns. Others found enough buffaloes left in Kansas, Nebraska, and eastern Colorado to keep them busy during the fall and winter.

One pair of hunters, though, refused to be deterred. They were Dick Bussell and his brother, who had been hunting in Kansas for three years. They had been unable to go down to the Texas Panhandle in the spring of 1874 because they still had about fifty thousand hides stacked in their camp some eighty miles northeast of Dodge City. They had to haul and sell those hides, the results of two years of hunting, before they could leave for Texas.

Soon after Independence Day of 1874, with their Kansas hides disposed of, the Bussells set out for Texas with a two-wagon outfit. On the first night out, they camped beside Mulberry Creek, about twelve miles from Dodge. There they found another hunting party, headed north toward Dodge. From its members they heard the exciting but discouraging news of the fight at Adobe Walls. Immediately the skinner and cook hired by the Bussells deserted the outfit and headed back for Dodge City.

When the hired hands had gone, Dick Bussell heard his brother ask: "What are we going to do now?"

"We're going to Texas," he answered. So the two went on to the southern ranges, taking a roundabout and safer trail.

Left alone with their teams and two wagons and one saddle horse, the pair traveled east to the Arkansas River, crossed it, and followed it down to the eastern part of the Indian Territory. Near Fort Gibson they struck the old Texas Road, used by many emigrant families in covered wagons. In earlier years it also had been followed, northward, by many Texas cattle drovers, who knew it as the Shawnee Trail. Now it was paralleled by a railroad, the Missouri, Kansas and Texas, known familiarly as the Katy.

Down the broad wagon road the Bussells drove until they reached the Red River, which they crossed into Texas just above the new and bustling railroad town of Denison. From there they went ten miles southwest to Sherman, where they turned west, over the old Butterfield Trail, to-

ward the range country. Tediously they rumbled on, through
wilder surroundings. After pausing at Fort Belknap, they
went on to Fort Griffin, perched on a hill overlooking the
Clear Fork of the Brazos River, which they reached about
the first of August. This outpost of log and frame buildings
had been established in 1867 for protection from the Indians.

With its rolling prairies of lush grass, its wooded hills,
and its running creeks, the valley of the Clear Fork was an
inviting country, one from which the buffaloes had been
pushed west only a few years before. To the Bussells it appeared much as it had, in an earlier August, to an Army explorer, Captain Randolph B. Marcy. "We entered," wrote
Marcy, "a section covered with large mesquite trees, beneath which were innumerable large sunflowers spreading
over the entire country as far as we could see and giving it
a brilliant yellow hue."

At Fort Griffin the Bussells again were near buffalo
ranges. In the rough frontier village that was springing up
on the flat below the fort, a storekeeper named Clark sold
them provisions and ammunition, along with corn for their
horses. He said he would buy their buffalo hides, haul them
over the long road to Denison, and ship them to W. C. Lobenstein in Leavenworth.

So, early in the fall the brothers drove about twenty
miles north of Fort Griffin, where they found buffaloes on
Elm Creek. Working alone and doing their own skinning,
the pair killed about twenty-five hundred in the fall and
winter. There were scarcely any other hunters on the ranges
in that section.[1]

Meanwhile, the Mooar brothers stayed in Kansas during
the fall and winter, helping to clean out small bunches of

[1] Richard Bussell to J. Evetts Haley, Canadian, Texas, July 19, 1926,
MS. transcript in Panhandle-Plains Historical Museum, Canyon, Texas;
Richard Bussell: "Buffalo Hunting in the Panhandle," MS.

buffaloes that remained there and in the northern edge of the Indian Territory. From Dodge City, John Mooar wrote to his mother on October 31: "Have no fear about Wright and me. We are on the frontier and have to put up with what is here. But we think the Indian trouble is nearly over as far as the hunting outfits are concerned. The Indians have not brought on a fight for more than two months; and in every one they did bring on, they were badly whipped.

"Times look promising here now. Have great hopes, if our lives and health are spared, to see you before many months. We are bold, tough, hearty, and rugged. I would not give myself today for four such men as I was the day I left New York. We have some hardships to endure and also some good times. We can't set a nice table, but our food is of the best in the way of meat that the world affords. The things we sit down to eat in camp would make a meal for a king.

"Wright and I have been rigging ourselves out with new winter clothing. The first cold storm, I will put on the socks you sent last winter. Shall expect to hear from you the next time we come in." [2]

On their hunts that fall, the Mooar brothers took along a large black dog named Towser. When John Mooar had come up from Adobe Walls to Dodge City in the spring to sell hides and buy provisions, a soldier had put a chubby, brown-eyed pup in his pocket. The pup, said to be half shepherd and half wolf, grew fast. The Mooars fed him not scraps but the same bread and meat that they ate. In bitter cold weather John would wrap Towser in a coat.

The alert Towser knew all the men in the outfit and, in the evening, would check to make sure that each was back in camp. Sometimes he would go out on the prairie to play with the wolves, but always he was back in time to keep

[2] John W. Mooar to his mother, Dodge City, Kansas, October 31, 1874, MS. in John W. Mooar Papers.

watch over the camp while the men were asleep. If an Indian or an outlaw approached to try to steal the horses,
Towser would not bark but would go to each sleeping man in
turn and lick his face to wake him.

Once, while the Mooars were in Dodge City, an Englishman visited the fort and was overly boastful of the fighting
ability of the bulldog he had with him. He told the Army officers his dog never had lost a fight and never would lose one.
Without bothering to ask the Mooars, one of the officers sent
a soldier to the wagon yard for Towser, and a crowd began
to gather in the street. Confronted with the English bulldog,
Towser at first tried to play with him. When convinced of
the other's hostility, he bristled and tore into him before a
cheering crowd. A few minutes later he picked up the bleeding bulldog by the back of his neck and dropped him at the
feet of his owner.

The enraged Englishman insisted that Towser be killed,
but the crowd refused. "No, sir," said one. "It was a fair
fight. You will have to admit that John Mooar has the better
dog." [3]

## II

While the Mooars and others were engaged in skimpy
hunting in the relative safety of the Kansas plains, United
States soldiers were clearing the Texas ranges of hostile Indians. The attack on Adobe Walls spurred military action
that had been under way for several years. Most often the
roving bands of marauders had eluded the troops sent
against them. In the skirmishes that did take place, the soldiers, not well adapted to Indian methods of warfare,
achieved only indifferent success. But now the commanders
were making a more determined effort.

[3] Louise Mooar: "Towser, the Pioneer Dog," MS. in John W. Mooar Papers.

Roaming about in the southeastern Panhandle in late September 1874, far from their reservation, was a large band of Comanches led by Chief Quanah Parker. The tribesmen had received their full rations, but were too restless to stay on their reservation. While they were out after buffalo robes and meat, they were not averse to stealing horses, pillaging settlers' cabins, and destroying any wagon trains or hunters' camps they might find.

Out looking for the truant Comanches was a military force commanded by young Colonel Ranald Slidell Mackenzie. Under him were seven troops of the Fourth Cavalry and five companies of the Tenth Infantry. He also had Seminole and Tonkawa scouts who knew the country. Early in September, Mackenzie made a temporary camp near Mount Blanco, 180 miles west of Fort Griffin. When the scouting parties he sent out in all directions failed to find any Indians, he moved north to the Quitaque, ascended to the Staked Plains, and headed west.[4]

Mackenzie's scouts reported that the Indians were encamped in Palo Duro Canyon, through which flowed the Prairie Dog Fork of the Red River. This was the Deep Barranca in which Coronado and his Spanish conquistadors had camped in 1541 while searching for legendary cities of gold. Its rugged walls and high turrets of many-hued stone made a picturesque backdrop for the hundreds of Comanche tepees.

On the night of September 25 the Mackenzie force was encamped at the head of a small draw, a tributary of Tule Canyon, which led into the Palo Duro. There, at about ten o'clock, the full force of the Comanches attacked. But the soldiers were ready, and they fired back with such vigor that the onslaught was repulsed without loss to the whites.

The next day Colonel Mackenzie sent a captain with a part of his force in pursuit of the six hundred attacking In-

4 H. H. McConnell: *Five Years a Cavalryman*, p. 232.

dians. Supposing that the main body of the troops would follow, the Indians fled to the southwest to draw the soldiers
away from the camp in the Palo Duro, to which the warriors
secretly returned that night. But Mackenzie had not been
fooled. At dawn on the morning of September 27 his columns reached the rim of the canyon, and the men looked
down on the big, unguarded camp. Quickly the riders dismounted and, in single file, began to scramble down the
steep cliffs of the canyon. Three companies reached the
bottom and others were on the way before the Indians awoke
and realized what was happening.

In the Comanche camp, women and children ran about,
screaming in confusion. The warriors found shelter behind
cedars and boulders along the sloping sides of the canyon
and began firing at the soldiers. Colonel Mackenzie, aware
of the danger to his men out in the open, devastated the
camp rather than try to force the braves to come out from
their hiding. He burned the tepees and destroyed a large
supply of provisions, which included dried buffalo meat,
flour, and sugar. More important, the troops captured from
the camp 1,424 ponies and mules.

The next day Mackenzie turned over some of the better
Indian horses to soldiers and scouts who needed new
mounts. The other 1,048 he ordered shot to keep them from
being recaptured by the redskins. Most of them were pack
animals of little value.

In the Palo Duro clash the only casualty of the white
troops was a wounded bugler. The soldiers found four dead
Indians—one after the night attack and three in the canyon.
They did not know how many others, if any, they might have
killed.

Although the Comanches did not suffer heavy casualties
from the attack on their camp in Palo Duro Canyon, the loss
of their tepees, their food, and especially their horses was a

severe setback. As they went plodding back toward their reservation, looking for game along the way, much of the fight was out of them.[5]

## III

With most of the hostile Indians gone from western Texas, hunting parties from various Texas frontier towns began to venture into the buffalo country.

Sport and meat were the objectives of six men who left the town of Comanche in October 1874. They had two mule-drawn wagons and two saddle horses. Their arms were rim-fire Winchesters and cap-and-ball pistols.

This party found buffaloes at Caddo Peaks, about sixty-five miles from Comanche, but did not get a shot at them. Next they moved their camp to Buffalo Gap, in what later became Taylor County. There they found more buffaloes, a few of which they were able to shoot. They might have killed more except that, inexperienced in the methods of the professional hunters, they did their shooting from horseback. This quickly winded their mounts and drove the buffaloes away.

One member of the party, John Moore, riding a fast mustang pony, was chased by a wounded buffalo bull. With head lowered and tongue hanging out, the snorting bull charged the horse and rider. Moore, who was down to his last cartridge, quickly raised his Winchester and fired. He aimed well, and the shaggy fell at his feet.

From Brownwood, in an adjoining county, a party of five men left in October to hunt buffaloes for meat. They

[5] Annual Report of the Commissioner of Indian Affairs, 1874; Robert G. Carter: *The Old Sergeant's Story*, pp. 103–11; Carter: *On the Border with Mackenzie*, pp. 488–92. A two-room log cabin in the Palo Duro Canyon became the first headquarters of the JA Ranch, established in 1877 by John Adair and Charles Goodnight. Later much of the scenic canyon was included in a state park.

had two wagons drawn by eight-yoke ox teams and a lighter one pulled by a span of mules. For winter protection in their camp, they built crude huts of poles and covered them with buffalo hides. They also fastened hides on the inside and placed them on the floors. They found thousands of buffaloes and also saw enough Indians to cause them to keep close guard on their mules at night.

Frank Sherrod, an eighteen-year-old youth who was a member of this outfit along with his brother Noah, recalled that the men easily butchered and dried enough meat to fill the three wagons. Most of it was from yearlings and two-year-olds. In a wash kettle they had brought along, the men rendered thirty-two kettles full of marrow and tallow. This became so hard in the winter that it could be thrown about like chunks of wood. "We would take an ax, break the bones, and then scrape out the marrow," said Frank Sherrod. "The marrow and tallow were used for cooking and for making soap."

That winter, he added, "we killed enough buffaloes to furnish Brown County with meat all the next year. Twelve months later the meat would be hard as stone on the outside but good and fresh when cut into. We didn't salt our meat. Most of the meat we cut in large chunks, as big as a ten-pound bucket, and dried. Some we carried back in whole hams."

The Sherrods found that the Indians weren't the only hazard of the buffalo country. On one cold night Noah became lost and nearly froze. He was afraid to fire a signal shot because there were Indians about. He covered himself with sage grass for a bit of warmth, but coyotes pulled it off several times before morning. On another night that winter, when the ground was covered with snow, darkness overtook the two Sherrods and one of the other men on the range. Noah became so numb from cold that he fell to the ground and couldn't get up. The others saved his life by quickly skinning a buffalo and wrapping him in the fresh hide.

In Brownwood, too, the Causey brothers, who had hunted in Kansas, formed a small outfit in the fall and went out for hides. They took along as a skinner twenty-two-year-old Bob Parrack, who had come to Texas from Missouri in 1870 and had worked for cattlemen around Brownwood. The Causeys paid him twenty to twenty-five cents a hide. They located their main camp on Duck Creek, in what later became Dickens County, and found a good supply of buffaloes.[6]

Another veteran of the Kansas buffalo ranges, rawboned Jim White, also was ready to hunt in Texas, in spite of the abandonment of Adobe Walls. In the fall of 1874 he arrived at Fort Griffin, which was becoming a gathering place for hunters. There he found a stout Missourian, Windy Bill Russell. Soon afterward the two drove out to the plains to the west after hides. But the danger of Indian attack was so great that they moved cautiously and did not go as far from Fort Griffin as they would have liked.

During the fall and winter the primitive town on the flat below the fort drew other hunters from Kansas and a sprinkling of youths in search of adventure. Among the latter was Frank Collinson, who had come over from Yorkshire to Galveston and San Antonio two years earlier. He had worked as a cowhand on the Noonan Ranch and, in the spring of 1874, had gone to Nebraska with a herd of Longhorns. Now he wanted to shoot buffaloes.

Collinson had saved some of his earnings and had money in a bank in Fort Worth. While there he had bought a horse and a good saddle. He also had a bedroll and a twelve-pound Sharps .44 rifle, with a supply of ammunition. From

[6] Frank M. Sherrod to J. Evetts Haley, Tahoka, Texas, October 20, 1926, MS. transcript in Panhandle-Plains Historical Museum, Canyon, Texas; W. C. Holden: "Robert Cypret Parrack, Buffalo Hunter and Fence Cutter," pp. 29–32.

Frank E. Conrad, who ran the sutler's store at Fort Griffin, he obtained a center-fire Winchester carbine and a thirty-five-dollar Colt .45 single-action, white-handled pistol.[7]

This store at Griffin was a popular outfitting point for hunters. Conrad, who was thirty-three, was a native of Illinois, but spent much of his childhood in Florida. At the outbreak of the Civil War he was a clerk in his uncle's store, but he left to serve in Hood's Texas Brigade. After the war he became the post trader at Fort McKavett, but in 1870 he shifted to Fort Griffin. Often he grubstaked hunters with equipment and provisions and, at times, advanced cash to pay their skinners. His safe became the bank of the frontier town.

[7] Frank Collinson, reminiscences, MS.

## ── ◄ 12 ► ──

# BEYOND CLEAR FORK

**B**y the fall of 1874 the village of Fort Griffin, on the flat below the fort on Government Hill, was becoming a popular outpost of the Texas frontier. It had three stores and three saloons. It was frequented by woodchoppers and freighters for the fort, men who hunted wolves and other animals for their pelts, and the few hardy families who were establishing farms and ranches in the neighborhood. It was a convenient point from which the Texas hide hunters could take off for the buffalo ranges to the west and northwest.

From Fort Griffin a small party of hunters set out on Christmas Day of 1874. It was made up of two former Kentuckians, John William Poe and John C. Jacobs, and Joe S. McCombs, who had come from Alabama. Poe—twenty-nine, tall, and muscular—had worked on near-by ranches and had gone into a farming partnership with Jacobs. The latter, who was twenty-three, was locally called John Jay. When grasshoppers ate their crops, the pair turned to shooting and skinning wolves. Before long they had 489 pelts, which they sold to Frank Conrad at a dollar apiece. McCombs, a youth of twenty who was full of witticisms and pranks, had been up the Chisholm Trail with cattle and had worked on ranches and farms near Fort Griffin. One year he ran the government woodyard there, and later he worked with a party surveying railroad lands on the plains to the west and southwest.

After putting together a small outfit, the trio headed west over the Mackenzie Trail. In Haskell County they found plenty of buffaloes and pitched their camp beside Paint Creek, near Mockingbird Springs. There, far beyond the settlements, they soon began to acquire piles of hides. McCombs, who was a good shot and had killed buffaloes on his surveying trip, did much of the shooting at first, then helped his older partners with the skinning. He approached each bunch by creeping through the grass and always tried to kill the leader first.

In two months, during which they saw no other persons, white or Indian, the three took seven hundred hides. Leaving Jacobs to haul the hides to Fort Griffin, Poe and McCombs rigged a pony team and went on west. They headed up the Clear Fork, passing Fort Phantom Hill, and made camp near the future site of Rotan. Jacobs, after delivering the hides from the first hunt, followed their wagon tracks.

"We were glad to see him," recalled McCombs, "as we had been out of bread for ten days. On this hunt, one of our ponies slipped a shoulder, so we had to haul our hides into camp. We would just skin and peg the hide on the ground; and when Jacobs arrived, we hauled them in."

During this hunt Poe learned about the anger of a wounded buffalo bull. "I had downed several bulls together," said McCombs. "Poe, only a short distance away, came over; and we approached the kill. When we were about fifteen feet from a downed bull, up he got and charged straight at

Poe. I was behind Poe and shot past him, dropping the bull at his feet. Poe was shooting with a pistol as the bull fell."

By May 1 this small outfit had thirteen hundred hides, making two thousand for the two hunts since Christmas. The men sold all of them to Frank Conrad, obtaining $2.00 each for those suitable to be made into robes and $1.50 each for the others.[1]

From various directions, other outfits also were pushing into the buffalo ranges of western Texas, looking for hides. The routing of the Comanches by Mackenzie's troops in Palo Duro Canyon had made the country seem a bit safer. While traveling across the Panhandle in November 1874, John R. Cook became lost from his companions. After several days he reached the ruins of Adobe Walls, where a family of buffalo hunters was living. He stayed through the winter and hunted with the men of this family—tall Buck Wood, his father, and his brother-in-law, George Simpson. They sold their hides at the stockaded Springer Ranch, receiving $3.00 each for the choice robe hides of cows and $1.75 each for the others.

In the spring of 1875, Dick Bussell and his brother, who had been hunting out of Fort Griffin during the fall and winter, set out again. They headed northwest, along the Pease River and the Prairie Dog Fork of the Red. Camping on Mulberry Creek, they found all the buffaloes they could handle. Later they moved north to Sweetwater Creek, where they varied their diet with fish.

While on the Sweetwater, the Bussells saw about 150 loaded wagons and several hundred soldiers arrive to build a new fort for protection against the Indians. This was the Cantonment of Sweetwater, established on June 5, 1875, and soon afterward named Fort Elliott. Before long the new fort had a rectangle of rambling buildings of frame and adobe.

With the military equipment and supplies came those of Lee and Reynolds, the fort sutlers. Until they could build a store, they set up a big tent on Sweetwater Creek. There they sold provisions and whisky and beer, although at first they had no ice. They also were ready to buy the hides that hunters brought in.

In June the Bussells, with four others, pulled out down the Red River and killed about two hundred buffaloes. Next they moved up to Red Deer Creek and butchered about twelve hundred more. They hauled their hides to the mouth of Boggy Creek, where the trail crossed the one leading to Fort Supply.[2]

## II

While this nibbling at the big Texas herds was being started from various directions, those hunters who still made their headquarters at Dodge City were cleaning out the bunches north of the Cimarron River. But they were acting more cautiously. They had their horses herded by day, and at night drove them into Tom Nixon's big corral, where guards kept watch against marauding Indians.

For safety, the hunters worked in larger outfits. Twelve of them, including Wright Mooar and Steel Frazier, formed an outfit to hunt along the Cimarron. With a dozen wagons, they drove south and soon had four hundred hides stacked in their camp. Next the hunters followed the herd to Beaver Creek, in No Man's Land, where they took many more hides. Then they decided to begin hauling the dried hides back to Dodge. While nine men stayed to hunt and skin, Mooar and

2 John R. Cook: *The Border and the Buffalo*, pp. 60–96; Richard Bussell to J. Evetts Haley, Canadian, Texas, July 19, 1926, MS. transcript in Panhandle-Plains Historical Museum, Canyon, Texas.

two others started north in a howling sandstorm with two loaded wagons.

They camped the first night near a spring at the head of a stream called Stumpy River, in what later became Meade County, Kansas. As they left early the next morning, traveling along a ridge toward Crooked Creek, they heard the shooting of small-caliber rifles in the distance. Mooar thought maybe some of the men from Dodge were shooting small game. When the drivers reached Crooked Creek, near sundown, Mooar insisted on going on to Mulberry Creek before making camp. Later they learned about the shooting they had heard. A band of twenty-five to thirty Indians had attacked a party of six surveyors camped on Crooked Creek. All the surveyors were killed and scalped and their bodies were mutilated. Later some hunters found near Beaver Creek a compass and other instruments that the Indians had thrown away.

In November 1874, Wright Mooar and others drove as far south as Francisco Creek, in the Texas Panhandle. After taking many hides, they dropped back north to Beaver Creek in December. There, in the Neutral Strip, they spent the winter, acquiring more hides and a supply of meat. In March 1875 they loaded their wagons and headed north again. They sold the hides in Dodge City and the meat in Wichita and El Dorado.

By this time the buffaloes in the familiar hunting grounds were so scarce that the Mooar brothers decided to go to Texas and make new headquarters there. So, with two lumbering wagons drawn by mules and loaded with ample provisions, they started southeast, on the route that the Bussells had used eight months earlier. They drove along the Arkansas River, and then south over the old Texas Road. They crossed the Red River by Colbert's Ferry on the last day of April and camped beside a creek between the river and the rip-roaring town of Denison.

Denison, which had sprung up to greet the coming of the railroads in 1872, had become one of the toughest towns on the frontier. Lee (Red) Hall, who had just served a term there as deputy sheriff, had driven out some of the worst criminals; but the town still had more than its share of thugs, gamblers, and loose women. Main Street was fairly respectable—except on Sundays, when the "soiled doves" donned their finery and paraded there or rode back and forth in livery rigs. Hogs wallowed in mudholes; but the Crystal Palace and other Main Street saloons kept fair order, as did the pool halls and dance houses. But on Skiddy Street, one block south of Main, almost anything went.

Skiddy Street, named for a director of one of the railroads, was a ravine with the underbrush cleared away. It was lined on both sides with tents and shacks that housed low-class bars, gambling joints, cocking pits, hurdy-gurdy dance halls, and "dovecotes" whose inmates were ready to serve men of every race. Among the more notorious dives were the Palace, the Park, and the Sazerak. The Sazerak was run by Rowdy Joe Lowe and his wife, Kate. They had left Wichita after soldiers burned their dance hall on the outskirts of that cow town. Cowboys often shot up the Denison streets; and Indians from across the Red River, after a few drinks of firewater, filled the night with their whoops. Brawls and holdups were almost everyday events.

By the time the Mooars arrived, Denison was shipping large numbers of Longhorn cattle and was becoming a market for buffalo hides hauled in from the west. W. C. Lobenstein of Leavenworth had an agent there, as well as one in Dallas. On the day before the Mooars reached Denison, the Lobenstein agent, A. S. Holland, had bought a batch of buffalo hides from a group of Denison men who had been hunting at the foot of the Staked Plains. On May 21 he bought 691 large hides from a hunter named Van Ostrand, who had been butchering two hundred miles to the west. Van

Ostrand had tried to sell his hides in Sherman, ten miles to the southwest, but no one there would buy them.

The Mooars stayed in Denison long enough to trade some of their mules for oxen, buy extra wagons, and hire Ben Griffin and other teamsters. Their big freighting outfit would enable them to take in cash until they could become well established as hunters on the Texas ranges. When they left, they had a dozen large wagons, half of them filled with their own equipment and provisions and the others with government freight for Fort Griffin and other military outposts on the frontier. One wagon had an unwieldy load of stovepipes that had gathered dust and rust in Denison for a year because no other freighter would haul them.

As the caravan moved slowly west across the rolling prairies and through a belt of timber, Ben Griffin, who knew the trail, picked the best places for camping. After passing through the village of Decatur, the travelers saw the lone stone chimneys of pioneers' cabins that had been burned by Indians. Many of the settlers who built them had been killed and scalped, and their wives and children carried off into captivity.

Early in July the Mooars were back in Denison. "Wright and I came in here a few days ago after an absence of nearly a month," John wrote to their mother on July 3. "If you are asked what we are doing, you can say we have teams freighting for the government in the summer and packing meat and buying hides in the winter."

Soon the Mooars had their hunting outfit at work in the valley of the Brazos River, northwest of Fort Griffin. They found an abundance of buffaloes and made their winter camp on Mule Creek, at the future site of Weinert. Jim White and Windy Bill Russell had thrown in with the Mooars for a while. Other hunters in the big outfit of the Mooar brothers included John Goff and Mike O'Brien.

By November the Mooars had four thousand hides ready

to sell. They loaded them in wagons, and John Mooar, accompanied by W. H. (Pete) Snyder and other freighters, started off with them. The long caravan was made up of eighteen teams of six yokes of oxen, each team drawing three wagons. This wagon train of hides, the like of which had not been seen in northern Texas, drew much attention along the way. After stagecoach drivers had spread the word, many frontier families came out to watch it rumble past. Some dogs, instead of barking, ran under the houses with their tails between their legs. Some of the Sherman people who came out to see the caravan as it camped on the outskirts of the town had never before seen a buffalo hide.

A. S. Holland, the Lobenstein agent at Denison, was unprepared to buy so many hides. Besides, he wasn't sure just what they were worth. So John Mooar telegraphed W. C. Lobenstein in Leavenworth, who bought the whole shipment and wired the money. This purchase induced Lobenstein to establish agents in Fort Worth and Fort Griffin, closer to the hunters' camps.

In Denison, John Mooar bought a month's supplies for the outfit and, on November 23, ordered ten thousand primers, to be sent to him in care of a Fort Griffin dealer, T. E. Jackson and Company.[3]

## III

While some of the Kansas hunters, like the Mooars, went to Texas in 1875, others traveled north to hunt among the vast herds that grazed on the upper ranges. They were especially plentiful in northeastern Wyoming, southeastern Montana, and western Dakota. Hunters in that area shipped be-

---

[3] John W. Mooar to his mother, Denison, Texas, July 3, 1875, MS. in John W. Mooar Papers; John W. Mooar, MS. letters in correspondence of Sharps Rifle Company; J. Wright Mooar, as told to James Winford Hunt: "Buffalo Days," *Holland's*, April 1933, pp. 5, 22; Louise Mooar: "The Mooar Family," MS. in John W. Mooar Papers.

tween fifty and one hundred thousand hides east in 1875, in addition to those from Canada. Among other dealers, the I. G. Baker Company of Fort Benton forwarded about twenty thousand hides and the T. C. Price Company, of the same Montana outpost, about twenty-five thousand.

Some of the hunters, in addition to taking hides, dried meat to be sold in the mining camps that had sprung up in Montana and the Black Hills and were attracting many adventurers.

In Texas, Jim White and Windy Bill Russell formed their own hunting outfit. It was a large one, with heavy hide wagons drawn by twenty-five yokes of oxen and lighter wagons pulled by six mules. The latter were used in skinning and in moving camp. As one of their skinners, White and Russell hired the English-born Frank Collinson, who had been staying at Fort Griffin in the hope of joining a hunting party.

From Fort Griffin the outfit of White and Russell followed the Mackenzie Trail west for several days and made camp on Kiowa Creek. There the men found an abundance of buffaloes and began hunting. They were well supplied with flour, corn, and other provisions. Their ammunition included 425 pounds of Du Pont powder, 400 pounds of lead, and the necessary patch paper and other supplies. For camp shelter they built a tepee of poles and buffalo hides, but in good weather they cooked and ate in the open.

Although the hunting was good, Russell became dissatisfied after about a month. He had a wife and children living near Kansas City, and he wanted to go back to them. Frank Collinson then told White that if White would have him for a partner, he would try to buy out Russell. As that was agreeable, Collinson, a few days later, drove with Russell to Fort Griffin in the one wagon that Russell retained; and Collinson wrote a check on a Fort Worth bank for fifteen hundred dollars for his share in the outfit. Then Collinson rode back to the plains and to his hunting with Jim White. The slaughter was all that a hide man could ask. In one stand, White downed forty-six buffaloes with forty-seven shots.

Among the Kansas hunters who had gone to Texas, the Causey brothers were out on the range again. One evening George Causey was alone in his camp between Little Duck Creek and Stinking Creek, near the foot of the Staked Plains. That night three rough-looking men rode into the camp. With the usual hospitality of the West, Causey shared his food with them, without asking their names.

After supper, other horsemen arrived. They were a band of vigilantes from Fort Griffin. They had been trailing Causey's visitors, who were notorious horse thieves. As they didn't know Causey, they arrested him, too, despite his protests. The next evening the party stopped at the hunting camp of Jim White and Frank Collinson, then on Duck Creek. The leader brought up Causey and asked White: "Do you know this man?"

"Yes," answered Jim, "he is Jim Causey. I knew him in Dodge City. He's a buffalo hunter and was on the Kansas range for several years. I didn't know he had come to Texas."

At that, the vigilantes released Causey, who later went into partnership with White and Collinson. The next day the bodies of the three horse thieves were found with their throats cut.[4]

## I V

Young Frank Sherrod, who had gone out with a Brown County outfit a year earlier, was on the range again in 1875. This time he saw fewer coyotes and Indians but more white hide hunters. "There were places on the plains where

[4] *Benton Record*, Fort Benton, Montana, February 1, August 7, 1875; Frank Collinson, reminiscences, MS.

you could almost walk on the buffalo carcasses," he said. "We came up the Jim Ned Creek, through Taylor County, and up to the head of the Colorado River, where we camped and made a pole house. We cut forked poles, placed them in the ground, and covered them with green hides. We made our house eight or ten feet wide and real long, with the south side open. When we built a fire in front, we were warm inside."

This outfit stayed on the range about six and a half months, hunting mainly in the valley of the Colorado River of Texas. One of the parties it met, out from Fort Worth, was killing buffaloes for only their tongues, which brought fifty cents each.

Joe McCombs, who had been hunting with John William Poe and John Jacobs, formed an outfit of his own in the fall of 1875. As skinners he hired Bob Pitcock, Wesley Tarter, and Sol Pace. The four left Fort Griffin with a wagon drawn by a span of mules. They had eight hundred pounds of lead, five kegs of powder, a reloading outfit, and a Sharps sporting rifle that weighed sixteen pounds.

This party struck out by Phantom Hill, going to the future site of Sweetwater, in Nolan County. Camping there, McCombs recalled, "I killed several hundred buffaloes before moving on to Champion Creek, near Colorado, Texas. There we made a permanent camp and stayed until April 1. Our total kill was a little more than two thousand hides. During this entire hunt of more than six months, we did not see anyone outside of our outfit. There were no settlers in that country. On our return to Fort Griffin, I hired five or six wagons to go out after the hides. Each wagon had a trailer and six yokes of oxen. They made two trips for the hides."

Meanwhile John William Poe and John Jacobs continued to hunt, hiring Thomas Kilpatrick as a skinner. Tom was a fast worker who could skin fifty to sixty buffaloes a day when the hunters killed that many and left them close together on the prairie. The outfit found plenty of shaggies and soon had a big stack of hides to haul back to Fort Griffin.

All the hides sold to dealers in Fort Griffin had to be freighted by wagon train to some rail point. Some of them were hauled northeast to Denison. Others went east to Dallas, which had taken a spurt in growth after obtaining one railroad in 1872 and a second one a year later. But hogs still wallowed in mudholes in the streets, and dogs barked at every new arrival.

The Dallas *Herald,* besides chronicling such events of 1875 as a visit to the city by Jeff Davis and the opening of the new Le Grand Hotel, found space to mention some of the arrivals from the west. "The buffalo meat cured on the frontier and brought in here by old hunters," the newspaper noted on February 27, "is the sweetest kind of meat and is tender." On March 11 it reported the arrival of more buffalo meat, and on the 28th it mentioned that "hides continue to arrive in large quantities." Some of the hides went to W. C. Lobenstein's hide house on Elm Street, while others were sold to S. T. Stratton or other local commission merchants.

On April 4 the *Herald* reported: "Buffalo meat is becoming plentiful. Two more wagonloads arrived in town yesterday." And on September 11: "A large wagon train arrived in the city yesterday, loaded principally with lumber and hides." Some of the caravans from Fort Griffin might contain as many as forty wagons, each drawn by six or eight mules or oxen. The hides were piled high and were held in place with ropes and poles. Buffalo hides sold in Dallas at a dollar to a dollar and a half, and one could buy a good doeskin suit for twelve dollars. Jerked buffalo hams brought three cents a pound, while a saddle of venison sold for forty cents.

Yet not all the hides taken in Texas were shipped from

Texas railroad towns. Some of the men who hunted in the Panhandle found it more convenient to sell their hides in the new village that had sprung up on Sweetwater Creek below Fort Elliott. From there the hides were hauled north by wagons to towns on the Santa Fe Railroad in southern Kansas.

This village, which was started in June 1875 with the tent store of Lee and Reynolds, had grown much by the end of the year. At first it was called Hidetown, then Sweetwater —a name destined to be changed in 1879 to Mobeetie. The sutler's store carried supplies for hunters and was surrounded by acres of high piles of hides. "It was a wild and woolly place," said John R. Cook, who visited it. "It had a large dance hall, two restaurants, and three saloons. Big hunting outfits were coming and going—from ten to fifteen outfits there nearly every day." The hide hunters were ready to leave the Texas ranges as clean as those of Kansas.[5]

[5] Frank M. Sherrod to J. Evetts Haley, Tahoka, Texas, October 20, 1926, MS. transcript in Panhandle-Plains Historical Museum, Canyon, Texas; McCombs: op. cit.; Poe: op. cit., p. 59; Cook: op. cit., p. 104.

## ── 13 ──

# VOICES IN PROTEST

As millions of carcasses rotted on the Western plains in the 1870's, reports of the buffalo slaughter shocked people in the East. Many protested against the butchery on sentimental grounds. Others objected to the waste of meat, especially in a period when thousands of industrial workers were jobless and their families hungry. There was fear in some quarters that the herds might be completely wiped out.

State and national lawmakers began to receive pleas to halt the killing. Indian tribes on the plains sent bonneted chiefs to Washington to complain that they were being deprived of their traditional food. Other protests came from whites, even from Army officers. They demanded laws to restrain the hide hunters.

Bills to check the shooting came up in the state and territorial legislatures in the West and in Congress. Idaho had passed such a measure in 1864. Wyoming followed in 1871 and Montana and Colorado in 1872. The Colorado game law provided that hunters should not leave any flesh to spoil. Yet, regardless of laws, the slaughter went on as before. In

1872 the Kansas legislature passed a bill "to prevent the wanton destruction of buffaloes," but the Governor killed it with a pocket veto.

Columbus Delano, who became Secretary of the Interior under President Grant in 1871, had no sympathy with those who wanted to check the killing of buffaloes. He held that if the government should encourage the hunters by ignoring them, soon the plains would be cleared and the Indians starved into submission. When visited by a delegation of Sioux in 1871, Delano refused to promise to keep white hunters out of their country. In his report for 1873 he wrote: "I would not seriously regret the total disappearance of the buffalo from our western prairies, in its effect upon the Indians. I would regard it rather as a means of hastening their sense of dependence upon the products of the soil and their own labors."

Debate in Congress on the wholesale killing of buffaloes in the West began in 1871, when the slaughter in Kansas was becoming heavy. On March 3 of that year, R. C. McCormick, a delegate from Arizona and former Governor of that territory, sponsored a bill aimed to limit the butchery. It provided that, "excepting for the purpose of using the meat for food or preserving the skin, it shall be unlawful for any person to kill the bison, or buffalo, found anywhere upon the public lands of the United States." It provided further that "for the violation of this law the offender shall, upon conviction before any court of competent jurisdiction, be liable to a fine of $100 for each animal killed." One half of the fine, upon its collection, would be paid to the informer.

This was a weak measure in that it would not have interfered with hunting for hides. The bill was ordered printed and was approved by the Committee on Public Lands, then quickly was forgotten. But public agitation for a law to hold back the riflemen continued. Henry Bergh, president of the American Society for the Prevention of Cruelty to Animals, gathered from Army officers and others in the West letters to back his plea for protection of the remaining herds. In one such letter Colonel W. B. Hazen, stationed at Fort Hays, Kansas, wrote in part:

"The introduction of railroads into and across the wilds of our country has made the vast herds of buffaloes accessible to all classes of people. Each year vast numbers are slaughtered for sport and a great number for their hides, which net about one dollar. I have seen men this winter who have in the past season killed one thousand each for the paltry sum of one dollar apiece, the carcasses being left to rot on the plains.

"The buffalo is a noble and harmless animal, timid, easily taken for a cow, and valuable as food for man. It lives upon short grass, which grows luxuriantly upon the high, arid plains of this middle region that is, from dryness, unfit for agriculture. The theory that the buffalo should be killed to deprive the Indians of food is a fallacy, as these people are becoming harmless under a rule of justice. I earnestly request that you bring this subject before Congress with the intention of having such steps taken as will prevent this wicked and wanton waste, both in the lives of God's creatures and of the valuable food they furnish." [1]

In another letter, Lieutenant Colonel A. G. Brackett of the United States Second Cavalry, stationed at Omaha, wrote: "All the reports about fine sport and good shooting are mere gammon. It would be equally good sport, and equally dangerous, to ride into a herd of tame cattle and butcher them indiscriminately. The wholesale butchery of buffaloes upon the plains is as needless as it is cruel."

A third letter to Bergh came from Colonel E. W. Wynkoop, who had spent thirteen years on the plains as an Army

[1] *Rocky Mountain News*, April 13, 1871, February 3, 1872; Ellsworth *Reporter*, March 7, 1872.

officer and as an Indian agent. "There is another strong reason, apart from cruelty," wrote Wynkoop, "which should compel Congress to take action. It is one of the greatest grievances the Indians have and, to my personal knowledge, frequently has been their strongest incentive to declare war. Little Robe, the Cheyenne chief who recently visited Washington, at one time remarked to me after I had censured him for allowing his young men to kill a white farmer's ox: 'Your people make big talk, and sometimes make war, if an Indian kills a white man's ox to keep his wife and children from starving. What do you think my people ought to do when they see their cattle—the buffaloes —killed by your race when they are not hungry?'"

On February 14, 1872, Senator Cornelius Cole of California, who had gone west as a forty-niner, introduced a resolution on game conservation. It directed the Committee on Territories "to inquire into the expediency of enacting a law for the protection of the buffalo, elk, antelope, and other useful animals running wild in the territories of the United States against indiscriminate slaughter and extermination." It instructed that group to report to the Senate by bill or otherwise. The Senate approved the resolution, but apparently the committee pigeonholed it.

Two days later, Senator Henry Wilson of Massachusetts, who was to become Vice-President the next year, introduced a bill that would have restricted the killing of buffaloes upon the federal lands. It was read twice and referred to the Committee on Territories. On April 5, Delegate McCormick of Arizona, who had revived his bill of more than a year earlier, made a speech on the proposal to restrict the killing.

McCormick called the buffalo "the finest wild animal in our hemisphere." He related that, while he was on one of the trains snowbound on the Kansas Pacific Railroad in December 1870, buffalo meat had kept him and the other passengers from going hungry. He cited pictures in *Harper's Weekly* depicting the slaughter of the shaggies, read some of the letters gathered by Henry Bergh, and told of one hunter who had downed nearly a hundred buffaloes in a single day.[2]

Nothing came of these initial efforts in Congress, but public agitation for checking the slaughter continued. Some of the protests came from the buffalo country. In May 1872, Denver's *Rocky Mountain News* denounced the shooting of buffaloes from trains. "The carcasses of the animals, in every stage of decomposition, which have been wantonly shot from the passing trains, are seen on either side of the track, all along where it passes through the buffalo ranges. It would be a good idea for the general division superintendents to enforce a rule prohibiting the firing of guns from the train."

Writing from Denver in the following autumn, the associate editor of the *American Agriculturist* said: "Our pioneers want meat in the first years of their settlement. There is no good reason why the idlers and the rich men from our Eastern cities should take it from their mouths. There should be a closed time for the buffalo as there is for the deer and other large game—six months at least, including the breeding season—in which it shall be unlawful to kill them in any part of our territory. Our sporting clubs in the East could not do a better thing than to memorialize Congress upon this subject the coming season."

In March 1873 the Wichita *Eagle,* after reporting the shipment of an average of two carloads of hides a day in the preceding two months, commented: "The destruction of these animals for the last winter has been fearful. A congressional law should be enacted against the wanton destruction of these monarchs of the plains." [3]

[2] *Rocky Mountain News,* February 17, April 14, 1872; Congressional Globe, April 6, 1872, Forty-second Congress, second session.
[3] *Rocky Mountain News,* May 11, October 16, 1872, January 12, 1876; Wichita *Eagle,* March 20, 1873.

II    CAPTURING ANIMALS FOR A CIRCUS

12    ON THE KANSAS PACIFIC

## II

Early in 1874, with nearly all the Kansas buffaloes gone, Congress again took up the pleas to halt the slaughter. On January 4 of that year Representative Greenburg L. Fort of Illinois, a veteran of the Union Army, introduced a bill to restrict the killing of buffaloes in the territories. After being read, it was referred to the Committee on Territories, which on March 10 recommended its passage. On February 2 of the same year Fort introduced another bill to tax buffalo hides. This was referred to the Committee on Ways and Means, which reported it adversely on June 10. On the same February 2, McCormick of Arizona revived his bill, which was referred to the Committee on Public Lands and never heard of again.

When the original Fort bill reached the floor, with committee approval, it evoked considerable discussion. This measure would have made it unlawful for any person not an Indian to kill any female buffalo in any of the territories of the United States. It also provided that no more buffaloes should be killed than were needed for food or for curing or preserving meat for the market. The penalty was one hundred dollars for each buffalo unlawfully killed.

One member objected to the preference given to Indians. He also said that hunters had told him it was impossible to tell the sex of a running buffalo. But others assured him that any but the greenest hunter could distinguish the sex of buffaloes while they were running.

During the debate on the Fort bill, McCormick had the clerk read into the record an item from the Santa Fe *New Mexican:* "The buffalo slaughter, which has been going on the last few years on the plains and which increases every year, is wantonly wicked and should be stopped by the most stringent enactments and most vigilant enforcements of the law. Killing these noble animals for their hides or to gratify the pleasure of some Russian duke or English lord is a species of vandalism which cannot too quickly be checked. United States surveying parties report that there are two thousand hunters on the plains, killing these animals for their hides. One party of sixteen hunters reports having killed twenty-eight thousand buffaloes during the past summer. There is as much reason why the government should protect the buffaloes as the Indians."

McCormick also read part of a letter he had received from Colonel W. B. Hazen, who wrote: "I know a man who killed with his own hand ninety-nine buffaloes in one day, without taking a pound of meat. The buffalo for food has a value about equal to that of an average Texas beef, or twenty dollars. There probably are fewer than a million of these animals on the western plains. If the government owned a herd of a million oxen, it would take steps to prevent their wanton slaughter. The railroads have made the buffalo so accessible as to present a case not dissimilar."

After further discussion, the House passed the bill, with 132 favorable votes and the opposing ones not counted. It came up in the Senate on June 23. After a few objections to favoring the Indians were made and withdrawn, the Senate passed the measure and, a few days before the session ended, sent it to the White House for signature. But President Grant, possibly on the advice of his Secretary of the Interior, let it die for lack of his signature.[4]

Yet the President's pocket veto failed to halt the movement to check the slaughter of the buffaloes. In 1875, William Weston, traveling passenger agent of the Kansas Pacific, discussed with the management of that road the shooting of buffaloes and other game from its trains. The railroad, which at first had encouraged such shooting and had publicized it

[4] Congressional Record, Forty-third Congress, first session, Vol. II, part 1, p. 371, Vol. II, part 3, pp. 2105, 2109.

to attract excursionists, issued orders forbidding this un-sportsmanlike practice.

Early in 1876, with the hunting in Texas at its height, Congress again considered the subject. On January 31, Representative Fort reintroduced his bill to make unlawful any killing except for meat and any killing of female shaggies. The bill was referred to the Committee on Territories, which reported it back without change on February 23.

When the bill reached the floor, Fort spoke strongly in its support. The aim of the measure, he said, was to preserve the buffaloes "for the use of the Indians, whose homes are upon the public domain, and the frontiersmen who may properly use them as food. They have been, and are now being, slaughtered in large numbers. Thousands of these noble brutes are annually slaughtered out of mere wantonness. This bill, just as it is now presented, passed the last Congress. It was not vetoed but fell, as I understand, merely for want of time to consider it after having passed both houses."

Fort called attention to the fact that the government was spending large sums to buy cattle to feed the Indians on the reservations. He argued that this money could be saved if Congress would preserve the buffalo herds and allow the Indians to kill what they needed for meat. Another member, supporting the bill, presented a letter from Lieutenant Colonel A. G. Brackett of the Second United States Cavalry. Brackett asked Congress to stop the wholesale slaughter still going on.

Although Texas did not come within the scope of this bill, several members of the House from the Lone Star State took part in the debate. John H. Reagan, who had been Postmaster General of the Confederacy, said he viewed the bill as proper and right. From personal experience, he added, he knew that wanton slaughter was going on and that the Indians were not the ones who did it.

Speaking in opposition to the bill were two other Texas members, stalwart John Hancock and James W. Throckmorton, a former Governor known as Old Leathercoat. Throckmorton agreed that the intent of the bill was good, but he viewed it as mischievous and difficult to enforce. He believed it would bring hardship to a large number of people on the frontier. He also thought that, at a distance, a buffalo cow could not be distinguished from a bull.

Hancock denounced the bill as embodying a bad policy and said that the sooner the buffaloes were exterminated the better. He moved that the bill be tabled. This proposal was defeated, as was the amendment offered by another member that would have limited the ban to "wanton" killing.

The House passed the bill by a vote of 104 to 36 and sent it to the Senate. It was reported there on February 25 and referred to the Committee on Territories, from which it never emerged. On March 20, Fort introduced again his bill to impose a tax on buffalo hides. It was referred to the Committee on Ways and Means, which pigeonholed it to quiet oblivion. Thus ended the efforts in Congress to save the buffalo herds that were being rapidly swept from the Great Plains by the booming guns of the hide hunters.[5]

### III

But discussion of the issue continued in the state legislatures. Nebraska had passed a protective law in 1875, and lawmakers in several other states were debating similar proposals.

One such bill came up in the Texas legislature in Austin while the hunters were leaving the western ranges strewn

[5] Congressional Record, Forty-fourth Congress, first session, Vol. IV, part 1, p. 773, part 2, pp. 1237–41; Dallas *Herald*, February 15, March 2, 1876; *Rocky Mountain News*, February 27, 1876.

with rotting carcasses. Local opinion was divided. Some Texans, like the editor of the Weatherford *Times*, demanded a law to ban the slaughter of buffaloes for their hides alone. But others wanted the plains cleared for ranching. On the course of this Texas measure, surviving records and newspapers are strangely silent. But an often quoted account in the reminiscences of one of the Texas hunters, John R. Cook, may be mainly reliable.

General Phil Sheridan, Cook noted, "was then in command of the military department of the Southwest, with headquarters at San Antonio. When he heard of the nature of the Texas bill for the protection of the buffaloes, he went to Austin and, appearing before the joint assembly of the House and Senate, so the story goes, told them that they were making a sentimental mistake by legislating in the interest of the buffalo. He told them that, instead of stopping the hunters, they ought to give them a hearty, unanimous vote of thanks. He suggested that they appropriate a sufficient sum of money to strike and present to each one a medal of bronze, with a dead buffalo on one side and a discouraged Indian on the other.

"He said: 'These men have done in the last two years, and will do in the next year, more to settle the vexed Indian question than the entire regular Army has done in the last thirty years. They are destroying the Indians' commissary; and it is a well known fact that an army losing its base of supplies is placed at a great disadvantage. Send them powder and lead, if you will; but, for the sake of lasting peace, let them kill, skin, and sell until the buffaloes are exterminated. Then your prairies can be covered with speckled cattle and the festive cowboy, who follows the hunter as a second forerunner of an advanced civilization.'"

The Texas lawmakers followed General Sheridan's advice, with the result that for the next three years, as John

Cook put it, "the American bison traveled through a hail of lead." [6]

Some of the other Western legislatures still debated the issue. New Mexico passed a protective law in 1880, and Dakota Territory enacted one in 1883; but those measures came too late to have much effect, even if they could have been strictly enforced. The hide hunters could not be bothered with sentiment for an animal that seemed noble at a distance but that, close at hand, proved to be stupid, smelly, and infested with lice.

---

[6] John R. Cook: *The Border and the Buffalo,* pp. 113–14. General Sheridan was proved correct in that the westward spread of Texas cattle ranching followed closely the wiping out of the buffalo herds.

# HIGH TIDE

# AT FORT GRIFFIN

Over the dusty prairie trail, in slow procession, came the creaky freight wagons, their underparts spattered with mud from streams forded farther back. Each wagon was drawn by several spans of mules or oxen and was piled high with dried buffalo hides that poles and ropes kept in place.

The men who held the lines were as weatherbeaten as the wagons, their whiskered faces almost as blank as the clumps of prickly pear they passed. Yet half-closed eyes saw every rut in the trail and the fall of every hoof. Occasionally the monotony was broken by a sharp report like that of a pistol shot. This crack of a long rawhide whip kept the teams in line, but didn't seem to affect their leisurely gait.

The wagon trains were headed from Fort Griffin east to Fort Worth, which had acquired a railroad in July 1876. There, along a siding of the Texas and Pacific, were stacked in tiers the bales of odorous hides, often tens of thousands on a single platform. Soon they would be hauled east to be made into leather for saddle trimmings, jackets, luggage, or other items.

Except for the whitening bones on the ranges, the hides were all that remained of the buffaloes that had borne them a few weeks earlier. The flesh of the carcasses left by feasting wolves had rotted away. The herds that had grazed on the plains as far as anyone could see were being wiped out.

The slaughter in Texas reached its peak in the winter of 1876–7, when an estimated fifteen hundred hunters and skinners were out on the ranges. "There were hunters everywhere," said a frontiersman from Arkansas, S. P. Merry. "You could hear guns popping all over the country."

Hunters and teamsters who dropped into Fort Worth, the cowboy capital of Texas, found much to entertain them. The rough town was well supplied with saloons, gambling casinos, variety theaters, and dance halls. Sporting women roamed the streets, eager to trade their charms for cash. On Saturday nights, cowhands in from the range or the trail sometimes shot up the streets and popped a few lights. Occasionally some of the more exuberant sobered up overnight in the log jail at Second and Commerce streets. The new marshal, Long Hair Jim Courtright, didn't mind a bit of celebration as long as no one was hurt.

Yet Fort Griffin, the smaller town to the west, was where the hunters felt most at home. Griffin, which outfitted nearly all the hunting parties, had become one of the toughest towns on the rampaging Texas frontier. Its merchants sold guns and ammunition and camp provisions. They bought the flint hides and forwarded them to the railroad. To take the money the hunters obtained for the hides, the town was filled with hastily built saloons, gambling rooms, dance halls, and bagnios.

Griffin sprawled over a site called the flat, at the foot of the hill on which the fort stood. Its main street led from the hill to the woods-lined Clear Fork of the Brazos. Often the street, either muddy or dusty, was filled with wagons and other vehicles drawn by oxen or mules. Along each side, in front of the stores and saloons, were hitching racks for the saddle horses of visitors.

By day and night the streets echoed the whoops and curses of cowboys, bullwhackers, hide hunters, off-duty soldiers, and Tonkawas—all showing the effects of firewater. From some of the saloons came the sounds of pianos, fiddles, and guitars aimed to entice customers inside. The bars were the scenes of frequent brawls and occasional killings. The one-story Bee Hive—a combination saloon, gambling house, and dance hall—had this swinging sign out in front:

> *In this hive we're all alive;*
> *Good whisky makes us funny.*
> *If you are dry, step in and try*
> *The flavor of our honey.*

Nearly every saloon had a gambling room in the back, and most of the games were crooked. "I saw a buffalo hunter come to town and market his season's kill for $1,500," said Henry Herron. "The next morning he had to borrow money for his breakfast. The gamblers had taken all of it."

The amusement places for mixed company were notorious dives. Young J. W. Woody, fresh from Missouri in the fall of 1876, viewed performances that made his eyes pop. In the dance halls, he said, "I saw men and women dancing without a stitch of clothing on."

Not only in the dance halls but also in the bars and in the streets luridly dressed women flaunted their charms. The soiled doves, as some frontiersmen called them, were virtually licensed by fining each one a hundred dollars once a year for running a bawdy house. Among those who paid such fines were redheaded Lottie Deno and enterprising Mollie McCabe. Mollie had not been deterred by a misfortune

that struck in the fall of 1875. "Last Friday night," reported
the *Frontier Echo* of November 19, "a fire broke out in Mollie McCabe's Palace of Beautiful Sin. She owned the building, which was entirely consumed, together with her household goods and clothes. The fire was caused by one of the
damsels of spotted virtue." Two other sporting women,
known as Minnie and Long Kate, were tried for fighting in a
grocery store.

Most of the saloons and other places of business were
flimsily built frame structures. C. G. Convers, T. E. Jackson, and S. T. Steierson ran stores in the flat; but the biggest and busiest one was that of Frank E. Conrad. W. H.
Hick had become trader at the post, whose force had been
reduced to a single company of Negro soldiers.

On the evening of January 13, 1877, Bill Akers and
Captain James Montgomery drove into Fort Griffin and
stopped at Charlie Sebastian's Bison Hotel. There they
feasted on buffalo, venison, and antelope. The next morning they went out to see the town. Akers was disappointed,
finding little besides "a few adobe and picket houses, corrals, and immense stacks of buffalo hides."

Akers was impressed, though, by Frank Conrad's store.
There, he wrote, "the hunters procure their supplies and deliver most of the hides." He described the place as "an immense house of rooms, crowded to their utmost with merchandise, with forty or fifty wagons waiting to be loaded and
perhaps a hundred hunters purchasing supplies. I was told
that yesterday Mr. Conrad's sales amounted to nearly $4,-
000, about $2,500 of which was for guns and ammunition
just received."

Akers and Montgomery also visited the Tonkawa village
east of the flat. They found the Indians living in conical tepees with holes at the tops to let out the smoke. Some of the
children wore only clouts, despite the season, while others
ran about in dirty red flannel leggings. The older boys and

the young squaws wore skins and ornaments. The men sat
about idly while the women worked at tanning skins.[1]

## II

In addition to being the chief outfitting point for buffalo
hunters and market for hides, Fort Griffin had become one
of the stops on a new cattle trail. From the fall of 1867
through 1875 most of the Longhorn cattle trailed from
Texas north to Kansas went up the Chisholm Trail through
Fort Worth. But in the late spring of 1876 some of the drovers opened the new Western Trail, which led past Fort
Griffin to the new market at Dodge City.

The new trail, rivaling the older one, added to the outfitting and entertainment business of Fort Griffin. It brought,
in the trailing season, a crowd of boisterous cowboys who,
like the buffalo hunters, wanted the crude amusements
that the frontier town could offer. Soon this demand was
met by a new influx of professional gamblers and ladies of
easy virtue.

The trail drives, along with the beginnings of ranching
in the area, also increased the number of horses in and
about Fort Griffin. This brought a rise in the number of
horse thieves at work in the neighborhood. The outlaws
would steal horses at night and by morning would be well on
their way toward Kansas, where they would sell to men
who didn't ask questions. Then they would steal Kansas
horses to sell in Texas.

Soon this thieving aroused some of the leading citizens
of Fort Griffin and, even more, the cattle raisers in the surrounding country. To them, a horse thief was even worse
than a murderer. The man who took another's horse de-

[1] Fort Worth *Democrat*, January 25, 1877; J. W. Woody to J. Evetts Haley,
Snyder, Texas, October 19, 1926, February 11, 1928, MS. transcripts in Pan-
handle-Plains Historical Museum, Canyon, Texas; Carl Coke Rister: *Fort
Griffin on the Texas Frontier*, pp. 128–39.

prived his victim of the means of travel and of making a
living. So in Fort Griffin in the spring of 1876 a group of
stockmen and others banded into a committee of vigilantes
to rid Clear Fork of horse thieves. After warning some of
the known outlaws and the loose women who had been tipping them off, they began night rides that left notorious
thieves dangling from the limbs of trees. The activities of
the committee made horses safe around Griffin for some
time.[2]

### III

The abundance of buffaloes in Texas brought a whole
army of hunters swarming into Fort Griffin early in 1876.
True, there still was good hunting in some other parts of the
Great Plains. Far to the northwest, Fort Benton alone sent
eighty thousand hides down the Missouri River to the St.
Louis market that year. But the Indian menace kept most of
the white hunters away from the northern plains. Western
Texas was their paradise. It attracted veterans of the Kansas ranges, adventurers from the East, and ne'er-do-wells
and fugitives who wanted a change of scene. Some frontier
farmers and ranchmen found buffalo hides and meat a convenient source of cash until they could make their land more
productive.

Often men left other occupations for the adventurous
life of the buffalo range. One such was Robert Truby, a Fort
Griffin butcher. Truby not only headed west with a hide
wagon, but, unlike the other hunters, took his wife with
him. She was willing to face the dangers of the wilderness
even though she expected a baby soon.

The Trubys camped in Randall County, just above the

2 Dallas *Daily Herald*, April 23, 1876; *Frontier Echo*, April 28, May 12,
June 9, 1876; Denison *Daily News*, June 4, 1876; Wayne Gard: *Frontier Justice*, pp. 202–3.

scenic Palo Duro Canyon from which Mackenzie's troops had routed the Comanches less than two years earlier. While Robert Truby hunted, his hardy wife did the strenuous work of skinning. She still was skinning buffaloes the day before the baby was born. Then, on the day after giving birth to a boy, she went back to the skinning. This child, Hank Smith Truby, brought into the world without the help of a doctor or midwife, was the first white child born in Randall County.[3]

Among the more successful outfits at work west of Fort Griffin in the early months of 1876 was that headed by a noted marksman, Charles Hart, a veteran of Shiloh and Andersonville. As skinners he had John R. Cook, who had hunted in the Panhandle, Warren Dockum, a Union veteran from northern Kansas, Cyrus Reed, and Reed's brother-in-law, Frank Williamson, a green, gawky youth of seventeen. A sixth man drove six yokes of oxen hitched to a freight wagon. The party also had two two-horse teams pulling light wagons. The equipment included two Dutch ovens, other cooking equipment, bedding, extra guns, ammunition, and a grindstone.

Leaving Sweetwater, near Fort Elliott, in January 1876, the party had headed south to the Pease River country and the Salt Fork of the Brazos, where they found buffaloes plentiful. In three months they had 3,361 hides, which were hauled into Fort Griffin. Usually Hart and his men were not far from the camps of other hunters. One day Cook rode to that of John Goff to borrow some flour. His description of Goff could be applied to many of the hide hunters: "He had long hair and was the dirtiest, greasiest, and smokiest mortal I had ever seen. He sat on a fleet horse, holding carelessly

[3] Hamlin Russell: "The Story of the Buffalo," p. 797; Charles Boone McClure: "A History of Randall County and the Anchor Ranch," thesis, pp. 58-9.

in his hands a .44 Sharps. After we reached his camp, he treated me like a nobleman." [4]

<h1 style="text-align:center">IV</h1>

The spring of 1876 found the Mooar brothers as busy as ever. Bills of sale saved by John Mooar give some indication of their activities. In Fort Griffin on March 18 the Mooar partners sold to C. G. Convers and Company thirty pounds of buffalo meat at six cents a pound and 164 tongues at twenty cents each. Supplies bought then included sugar, canned tomatoes, and an ax handle. On the 30th the Mooars paid W. H. Hick, the post trader, for supplies they had bought earlier, including four skillets, a coffeepot, yeast powder, molasses, and a keg of nails. Later in the spring they bought from Hick crackers, beans, corn, sugar, molasses, tea, lard, rope, and three cans of bug poison at eight dollars each. From Convers they obtained bacon, corn, and flour.

In April, when the Mooars were encamped on Mule Creek, they had two visitors from Dodge City. They were W. H. West and John Russell. West told the Mooars that a new trading firm had been formed in Dodge. The partners were Charles Rath, Robert M. Wright, the former sutler at Fort Dodge, and Lee and Reynolds, sutlers at Fort Supply and traders at the Cheyenne agency. The partners had named West as business manager and Russell as wagonmaster. They had sent the two south to blaze a trail and to see about locating one or more trading posts in western Texas in the fall.

From the Mooars, West bought 450 choice hides suitable for being made into robes. The Mooars were to deliver them to Chief Whirlwind's camp at the Cheyenne agency in the

---

[4] John R. Cook: *The Border and the Buffalo*, pp. 110–50. Cook says this hunt started in January 1875, but other evidence in his book indicates the following year. Sweetwater, from which the party left, was not established until June 1875.

Indian Territory. There, for a fee, the Cheyenne women would process them for the new firm. Wright Mooar left with the hides on May 1.

When Wright arrived back at Fort Griffin early in June, he found John preparing to leave for Dallas with a wagon train of hides. John had paid the Hick bill on the 3rd and the Convers one the next day. On the 16th, through T. E. Jackson, he engaged a freighter with an ox wagon to deliver a load of hides to him at J. J. Crowell's place in Dallas. Four days later he hired several others.

As Wright Mooar had not seen his family in the East since he had left there more than six years earlier, he decided to visit them. He rode with John on one of the wagons part of the way to Dallas, then mounted his saddle horse and went on ahead along the prairie trail. In Dallas he left his mount at a livery stable and boarded a train for New York. There he visited his sister, then went to Vermont to see his parents. On his return trip, he stopped in Philadelphia to see the colorful Centennial Exposition. Joining in the throng of visitors, he marveled at such inventions as the high-wheel bicycle and Alexander Graham Bell's newfangled telephone.

In Dallas, John learned of the wiping out of Custer and his force by Indians on the Little Big Horn on June 25. He stayed in town until late in July, laying in a winter's supply of groceries, ammunition, rope, and other items. He bought spare parts of harness from the pioneer firm of Padgitt Brothers at 603 Elm Street. Not wishing to return any of the wagons empty, he arranged with Mayfield and Cowan to haul lumber to the frontier town of Graham, in Young County. On August 3 he bought more supplies in Weatherford. From his camp on Shirley Creek, four miles east of Fort Griffin, John wrote his mother that he expected Wright back any day.

Soon afterward Wright rejoined John, and the hunters

camped on Foil Creek. For the winter killing, John had gathered a large outfit that included four nine-yoke teams of
steers and thirteen wagons for hauling hides. In addition,
there were two four-mule teams with two wagons each. He
had engaged nine men as skinners and teamsters.

After two days at Fort Griffin, the outfit moved slowly
west, past Fort Phantom Hill on the military road to Fort
Concho. Wright went ahead with the mule teams, while
John followed with the slower oxen. Wright thought he
would find plenty of buffaloes in the open country along the
divide between the Brazos River and the Colorado.

With him and the mule teams were four men who had
not been in his outfit before. One night he overheard two of
them talking in their bed under his wagon. "Wonder how
much farther that kid is going," said one, "to try to find
where the sun goes down."

"I don't know," said the other. "But I'd be ashamed not
to follow when he volunteers to lead and find the way. Especially in these ravines that might be full of Indians."

On the prairies of Nolan County, near the future site
of Sweetwater, the Mooar outfit found a fine country almost
covered with buffaloes. With the grass luxuriant and lakes
offering plenty of water, this looked like a good place to hunt.
So Wright drove on a little farther west and south to make
camp along Deep Creek. The men pitched camp about ten
o'clock on the morning of October 7, 1876. Wright then
rode off to the west and southwest to look at the country
and the buffaloes, returning just before sundown.

As he neared the new camp, he saw something that startled him. From a ridge a mile and a half west of the camp,
he spied in the midst of a small herd a rare white buffalo.
He had killed one in Kansas, but had heard of only a few
others. Now maybe he could bag another—the first he had
seen in Texas.

Wright galloped into camp and asked how long the herd

had been there. It had been near for several hours, but no one had noticed the white cow. So Wright took Dan Dowd with him and went back, creeping through the grass to approach the albino. With his first shot, Wright downed the big white cow, which turned out to be a four-year-old; but the firing stampeded the herd. He had to shoot three bulls to keep the animals from trampling Dan Dowd and himself.

Wright had the white hide saved for mounting and told the men to hang the meat in near-by trees overnight. The next morning, while he did some more exploring, two men with a team went back to meet John and the ox wagons, taking along a hindquarter of the white buffalo. After the whole outfit was in camp, the Mooars began what became one of their most successful winters of hunting.[5]

## V

On the Texas ranges that winter, hunting outfits almost stumbled over each other. So many besides the Mooars found the hunting good along Deep Creek that an ox-team freighter, W. H. (Pete) Snyder, opened a supply store there. He built his place of chinaberry poles and buffalo hides and bought his provisions from Joseph H. Brown in Forth Worth. Soon his store was surrounded by dugouts and buffalo-hide tents. So many fugitives and other desperadoes gathered there that for a time the place was called Robbers' Roost.

One of the smaller outfits hunting in western Texas that winter was that of J. W. and A. B. Woody and Raymond and Matt Rumph. The Woodys, brothers, had arrived from Missouri in October. This party made its first camp at the head of Bull Creek in Garza County, at the foot of the high plains. The four men killed thirty-two hundred buffaloes during the winter, mainly between Yellowstone Creek and Muchaway Creek, four or five miles southwest of the future

[5] MS. in John Wesley Mooar Papers.

site of Gail. Their headquarters camp was at an old Indian burial ground six miles south of the site of Post. There they built a dugout with a rock chimney.

During the winter the Woodys and Rumphs went to the head of the Colorado River. Out in this arid country they discovered that they were far from water and didn't have even a drop in their canteens. But they went on, hoping to find a lake or a stream. When none appeared, they quit using tobacco and went without food. Each carried a bit of lead in his mouth to avoid spitting. But Raymond Rumph finally ate a piece of dried and salty buffalo meat. The four mules were played out and had lost their appetites.

The hunters and their mules had gone thirsty for nearly three days and nights when the party finally found water in Mustang Draw. By that time Raymond Rumph was suffering badly. His tongue had swelled until it pushed out of his mouth and became as thick as his hand. He ran ahead and fell into the water; but the others pulled him out and held him on the ground while they gave him small sips at intervals. After tying the mules to the wagon, they brought a bucket of water for each.

On this hunt, J. W. Woody did the shooting, while the other three skinned and pegged. Most of the hides were sold to buyers who made the rounds of the camps with big wagons. Prices ranged from 75 cents to $2.50. J. W. Woody recalled that some of the meat was freighted out, but that most of it was wasted. "Right around Big Spring for a mile, I've seen the carcasses so thick that you could jump from one to the other. We always saved the tongues. We'd parboil a lot of them in a big pot, take them out and skin them, then slice and fry them in marrow gravy obtained from cracking the bones open. They were the finest meat I ever ate."[6]

S. P. Merry, from Arkansas, was not quite twenty-one when he left Fort Griffin for the buffalo range in the fall

[6] Woody: loc. cit.

of 1876. He was cook and hide pegger for an outfit of six men. The party went past the ruins of Phantom Hill and found the first buffaloes north of Colorado City, near the future site of Roscoe. The men began killing on a tributary of Deep Creek, near the later site of Snyder. In December a large herd gathered in the creek valley for protection against a snowstorm. "You could stand on a hill and look down the valley, which was about a mile wide," recalled Merry. "It looked as if a man could walk on buffaloes." Early in March 1877, Merry began working for the Mooar brothers.[7]

John C. Jacobs and John W. Poe were partners again on the western ranges in the winter of 1876–7, and Joe S. Mc-Combs took out about the same outfit he had used a year earlier. McCombs made his winter camp on Morgan Creek, over the divide west of Colorado City. His season's kill was twenty-three hundred hides. He sold most of them in camp at the range price of $1.00 but obtained $1.50 for those he hauled to Fort Griffin.[8]

Another hunter was Windy Bill Russell, who had just come back to Texas. He camped that winter in a dugout on the Middle Concho in Tom Green County, near the town of Ben Ficklin. Russell, who was as good at hunting as at talking, made a big haul of hides. But one of his men, Robert C. Parrack, had an experience that he didn't want to repeat. Late one afternoon in November he was following a herd about three miles from camp. He noticed dark clouds in the north, but he wanted to down as many buffaloes as he could before dark.

Then a blinding snowstorm struck suddenly, and Parrack realized that he had waited too long to start back to the dugout. He set out, but the night quickly became blacker and the storm more intense. Finally he stumbled against the carcass of one of the buffaloes he had killed. Falling exhausted

[7] S. P. Merry, Amarillo, to J. Evetts Haley, August 21, 1926, MS. transcript in Panhandle-Plains Historical Museum, Canyon, Texas.
[8] Joe S. McCombs: "On the Cattle Trail and the Buffalo Range," p. 99.

in the snow, he crawled up against the dead animal for protection from the gale. Again and again he fired his rifle to signal the men in the camp, but he heard no response.

With all his rifle bullets gone, Parrack pulled out his six-shooter. "I first decided to save the shells," he recalled. "Then I thought that three shells wouldn't do a dead man any good, so I fired them. As soon as I shot the second time, I saw streaks of fire spurt a little south of me. Although I'd thought I was given out when I sat down there, I got up and ran all the way to the dugout. I had passed near the dugout and had gone beyond it. The men had heard my shots and had fired several times, but I had not been able to hear them because of the wind." [9]

## VI

While cumbrous wagons from Fort Griffin were being loaded with hides in the hunters' camps scattered over the ranges, the new trading firm in Dodge City was busy. The partners were taking steps to set up another outpost in the buffalo country of Texas, one that would give competition to Fort Griffin as a market for hides.

A long wagon train with lumber to build a trading post and supplies to stock it left Dodge City in the late fall of 1876. In December some of the merchandise was unloaded at the trading post of Sweetwater—later called Mobeetie —on the outskirts of Fort Elliott. There hunters who had been taking hides in the Texas Panhandle heard about the new venture, and many of them decided to go along. Some joined the caravan there, and others after it had crossed the Red River.

Charles Rath rode ahead on horseback. With a compass on the horn of his saddle, he struck out almost directly

[9] W. C. Holden: "Robert Cypret Parrack, Buffalo Hunter and Fence Cutter," pp. 34–5.

south. Behind him was a wagon drawn by mules and carrying a dozen men with picks and shovels. At the creeks and ravines they made easier crossings for the heavy freight wagons that followed.

The long caravan of the merchants was in charge of John Russell. Wright Mooar said there were twenty-six wagons drawn by mule teams and an equal number pulled by six-yoke ox teams. Some of the wagons, he recalled, had hind wheels seven feet high. Behind them came more than fifty wagons of the hunting outfits, ready to make use of the new trading post at its start.

In January of 1877 the wagon train reached its destination; and construction of the new post began, while the hunters scattered to look for buffaloes. The site was on the south side of the Double Mountain Fork of the Brazos River, in Stonewall County. It was twelve miles northwest of the future site of Hamlin and was near a point at which the northern boundary fence of the T-Diamond Ranch would join that of W. Pringle Moore.

Quickly the store and other crude buildings rose from the prairie. Some were formed of sod, and others of cedar pickets driven firmly into the ground, with the cracks between them chinked with mud. The new trading post would be convenient for many hunters who didn't want to take time to haul their hides all the way to Fort Griffin. Some referred to the outpost as Camp Reynolds or Reynolds City. Others called it Rath City. Charles Rath continued to live at Dodge City, where he still had a large store, but he made frequent trips to Texas, sometimes accompanied by his wife.[1]

Yet, although Rath City was to handle one hundred thousand dollars' worth of buffalo hides in 1877, its busi-

---

[1] Dodge City *Times*, May 12, June 23, July 7, September 8, October 20, 1877; Cook: op. cit., p. 181; Amarillo *News-Globe*, August 14, 1938. The Panhandle trading post of Sweetwater, whose name was changed to Mobeetie in 1879, should not be confused with the Texas town of Sweetwater, in Nolan County to the south, which retained its name.

ness didn't seem to diminish the prosperity of Fort Griffin. Frank Conrad sometimes had four acres covered with bales of hides waiting to be hauled to the railroad. The hides no longer needed to be taken to Dallas, since the Texas and Pacific Railroad had reached Fort Worth. That extension of the rails cut the wagon trip by thirty-three and a half miles each way.

So great was the demand of hunters for ammunition that Conrad sometimes had thirty tons of lead and five tons of powder stored in the warehouse and magazine attached to his store. The deluge of hides was pushing prices down; but, even at $1.25 each, the two hundred thousand marketed at Fort Griffin in the 1876–7 season brought the hunters a quarter of a million dollars.

In Fort Worth the hide wagons were becoming almost as common as the trail herds of Longhorn cattle. One morning in the spring of 1877 a newspaper reporter noted the arrival of a train of ten wagons from the west. "In front were eleven yokes of oxen, driven by one man and dragging after them four large new wagons, heavily laden. Two other teams, with seven yokes each, drawing three wagons, followed. There probably were 2,500 to 3,000 hides in the train." Later in the same spring another observer noticed sixty thousand baled hides piled high on a platform along the Texas and Pacific tracks.[2]

Besides all the hide hunting, there still was some shooting of buffaloes for sport. In November 1876 eight Dallas men headed for the ranges. One drove a two-horse wagon carrying a barrel of salt and other supplies, while the others rode horseback. The leader was Junius Peak, the city marshal and an expert marksman. Near the forks of the Little Wichita the men found plenty of buffaloes.

On their way home the Dallas party encountered, in a

[2] Fort Worth *Democrat*, May 3, August 10, December 2, 1877; Edgar Rye: *The Quirt and the Spur*, p. 220.

camp on the Little Wichita, five youths of fifteen to twenty years from the frontier town of Decatur. They had left home in October, with two wagons, to try their luck at shooting buffaloes. The Dallas men feared that the youths might fall victims to a large band of Indians believed to be camped on the Pease River. But, although the youngsters sighted one warrior, they suffered no harm. After killing more than a score of shaggies, they turned homeward, taking about two thousand pounds of the humps and hindquarters of fat calves and yearlings, which they had smoked and dried in camp. Their arrival was a relief to their parents, who had heard a rumor that all five had been captured by Indians.[3]

Some sportsmen still came from the East. Early in January 1877 a party of eight adventurers set out for the headwaters of the Salt Fork of the Brazos. One of them was seventeen-year-old Elliott Roosevelt, a brother of Theodore. Another was a cousin, John Roosevelt. The outfit passed Fort Belknap and Stinking Creek and made camp in Blanco Canyon. The men shot a few buffaloes, in addition to antelope and other game. They had several narrow escapes from wounded animals and went through a few Indian scares. For two weeks they lived on buffalo meat alone, having run out of flour, vegetables, and even coffee. On their return, Fort Griffin looked to them like a highly civilized place.[4]

If the hide hunters were indifferent to the waste of meat on the plains, several farmers in eastern Texas took another view. They saw in the slaughter an opportunity for profit. Taking along their guns and wagons, they drove large herds of hogs to the buffalo range. While they filled their wagons with buffalo meat and hides, the hogs fattened on the carcasses. Then they drove the hogs back to their homes in the pine-woods country and slaughtered them. Never had they taken better pork to market.

[3] C. V. Terrell: *The Terrells*, pp. 139–45.
[4] Theodore Roosevelt: "Buffalo Hunting."

# ⎯⎯◀ 15 ▶⎯⎯

# YELLOW HOUSE DRAW

In the early months of 1877, buffalo hunters on Texas ranges remote from the fringes of settlement had to contend with more than blizzards. Indian troubles were breaking out again. The white hunters within reach of Fort Griffin still felt safe, but those farther west, using the Rath City trading post as headquarters, were becoming uneasy. Mackenzie's blasting of the Comanches from Palo Duro Canyon had not caused the redskins to forget entirely the Texas hunting grounds. Now the Sioux victory over Custer on the Little Big Horn was making them bold again.

From their reservation camp in the Wichita Mountains, about seventy-five Comanche warriors and their families rode south into Texas to hunt buffaloes and to kill white butchers. The rotting carcasses on the prairies and the piles of hides in the camps added to their fury. At about the same time a group of Kiowas left their Rainy Mountain camp to hunt along Elk Creek, an upper tributary of the Red River.

The moves of the two roving bands made blood-chilling news in the poorly defended camps of the white hunters.

Some of the smaller outfits joined forces for better protection. The men began keeping their horses close to camp at night and sleeping with their guns within easy reach.

On February 20 a lone horseman made the rounds of several hunters' camps in the upper Brazos country. The rider was Louis Keys, a skinner who worked for Marshall Sewell. Keys, who had some Cherokee blood, warned the hunters that danger was close at hand. Indians, he said, had destroyed the camp of Billy Devons, about forty-five miles west of Rath City, and had taken all the horses. Devons and his skinners barely had escaped. At another camp, two Englishmen who had been out hunting afoot had returned to find their horses and ammunition gone and their camp wrecked. The Indians had cut the best leather out of the harness. They had pulled both the wagons between two high stacks of hides, then thrown dry brush on them and set them afire.

One of the hunters reached by Keys was John R. Cook, who, with others, was encamped a few miles southwest of the Double Mountain Fork. While the other men loaded the outfit to return to Rath City, Cook rode west to carry the alarm to two outlying camps. In the first camp he gave the news to Mort N. (Wild Bill) Kress and Sol Reese, veteran hunters who had come down from Kansas. Kress, from Pennsylvania, had been a cavalryman in the Civil War. Reese, of Indiana birth, had gone to Kansas in 1866, but had returned east a decade later to attend the Centennial Exposition in Philadelphia.

On hearing the alarm, Reese left Kress and their helper to load while he rode with Cook over broken prairie to the camp of Alabama-born Pat Garrett. There he found tacked to a stake a card that read: "Gone to Rath's store."

From several directions, caravans of hunters were making their way back to Rath City, traveling together when they could. John Cook recalled that there were twenty-three men in his group as they followed the Mackenzie Trail down to Stinking Creek. They rode on through a mesquite flat and thickets of chaparral to the Double Mountain Fork. On this trip the men kept their water kegs filled and their horses tied or hobbled at night. They posted guards every night and avoided making campfires after dark.

The hide men were especially cautious after George Causey and Sam Carr, who had been hunting together, said they had seen sixty Indians in war paint between the Mackenzie Trail and the Double Mountain. The crude buildings of Rath City, their pickets and boards not yet weatherbeaten, looked good to the weary travelers as they arrived in the evening.

Nearly three hundred hunters and skinners had gathered at this frontier trading post. They overflowed the big Reynolds-Rath store, with its hide yard in the back, and the other hastily raised buildings. Their equipment filled the wagon yard of Smoky Hill Thompson, a veteran Rocky Mountain trapper and Kansas hunter. For safety, the men kept their horses together. Twice a day they herded them to the creek, a mile away, and let them drink. They hauled creek water to the post in barrels for use in cooking.

In the crowded saloon the grizzled hunters could get away from some of the smell of buffalo hides, hear the latest news from the ranges, and fortify their courage with firewater. Presiding temporarily at the bar was Limpy Jim Smith, late of Montana. Smith had been hunting since November and had two thousand hides ready to send to market.

For those who wanted entertainment of a kind that Adobe Walls had not afforded, a new dance hall adjoined the saloon. About forty sporting girls had come down from Dodge City to help the hunters spend their money. The crowding of the post as a result of the Indian scare gave the dance hall a capacity business.

Billy Devons, who had been a soldier, noted that the outfit of Marshall Sewell, which had camped near him, was not yet accounted for. Sewell, from Pennsylvania, was well liked by the other hunters. Devons suggested that some of the men ride out with a warning. Quickly eighteen volunteered and prepared to leave, with Devons as a guide. The party included John Cook, Joe Jackson, and Joe Freed.

Soon after the others reached the site of the Devons camp, which the Indians had destroyed a few days earlier, they were joined by a man who came in afoot, worn and hungry. He was one known as Wild Skillet, a skinner hired by Marshall Sewell. The party learned that Sewell had been killed and scalped by Indians two days earlier.

On the day of the raid, Sewell had left his camp and had found a herd of buffaloes about two miles to the west. After he had killed twenty-one, his two skinners, Wild Skillet and James W. (Moccasin Jim) Stell, started to drive out to take the hides. On approaching, they saw a band of Indians circling Sewell and firing at him. There seemed to be about fifty of the warriors. Quickly Wild Skillet and Moccasin Jim turned the team around and headed back toward the camp.

About that time the Indians saw the skinners and started chasing them. But Wild Skillet and Moccasin Jim drove into a bushy canyon, abandoned the team and wagon there, and escaped into the breaks. They heard several shots and stayed hidden until after dark. The next day Moccasin Jim went afoot to warn the two Englishmen, not knowing of the fate of their camp, while Wild Skillet went on a similar mission to the Devons camp.

The party from Rath City, guided by Wild Skillet, found and buried the body of Sewell, which had been scalped and otherwise mutilated. It looked as if the Indians had slipped up on Sewell when he was absorbed in shooting buffaloes and had waited until he was out of ammunition before attacking him. They took his .45 Sharps rifle, his team, and the ammunition they later found in his camp, some distance away. Not bothering to skin the buffaloes he had killed, they left the carcasses to bloat on the prairie.[1]

## II

Of the scouting party, John Cook was the first back at Rath City. The others had sent him on ahead to spread the news and to have provisions sent out to them at the camp of John (Buckskin Bill) Godey. As soon as he dismounted, questioners surrounded Cook and learned of the death of Sewell. In the saloon several volunteered to go out after the Comanches. But others were silent, and Tom Lumpkins drew sharp words on himself by saying: "I haven't lost any Indians, and I don't propose to hunt any."

Outside, a crowd gathered in front of the store. Tall Hank Campbell grasped the hand of Cook and said: "John, I'm going with you." W. H. West, manager of the store, climbed up onto the wagon of Buckskin Bill Godey, who had just driven in. He told the men that Godey had offered the use of his team and wagon for the trip to the camp. West said his company would provide whatever supplies were necessary. Then Smoky Hill Thompson, who took his name from the Kansas river along which he had lived, stood up in the wagon.

"Boys," he advised, "first start this outfit to Godey's. Then organize two separate companies—one to go out and fight the Indians, the other to stay here and defend this place and care for the extra stock. Some of you hunters have from four to eight head of stock. Those not taken on the expedition must be taken out of the country or be well guarded. This place most likely will be the storm center. Those Indians have seen the acres of hide piles. Their revenge will be terrible."

Quickly the men loaded the relief wagon with supplies,

[1] John R. Cook: *The Border and the Buffalo*, pp. 180–95.

and a small party set out for the Godey camp. Godey drove. With him were John Cook, Billy Devons, Charley Emory, better known as Squirrel Eye, and three others. Charlie Hart lent his hunting horse to Cook, whose mount, Keno, was exhausted from the long night ride from the camps.

The party arrived at the camp in the evening and found Joe Freed and the others who had gone out earlier from Rath's. With them were the two Englishmen, along with Moccasin Jim and Spotted Jack Dean, who was part Comanche and had been a guide for Mackenzie. That morning, while the relief party was on the way, Indians had attacked the camp and had made away with all the horses except three. The long-range buffalo guns of the white hunters had served well in their defense and enabled them to drive off the attackers. Spotted Jack had received a serious bullet wound in the thigh; but the ball had missed the bone, and he still was able to walk. Three others had slight wounds.

For the night, the hunters moved their camp to a place that might be defended more easily. The next morning all headed back to Rath City. Joe Freed and Squirrel Eye rode ahead to carry the news. The others arrived in the evening and found preparations under way for an expedition against the redskins.

Of the nearly three hundred men who had been at Rath City a few days earlier, at least one hundred and twenty-five had left for Fort Griffin or other safer places to the east. Pat Garrett was among those who had gone. Of the eighty-five hunters who had volunteered to go out to fight the Indians, only forty-eight were in the expedition that left for the west in the first week of March. They took four wagons to haul grub, camp equipment, and feed for the horses and to bring back any men who might be wounded. The store had donated the provisions. Conspicuous on one of the wagons was a fifty-gallon barrel filled with whisky. A hilarious drinking bout had preceded the departure.

The hunters had elected Jim White as their captain, but on the first day out he began bleeding in the lungs. So Bill Bronson took him back to Rath City, leaving only forty-six men in the expedition. The men then chose blustering Hank Campbell as captain, Limpy Jim Smith as lieutenant, and Joe Freed as third in command. Smoky Hill Thompson was wagonmaster, and Ben Jackson served as quartermaster. Bill Beldon and George Holmes said they would do the cooking if exempted from guard duty, but they agreed to fight along with the others.

Among those on the expedition was Bill Benson, who could aim a rifle better with his one arm than many another could with two. Another was Hiram Bickerdyke, a son of the famous Civil War nurse Mary Ann Ball Bickerdyke, better known as Mother Bickerdyke. Still others, all from the hunting ranges, were W. Skelton Glenn, of Georgia birth, John R. Cook, Spotted Jack Dean, Squirrel Eye Emory, Whisky Jim Greathouse, Louis Keys, Sol Reese, Bill Kress, Al Waite, Joe Jackson, Lee Grimes, and Frank Collinson.

Only twenty-six of the men were mounted. The others rode in the wagons. Nearly all of them had long-range rifles, with 250 rounds of ammunition for each. Between visits to the whisky barrel, they tried to keep a sharp eye out for Comanches and Kiowas.

The party had as its guide a Mexican, José Tefoya, who had traded with the Comanches on the high plains and had scouted for Mackenzie three years earlier. The route the avengers took was mainly west, past the Godey and Sewell camps. For three days they made their way through an enormous herd of buffaloes. They found a place where Indians had camped, but the warriors had left. Their trail led west through the breaks and up the escarpment to the Staked

Plains. The hunters had to double their teams and push by hand to get the wagons up the steep, winding trail; but finally they reached the high plains, which most of them were seeing for the first time.

The tableland on which the hunters emerged was even flatter than the plains of western Kansas that some of them had known. It was a grassy plateau of far horizons and frequent mirages, a land of sun and solitude. Hardly a tree, bush, or hill could be seen. Yet the eastern edge of this plateau was penetrated by several wooded canyons, no one of which the traveler was likely to notice until just before he came to its rim.

After reaching the South Plains, the fugitive Indians had divided into small bands; but the hunters followed their trail as best they could. Paralleling the deeply cut Casa Amarilla or Yellow House Creek, the tracks led across flat plains covered thickly with short, curly mesquite grass. The redskins appeared to have several hundred horses with them. From some of the camps the Indians had started dragging travois poles to the north, as if to give the false impression that they were heading back to Fort Sill. This tactic did not fool the pursuers.

Aware that they were coming closer to the Indians, the whites advanced cautiously but steadily, taking little time out to eat or sleep. Some of them vowed they would neither eat nor sleep until they had slain ten of the savages who killed and mutilated Marshall Sewell. On the evening of March 16 the weary, unshaven men were beside Yellow House Creek, a few miles below the future site of Lubbock. They pushed on through the night, without waiting for the wagons and food to catch up with them.

Early the next morning José, accompanied by John Cook and Louis Keys, rode on ahead for seven or eight miles. From a hidden point on the bluff, the trio saw Indian hunters going to and from a camp in a deep ravine known as Yel-

13    SCAVENGERS OF THE PLAINS

14　SKINNERS AT WORK

low House Canyon or Yellow House Draw, farther upstream. Squaws were bringing in packhorses loaded with buffalo meat.

Keys rode back about two miles and signaled for the rest of the party to follow. The hunters saw that a band of Apaches from New Mexico had camped just above the Comanches. Although the trees of the canyon screened the camps, the whites thought there must be 150 to 160 warriors, besides the women and children. Now the Texans were ready to take Indian scalps.[2]

## III

From their hiding places on the bluff, the hunters could hear the booming of stolen rifles as the Indians killed buffaloes on the other side of the creek. Since the redskins gave no sign of having seen their pursuers, Hank Campbell decided to make camp in the bed of the brushy canyon several miles below the Comanche camp. A bend in the canyon hid this site from the Indians. Campbell planned to make a surprise attack by going up the canyon at night. He ordered the men to fire no gun except at an Indian.

The captain took José, Cook, and Keys onto the bluff to watch the Indians. Soon afterward José spied a lone warrior —apparently a scout—riding toward them. Quickly Cook, on the borrowed chestnut sorrel he was riding, reported this news to Campbell.

"We must get him," the captain agreed, "or he will ride down, strike our trail, and give the whole thing away."

Cook rode back up the hill to the watching post, accompanied by Joe Freed, Al Waite, and one of the Englishmen whose camp had been plundered. The men divided and hid

[2] Cook: op. cit., pp. 195–212; Frank Collinson: "The Battle of Yellow House Draw," reminiscences, MS.; Rex W. Strickland, editor: "The Recollections of W. S. Glenn, Buffalo Hunter," pp. 42–52.

on each side of the trail that the Indian seemed to be taking.

"Where is the bloody cuss?" asked the Englishman, who
had an express rifle he had brought from the old country.
"I want to kill him myself."

The warrior, a Comanche, had a Winchester in his scab-
bard, but he had no chance to use it. When the Englishman
fired, the bronze scout fell dying. The pony bolted, but Cook
and Waite, after a chase, caught him a mile down the creek.
The hunters threw the body of the warrior into a clump of
tall reeds near a water hole.

Hiding in the canyon below the camp of the Indians, the
tired whites ate and rested in preparation for the night attack. Some found time for drinking and gambling, but Hank
Campbell kept guards posted on all sides. For the attack, he
divided the men into three groups. He and Limpy Jim Smith
each commanded a band of mounted hunters, while Joe
Freed took charge of those who were afoot. The captain assigned Cook and Godey to go ahead with José and find the
camp.

After dark, all the men advanced up the creek as quietly
as they could, hoping to make a surprise attack on the Indians about midnight. The stars were out, although there was
no moon. But at a place where the canyon forked, José mistakenly led the men up the wrong prong. This lost them several hours. The weary hunters grumbled at the delay, but
before daybreak the grease smoke from roasting marrow
bones told them they were near the Comanche camp.

At dawn the three men in advance saw a large band of
Indian ponies on the high plain ahead of them. Through the
cottonwoods in Yellow House Draw they could see the tops
of some tepees. José sent Cook back to bring up the hunters, who quickly made ready for the attack.

By this time the whites were footsore and hungry and in

considerable confusion. Some still felt the effects of their drinking. Campbell formed the men into an irregular line, with the unmounted ones in the center, about five paces apart. As they moved forward, Louis Keys, on the left, galloped ahead and began an old Cherokee war chant. Then Squirrel Eye chimed in with a Rebel yell.

As they approached the village, the hunters saw warriors pouring out of the tepees and running toward them. The Indians hurried to the crest of a slight rise between the camp and the attackers, dropped to the ground, and began firing. At first the truant Comanches thought they were being attacked by soldiers.

By the time the whites were in easy gun range of the Indians, Spotted Jack was in the lead. Some of the riders had dismounted to find better cover before they started firing. The squads became separated, and soon it was almost a case of every man for himself. The first hunter hit was Spotted Jack, who was knocked out of the fighting. Then Joe Jackson was shot in the groin and fell from his horse, and Billy Devons received a bullet in his arm. The horse of Hurricane Lee Grimes was shot from under him, and the fall broke Lee's left wrist. But, despite their own wounds, Devons and Grimes helped John Cook drag Joe Jackson back to safety.

The confusion of the hunters was becoming worse. Since the horses were easy marks for the Indians, Campbell ordered every sixth man to take the mounts back and hide them in the canyon. "As they started back," Skelton Glenn recalled, "it looked like two men to every horse."

As the fighting continued, Glenn and some of the others who had had battle experience in the Civil War began to make their shots count. Before long the Indians were forced off the knoll from which they had been firing. They carried back to the camp six warriors who had been struck. But most of the scattered hunters became so rattled that they shot at each other as often as at the redskins. Hank Campbell sent several bullets at Skelton Glenn before Glenn signaled to him with his hat.

The Indians driven from their knoll found other vantage points from which to fire. Hank Campbell decided to pull his men back to a safer place.

"Get back!" he yelled. "Back to the draw! They will kill us all!"

Most of the hunters complied with alacrity. "It was not a retreat," Frank Collinson recalled. "It was a stampede." Some of the men had not yet fired a shot.

After the attackers fell back to a more easily defended point in the canyon down the creek, the Indians became bolder. About a score, mounted on fleet ponies and strung out at intervals, rode past the hunters' camp, peppering more bullets at the whites. They kept this up for three hours without much result. Once five of the hunters crawled through the grass to get better shots at the Comanches. They knocked one off his horse and downed the mount of another. Glenn tried to set fire to the prairie and thus drive the warriors back, but the wind put out all his matches.

The early afternoon brought a lull in the shooting. José went out with some of the unmounted hunters to do a bit of scouting, but the Mexican came back with a painful bullet wound in his shoulder. Then a band of yelling warriors made a charge on the camp from below. Their attack apparently was a ruse to draw the attention and fire of the hunters while a larger force of Indians came down the canyon behind a screen of grass fire. But as the hunters suspected what was up and as the grass did not burn well, this stratagem failed.

Another lull gave the men a chance to look after their wounded, who were calling for water. Several men crawled down to the nearest water hole. They had no canteens, but John Cook had a pair of new boots that would hold water.

Those were used to carry water to the wounded. Then each man was given a drink from a bottle of brandy in Bill Kress's saddle pocket.

In the late afternoon the wagons caught up with the hunters, and everyone started talking at once. There had been no shooting for some time, but Hank Campbell feared that the Indians might be planning a night attack. So he sent two squads to take a look at their camp. "I will keep the rest and protect the wagons," he said. "We'll get on this hill and hold it till hell freezes over."

Approaching cautiously, the scouting parties found that all the Indians had departed. Not a tepee or a horse was in sight.

The white scouts returned to the camp an hour before sundown, bringing the saddle from Lee Grimes's fallen horse and a war bonnet that a Comanche brave had lost. The hunters fastened a blanket to two pieces of lodge pole to make a stretcher for the most seriously wounded man, Joe Jackson. Everyone was relieved that the Indians had gone. In attacking such a large camp, the Texans had taken on a bigger force than they had expected. Only with better leadership and less whisky could they have achieved a marked victory.

The men, who had not eaten since four o'clock on the afternoon of the preceding day, were ravenous. "I'm so hungry I could eat a raw coyote," said one. All were ready for a feast on the evening after the fight. They made two big kettles of oyster soup, opened two boxes of crackers, and carved a large cheese. In addition, they had pickles, canned peaches, and all the black coffee they could drink.

The next morning they started back toward Rath City, burning the prairie behind them to wipe out their trail and thus discourage pursuit by the Indians. Soon they found buffaloes and stopped long enough to butcher and cook. Except for those who scattered to the hunters' camps without going to Rath City, the party reached the trading post after four days of travel. They had been gone twenty-three days.[3]

## I V

At Rath City they found only forty-two men of nearly a hundred who had been there when the expedition left. Some had sought safety farther east; others had gone back to the range to shoot and skin. The wounded Joe Jackson was sent to Fort Griffin, where he died two months later—the only white fatality from the battle.

The hunters back from the South Plains had gone to their camps to bring in the hides they had left and to get more. But soon they learned that their attack on the Comanches at Yellow House Draw had not had the desired effect. Indians continued to raid the hunters' camps, even some within five miles of Rath City. On April 19, Captain P. L. Lee set out from Fort Griffin to drive them back to their reservations. With him were forty-five cavalrymen, five wagons, ten pack mules, and ten Tonkawa scouts. With this force and other cavalry detachments from Big Spring, he scoured the ranges in search of Indian camps.

On April 27, Rath City had other news. In the saloon, Tom Lumpkins made slighting remarks about the recent expedition of the hunters. When one of them, who was unarmed, reprimanded him, Lumpkins shot the man, breaking his arm near the shoulder. This was too much for Limpy Jim Smith, who pulled out his six-shooter and fired at Lumpkins but missed. Smith then followed Lumpkins out into the street, toward a wagon in which John Cook and John Godey were stacking dried buffalo tongues. Smith fired again, and Lumpkins fell. The grave of Lumpkins, marked by a buffalo skull, was the first in Rath City's Boot Hill.

    [3] Galveston *News*, April 5, 1877; *Frontier Echo*, April 27, 1877; Dodge City *Times*, May 26, 1877; Cook: op. cit., pp. 211–32; Collinson: op. cit.; Strickland: op. cit., pp. 52–63.

Captain Lee's two-pronged expedition brought in a few captives; but, like the earlier one by the hunters, it failed to halt the sporadic raids. Comanches wrecked several other hide camps, ran off stock, and killed three more hunters. From their camp forty miles northwest of Rath City, Bill Benson and Hiram Bickerdyke lost eight head of stock.

On April 29 a band of warriors attacked a camp that Skelton Glenn and the two Englishmen had made near Double Mountain, west of the trading post. Plundering the camp, they chopped spokes out of the wagon wheels, ran off the team, took two thousand rounds of ammunition, and seriously wounded Glenn. The next day George Cornett brought the news to Rath City. Quickly one of the hunters there started back with Cornett to bring help to the wounded man.

John Cook borrowed Charles Rath's buggy and fine team. The others, who included Charles (Squirrel Eye) Emory, were on saddle horses. The men found Glenn in a thicket near his camp and lifted him into the buggy. Starting back that night, they followed the trail by starlight. About four miles from the trading post, when streaks of light were beginning to appear in the east, they stopped to feed the horses and to eat a cold lunch.

While they were halted, the men heard a burst of gunfire from the direction of Rath City. Squirrel Eye galloped on ahead for about a mile, to a rise from which he could see the post.

"Boys," he yelled as he returned, "there are about seventy-five Injuns just over the hill. They're going west—and driving more than a hundred horses."

At Rath's, John Cook recalled, "we met a cheap-looking crowd. There were about fifty men—with two exceptions, all flat afoot. The Indians had made a clean job." The Dodge City *Times* said the raiders had captured twenty-five head of stock which Frank Foster was herding near by. Among the missing mounts were Cook's Keno and Sam Carr's prized

Kentucky gelding, Prince. Some of the Comanches had ridden through the empty street, shooting right and left at the
buildings and letting out blood-curdling yells. After sending
Glenn on to the hospital at Fort Griffin, the men talked of
pursuing the Indians, but they did not have enough horses
to set out at once.

Texas ranchmen who heard of the plight of the hunters
at Rath City gave them horses and offered money for supplies for a new expedition. Twenty-four started west in May,
with Jim Harvey as leader and José Tefoya as guide. Most
of the others had been in the fight at the Yellow House Draw.

They ascended to the caprock, as in March, and began
scouring the South Plains for Comanches. But wherever
they found a camp site, the Indians had just gone. In July,
on Bull Creek, a tributary of the Colorado River, they ran
into a force of about sixty cavalrymen under the command
of Captain Nicholas Nolan. The troops had left Fort Concho
on July 10, with the same aims as those of the hunters—to
punish marauding Indians and recover stolen stock.

Since Nolan had no guide, the two groups decided to
work together. But about a fortnight later, after running out
of water, they parted company. The hunters were disgusted
at the near-mutinous attitude of the soldiers and the stub-
bornness of Nolan, who refused to take expert advice on directions to water. The hunters, going their own way, found
water; but Nolan lost four men dead or missing, plus all of
his horses. Neither party shot any Indians, although the
hunters recovered a few horses and mules, including Sam
Carr's Prince.[4]

V

Despite the failure of the expeditions against them, the
Comanches were finding the Texas hunting grounds too

[4] Dodge City *Times*, June 2, 1877; Cook: op. cit., pp. 232–85.

hot for them. They were short of horses and had to keep on the move so much that they did not have enough time to hunt and butcher. Now, unwillingly, nearly all of them were reduced to staying on their reservation and eating beef issued by the government.

But, whether the Comanche raiders came back or not, the white hunters still were willing to risk their scalps for hides. Rath City, along with Fort Griffin, remained a popular outfitting point and market. On one occasion, girls from Fort Griffin rode the big blue hide wagons to Rath City to help entertain hunters and open-range cowboys at a gay fandangle. Cadmus Brown took out his fiddle and played such lively dance tunes as "Sally Goodins," "Sal, Spank the Baby," and "Turkey in the Straw." "The men went calicominded as soon as they got a whiff of Hoy't cologne," said one of them, "and they swung those gals so fast they got dust in their pockets."

In the fall of 1877, taking three skinners and a Mexican to peg hides, Joe McCombs again struck out west from Fort Griffin. He had a thousand pounds of lead and five kegs of powder. Following a trail he had used earlier, he made his first hunting camp at Big Spring. Later he moved to Mossy Rock Springs, near Signal Mountain, ten miles to the south. By the first of May he had made his biggest season's kill, taking 4,900 hides—all from his own shooting.

Not far to the north was the big outfit of John Jacobs and John W. Poe, which piled up 6,300 hides that winter. Several other outfits were hunting near by, and some of them stacked their hides in the camp of McCombs, asking him to sell them along with his own. At the close of the season he sold 9,700 to a Dallas dealer, W. H. Webb, at one dollar each, camp delivery.

The Mooar brothers continued to hunt from their camp on Deep Creek in the winter of 1877–8, sending the hides to Fort Worth. But they could see that the business of shooting and skinning was about to play out. In 1877 they began buying a few cattle, starting their herd on the open range near the mouth of Cottonwood Creek, in Fisher County. Their first brand was XTS, but later they changed it to SXT.

In April 1878, with a big wagon loaded with dried buffalo meat and drawn by eight mules, Wright Mooar headed west across the plains to Arizona. He reached Prescott after fifty-six days and stayed several months to engage in profitable freighting between that town and Maricopa. In Texas, besides looking after the hunting camp and the cattle, John cut hay to sell to the Texas and Pacific railroad, which was building westward.

In 1878, Frank E. Conrad, the flourishing hide merchant at Fort Griffin, where he had been post sutler earlier, bought the Lee and Reynolds interest in the Rath firm. Charles Rath bought the interest of Robert M. Wright. The company then became known as Rath and Conrad. Rath and his wife, who had been making frequent trips from Dodge City to Texas, moved to Fort Griffin. In October, Conrad had carpenters and painters busy altering and enlarging the building formerly occupied by the Wichita Saloon so he could bring the firm's forty-thousand-dollar stock down from the hill.

Fort Griffin, although still rife with vice and crime, was beginning to show a few signs of civilization. George Soule ran the Southern Hotel, the oldest in town. But those who could afford it patronized the new Planters House, managed by John Schwartz. It had two stories, seventeen rooms, and new furniture. Some called it the best hotel on the frontier. Other businesses were active, although some citizens were beginning to wonder what would happen when the buffaloes were gone. A Fort Griffin painter, Johnny Rodgers, was called the busiest man in town. Workmen had completed, in August 1878, a stone school building, with a second story to be occupied by the Odd Fellows. On September 26 a Masonic lodge was installed, with twelve members.

Fewer hide men were out on the Texas ranges in the winter of 1878–9, and not many of these found enough buffaloes to make their hunting pay. From September to March, Joe McCombs camped at Mustang Pond, at the future site of Midland, but his entire winter take was only eight hundred hides. "Buffaloes were scarce and wild," he explained, "and they started north on their last migration before the usual time. They never came back to the Texas ranges. Texas hunters ended their existence as herds on the one great range. All that remained of the vast herds of a few years back were a few straggling bunches, mostly calves." [5]

The Mooar brothers did some hunting that winter, still taking meat as well as hides. From Fort Griffin, on March 5, 1879, John Mooar wrote his mother that he expected Wright to start soon for Colorado City with a load of meat. But he wrote less about buffaloes than about cattle. "We have had good success with our little bunch of calves," he said. "We have fifty young calves in our yard and expect to have nearly a hundred more before many days."

Other hunters, too, realized that the Texas hide business was fading away. In Fort Griffin, hunters reported early in February that "the hunt had been much smaller than during the preceding season and that the buffaloes seemed to have moved northward out of Texas."

In Fort Worth, J. L. Hickey, agent for W. C. Lobenstein, still advertised for hides; and in Fort Griffin, Conrad and Rath had cash ready for all the loads brought them. But the business was dwindling rapidly. Frontiersmen who needed meat and sportsmen like the Earl of Aylesford still could find buffaloes in small groups; but not enough were left to make commercial hunting pay at the prevailing low prices for hides.

The groups of hide hunters whose guns had been boom-

[5] *Frontier Echo*, August 30, October 18, 1878; Joe S. McCombs: "On the Cattle Trail and Buffalo Range," pp. 99–100.

ing across the prairies melted away. Some followed the trail
of Jim White north to check on reports that a large herd still
was grazing in eastern Montana and northeastern Wyoming.
Others, like the Mooars, were eying cattle raising as a more
stable and probably more profitable occupation.

Fort Griffin quickly felt the falling off of the hide business, along with a slackening of cattle drives up the Western
Trail. The town had acquired a variety theater and a weekly
newspaper, the Fort Griffin *Echo*, but its population was de-
creasing, and cash was becoming scarce. Frank Conrad,
who had become postmaster, bought the old Southern Hotel.
He remodeled the building, establishing the post office and
a storeroom on the first floor and offices on the second. In
the spring a Chinese laundryman started business in the
abandoned tannery. The Cattle Exchange was closed and
the building offered for rent. A two-story building was about
to be dismantled and moved to Throckmorton to be used as
a temporary courthouse.

By midsummer of 1879, Charles Rath had seen what lay
ahead. He withdrew from the firm of Conrad and Rath and
went back into the freighting business. He obtained con-
tracts to supply hay to Army outposts—eight hundred tons
for Fort Elliott and six hundred for Camp Supply. He would
move to Sweetwater, the new town that had emerged from
a buffalo hunters' camp on the outskirts of Fort Elliott,
near the eastern edge of the Texas Panhandle. While he was
making this change, his wife went to Ohio to visit relatives
near Cincinnati.

The *Echo* lamented the departure of Charles Rath, not-
ing that "his worth as a businessman and his genial sociabil-
ity have endeared him to all." Rath had six five-yoke ox
teams and two six-mule teams. In addition, he and Henry
Hamburg, who was moving with him, engaged five five-yoke
ox teams from his old friends the Mooar brothers and two
six-mule teams from the Lewis brothers. The wagons would

carry household equipment, haymaking equipment, and other freight.

On July 15 the long caravan of creaking wagons, with the Mooar brothers among those holding the lines, left the flat and set out over the rutted trail northwest to Sweetwater. That new town, which was about to change its name to Mobeetie to avoid confusion with the newer Sweetwater in Nolan County, seemed to offer more promise than the declining Fort Griffin.

Rath was not with the wagons, but followed them two days later. His departure drew the curtain on the era of hide hunting in Texas.[6]

---

[6] Fort Griffin *Echo,* January 4, 11, April 12, May 24, July 5, 19, 1879; Fort Worth *Democrat,* February 5, 1879; John W. Mooar to his mother, Fort Griffin, March 4, 1879, MS. in John W. Mooar Papers. Early in 1880, Charles Rath moved back to Dodge City.

──── ◄ 16 ► ────

# REMNANT IN THE

# NORTH

**F**rom the Texas buffalo ranges the smoke had cleared. By the spring of 1879 the last of the hunters had to look elsewhere for a living. The herds that had darkened the southern plains were almost gone. The small, scattered bunches that remained were not enough to make the taking of hides worth while. The boom of the big Sharps rifles rarely was heard.

While most of the hunters turned to other occupations, those who still had hunting in their blood cleaned their guns and rode north toward the upper valley of the Missouri River. There, they were told, enough buffaloes remained to keep them busy for several seasons.

Among the hunters who went north were some of those who had been most successful on the Texas ranges. They included Hiram Bickerdyke, John Goff, John R. Cook, and Doc Zahl. They found Jim White already doing well at taking hides on the northern ranges, as were two brothers from Kansas, Bill and Steel Frazier.

On the northern plains the Indians had been hunting buffaloes longer than anyone could remember. As long as they hunted mainly for meat and robes for their own use, their killing did not make the herds noticeably smaller. Later, taking robes to sell to white traders increased the Indians' kill and lessened the supply. In 1875 a geologist estimated that the current rate of killing would denude the northern plains of buffaloes in twelve to fourteen years. But in 1879 a hide hunter could find plenty of stands without wearing out his horse.

As on the southern plains, the Indians resented the intrusion of the white hunters. Although their own killing often was wasteful, they never had engaged in wholesale slaughter to compare with that of the white men. Time and again they had been pushed off of hunting grounds promised them by treaty and had been forced to restrict their hunting to smaller areas.

A treaty of 1868 had granted good hunting grounds to the Sioux "as long as grass grows and water runs." It provided that they might hunt buffaloes "on any lands north of the Platte and on the Republican Fork of the Smoky Hill River as long as the buffaloes range thereon in such numbers as to justify the chase." But within five years two chiefs, Red Cloud and Spotted Tail, were complaining that the white settlers had crowded them from the Republican and denied them their treaty right of hunting.

Many of the Indians retaliated when they could. They killed and scalped some of the early settlers. One night in the spring of 1873, on Crow Creek about forty miles south of Cheyenne, they threw powder down the chimney of one of John W. Iliff's cattle herders and burned the cabin. The homeless cowman, Phil Bernard, escaped and ran barefoot for ten miles through the darkness to safety, his feet full of spines from the prickly-pear cactus.

From competing traders the Indians were obtaining

higher prices for dressed buffalo robes. In the 1870's a fine
robe often brought six dollars or a whole jug of whisky. Shipments of robes from Fort Benton ranged from eighty to one
hundred thousand a year between 1874 and 1877. Others
went to Hudson's Bay traders in the north, along with thousands of bags of pemmican.

Yet rising prices for robes did not blind the Indians to
the shrinking of their hunting grounds. In 1873 a commission from Washington asked the Sioux to relinquish part of
their land. Chief Red Cloud at first refused, but he consented
after being told that the land would be taken anyway. By
that time miners and railroad builders, as well as settlers,
were pushing into the northern buffalo country.

The Northern Pacific Railroad, started in 1870, crossed
the Red River of the North at Fargo two years later. Under
military protection, it was extended slowly westward across
the Indian country, reaching Bismarck, on the Missouri
River, in June 1873. There it began loading robes that had
been shipped down the Yellowstone and the Missouri. The
panic of 1873 halted construction, but building was resumed
five years later. In 1880 the rails reached Sentinel Butte,
near the Montana line. In the following year they penetrated
the plains to the rough town of Glendive and to Miles City,
the rip-roaring headquarters of many of the northern buffalo hunters.

The existence of this railroad encouraged the hunters.
It not only provided a quicker means for carrying hides to
outside markets, but also made the northern ranges safer.
It brought in settlers and forced the Army to give better protection. The annihilation of Custer and his troops on the Little Big Horn in 1876 had stirred a new determination to
tame the Indians on the northern plains. Chief Sitting Bull
of the Sioux had fled to Canada after the Custer massacre,
and subsequently there was less resistance to white hunters.

Some had invaded the northern ranges in the early

1870's, taking hides as well as robes. But, although they had killed several hundred thousand buffaloes, transport difficulties and the danger from Indians had been discouraging. Now the outlook was much better. In 1876 about fifty thousand robes and hides were shipped from Bismarck, some of them brought in from the west by white hunters. Buffaloes were plentiful in parts of the northern territories—in southeastern Montana, in northeastern Wyoming, and occasionally in western Dakota.[1]

## II

The boom of the buffalo guns became more frequent on the northern ranges in 1878. The Frazier brothers, Bill and Steel, veterans of the Kansas slaughter, made a successful hunt in Montana in the summer of that year. In September they sold their hides at Miles City and outfitted for a winter hunt.

Miles City, whose bedraggled appearance belied its name, was built in a cottonwood grove on the east bank of the Tongue River where it emptied into the Yellowstone. It was still a primitive village, with buffaloes roaming through its streets in the early morning. Called Milestown at first, it had been started in the fall of 1876 and named for Colonel Nelson A. Miles.

With six skinners, hired at fifty dollars a month each, and nine wagons, the Fraziers set out for the country drained by the Big Dry. While their outfit was encamped on Sunday Creek, a band of Sioux warriors rode pell-mell into the camp, yelling and brandishing guns and tomahawks. The Indians stampeded the four mules hitched to a wagon loaded with provisions and rode off with their loot. The Fraziers had to send the wagon back to town for more provisions. Hunting mainly on the divide between Sunday Creek

[1] Cheyenne *Leader*, April 22, 1873, January 5, 1876.

and the Little and Big Drys, they took five thousand hides that winter.[2]

One of the earliest of the Texas hunters to arrive in the northern ranges was husky Jim White. He had seen what was ahead in Texas and had left a year before the hunting ended there. With him in northern Wyoming he had a skinner, three sixteen-pound Sharps rifles, two mule-drawn wagons, seven hundred pounds of lead, and five kegs of powder.

While White was looking for a good place to camp and hunt, in September 1878, someone told him of Oliver P. Hanna, who had just settled on Goose Creek and built a cabin there. Hanna, who had been a scout for General George Crook in 1876, had liked the Wyoming country so well that he came back as soon as it was opened for settlement. Although he had been there only a month, he had obtained a contract to supply wild meat to Fort McKinney, being built on Clear Creek, forty miles away.

Hanna, worried about hauling meat to the fort, was glad to see Jim White and his wagons. The two men became partners and soon were delivering the required five thousand pounds of meat a week to the fort. They kept two teamsters busy hauling. Sometimes they killed enough in less than a day to load both wagons. The meat was that of not only buffaloes but also deer, elk, bears, and mountain sheep.

Hanna was amazed by White's marksmanship with a long-range rifle.

"Throw that little popgun of yours into the wagon," advised White. "Use one of my big guns and practice shooting at a long distance. In a short time you can kill game at 500 yards as easily as at 200. Being so far away, the animals can't see you and run away."

The pair hunted all that winter, during which White

[2] Usher L. Burdick: *Tales from Buffalo Land,* pamphlet, pp. 12–13.

claimed land on Hanna Creek. In the summer of 1879, White left the Big Horn Mountain country and went north into Montana. He drove down to the Yellowstone to pick a site for a camp for the next winter. Hanna would join him later. In October, White wrote Hanna that he had made a camp at the head of Sunday Creek, on the divide between the Yellowstone and the Missouri. That was fifty-five miles north of Miles City, on the Yellowstone, and two hundred and twenty-five miles from Hanna's cabin.

Despite the cold, stormy weather and the deep snow, Hanna set out, riding one of his ponies and leading the other with a pack. After crossing the Tongue River, he rode north toward the Wolf Mountains. When the snow, belly deep to the horses, kept him from going farther, he turned into a gulch that led to the Tongue River Canyon and followed it. The snow was deep there, too, and the sagebrush high. But, by traveling two and a half days on the ice, he got through.

The temperature was thirty degrees or more below zero, but Hanna had plenty of wood for campfires. Each evening he would climb cottonwood trees and chop the tops for his horses. They would browse on them all night. Hanna killed one buffalo, which provided enough meat for his trip.

Finally he arrived at Miles City, which by this time had acquired several blocks of cabins, stores, and honky-tonk dance halls. After leaving his ponies at a livery stable, Hanna inquired at a store about Jim White. Soon he found one of White's men, who took him to the camp.

The camp White had made was in a bleak country, far from wood and water. But thousands of buffaloes covered the prairies as far as any hunter could see. White had made a dugout on the slope of a hill, with buffalo hides inside and out and a fireplace chimney through the hill. Other hides served as rugs and bedding.

Although wood was scarce, White and Hanna found a

vein of lignite near their camp. As the lignite alone would not burn well, they saved buffalo suet, which they mixed with it. The combination made a satisfactory fuel.

After sending back to Miles City for more skinners and a cook, White and Hanna started shooting. They kept six men busy skinning and pegging the hides. They did their hunting afoot. When they saw a herd of buffaloes approaching, they hid in a gulch or behind some cover until they could shoot the leaders and obtain a stand.

The two took turns at killing. The one not shooting would cool the guns with water, clean them, and reload them. Sometimes the pair killed forty or fifty buffaloes in a day—as many as the men could skin. They did not want to leave any overnight, as the carcasses would freeze and be impossible to skin.

"We used the softest lead that we could buy," recalled Hanna. "When a bullet hit a buffalo, it would flatten out like a one-cent piece and tear a big hole in the animal. Generally it would stop on the opposite side against the hide, and the skinner would be able to save the lead and remold it. As lead was high, we reloaded all of our shells. After we had killed all the boys could skin in a day, we would go to our shack and reload ammunition for the next day."

Some of the men could skin twenty-five or thirty buffaloes in a day if they were killed close together. They began by skinning the head, Hanna explained. "Then they would cut off the head, lay it by the side of the buffalo, then turn him on his back with his legs straight up. The head under the side would keep him from falling over. They would skin the legs and half way down the sides, then pass on to the next carcass. Soon a man would follow with a mule and a chain. He would fasten the chain to the buffalo's tail and pull the hide off. That saved a lot of time. Then he would load the hide on a sled. When they had all the hides the mules could pull, they hauled them into camp."

After the hides were dried and stacked, bull freight teams hauled them to the bank of the Yellowstone River to await the boats that came up in June, during high water. The boats not only took down the hides, but also brought supplies for the hunters.

White and Hanna saved much of the best meat. "We built a smokehouse of rocks and dried tons of it," recalled Hanna. "Then we placed the fine meat under a bank where the snow would drift over it. We would send it in by ox teams and sell it to the soldiers and other people around Miles City. It had been in cold storage all winter and was the choicest of meat. We saved all the tongues, worth fifty cents each."

As the hunting progressed, the outfit made several branch camps, five or six miles from the main one. They used the smaller camps when the buffaloes happened to be near them. After two months they had about twenty-six hundred hides. They were becoming careless about watching for signs of Indians although they knew they were in dangerous country.

One day, after they had killed about forty buffaloes at one of the outlying camps, White asked Hanna to go back to this camp and start supper, as their cook was taking a vacation. White stayed to help the skinners complete their work.

About dusk, as Hanna was preparing the evening meal, White came in and asked if he had seen any of the eleven horses and mules.

"Yes," Hanna answered. "They were up on the flat when I came down."

"I don't see them," White said. Then Hanna went out with his rifle. He saw no horses or mules, but found many moccasin tracks in the snow. The two hunters followed the tracks to the top of a hill. From there they saw a band of Sioux warriors driving the horses and mules through a bunch of buffaloes. Afoot, White and Hanna had no hope of overtaking them in the snow.

Someone had to walk fifty-five miles through the snow to Miles City. Hanna volunteered, as he was only twenty-eight to White's fifty. After filling his pockets with dried meat and a little bread, and taking plenty of ammunition, he set out after dark, without any sign of a trail to guide him. The North Star helped him to keep his direction, but he knew that for thirty miles there would be no wood for a fire.

The trip was an ordeal. "Part of the time the snow would hold me up," he recalled, "and part of the time I would break through and would be knee-deep. I ran into several herds of buffaloes, and the wolves were howling on every side. About two o'clock in the morning a chinook came up, melting the snow as it blew against me and wetting my clothes."

Soon the wind became a northwester and brought more cold and snow. Although tired from walking, Hanna dared not stop for fear of freezing. Often he would stumble and fall. Just after daybreak, with the snow still blowing, he found a rocky cave, crawled in, and fell asleep. About two hours later he awoke to find rattlesnakes crawling over him. They were hibernating in the cave, but had aroused enough to investigate him. "I jumped ten feet to get out of there," he said.

Deciding that he hadn't been bitten, Hanna ate some lunch and walked on through the snow toward Miles City. Its snow-covered buildings and the smoke from their chimneys were a welcome sight. He arrived there twenty-two hours after leaving the camp. He was near exhaustion, for in some places the snow had been up to his waist.

Several hunters who arrived the next day had seen Indians cross the Yellowstone near the mouth of the Rosebud, driving a band of horses and mules that corresponded to Hanna's description. Later Colonel Nelson A. Miles at Fort Keogh offered help. "Some of the boys are eager for a little trip," he said. "So I have detached ten soldiers with ten days' rations and two packers to accompany you."

Hanna and the soldiers discovered the Indians' tracks and followed them. The next day they sighted the Sioux horse thieves in the pine timber above the mouth of the Lame Deer. But before the soldiers were ready to attack, the Indians discovered them and pulled out toward the Little Big Horn. The pursuers followed, sometimes coming close enough for a long shot. Hanna could see an old warrior riding his horse, Bones. Finally the Sioux dropped out four big mules. Hanna was glad to recover them, as they were worth four hundred dollars a span.

With the mercury twenty degrees below zero and the snow deep, the soldiers decided they had had enough of chasing Indians. So Hanna changed from his borrowed Army horse to one of the mules and headed back to the camp, about ten miles away. White and the others were glad to see him, as they feared he had perished in the storm. Hanna was so tired and stiff that he had to be helped off the mule; but coffee, food, and the warmth of the fire in the dugout soon revived him.

White and Hanna had to give up hunting for the rest of the winter, as the Indian scare became so bad that no skinners would work for them. But about the last of March a warm chinook melted the worst of the snow. Then the two hunters hired wagon freighters to haul their stacked hides to the bank of the Yellowstone near Miles City to await the steamers. There still was so much drifted snow in the gulches that the teamsters had to pile buffalo hides on the snow, three or four deep. The hides enabled them to drive the wagons across the top of the snow.

Meanwhile, in that winter of 1879–80, other hunters had been out on the Montana ranges. Some were professionals like the Frazier brothers and those who had come up from Texas. Others were homesteaders who saw in the market for flint hides an opportunity for easy cash. At Miles City the *Yellowstone Journal* reported on January 17 that more than a hundred local citizens were out after hides, worth $1.50 each. "One firm alone in this city already has on hand more than four thousand hides, and other houses have almost as many. There is much difficulty and expense by travelers in following roads along the Yellowstone valley, as trails are totally obscured in places by the immense herds of buffaloes."

A pioneer Montana ranchman, Granville Stuart, took note of the invasion of the northern ranges by hide hunters. Of the 1879–80 season he wrote: "The bottoms are sprinkled with the carcasses of buffaloes. In many places they lie thick on the ground, fat and the meat not yet spoiled, all murdered for their hides, which are piled up like cordwood along the way. Probably ten thousand buffaloes have been killed in this vicinity this winter. Slaughtering the buffaloes is a government measure to subjugate the Indian."

In Miles City, Hanna, White, and the other hunters and skinners waited for the river boats. They could find crude entertainment in the town's many saloons and its gambling rooms and hurdy-gurdy dance halls. Each dance cost a dollar, Hanna recalled. In addition, each wound up with an invitation for the men and their partners to gather at the bar for drinks. The merrymaking lasted all through the night. At the saloons, said Hanna, each dispenser of liquid refreshments had a formula for making tanglefoot from boiled mountain sage and a few plugs of tobacco steeped in water. If the whisky ran low, the homemade drink could be used to eke it out without many customers knowing the difference.

Now hides were competing with robes as cargo for the river steamers and were giving the new railroad some freight. Since 1876 the Northern Pacific had been receiving at Bismarck each year, from Missouri River boats, three to four thousand bales of ten or twelve robes each. In 1880 the boats began bringing down hides in large quantities.

Of one 1880 cargo the Sioux City *Journal* said that the

load "hid everything about the boat below the roof of the hurricane deck. There were ten thousand hides on that load, and they all were brought out of the Yellowstone on one trip and transferred to the *C. W. Peck.* How such a load could have been piled upon the little *Terry* not even the men on the boat appear to know. It hid every part of the boat, barring only the pilot house and the smokestacks." [3]

## III

After they had sold their hides in Miles City, Hanna and White returned to their homesteads in northern Wyoming. While Hanna spent the rest of the summer hunting in the mountains with a party of titled Englishmen, White settled on Soldier Creek, on land that later became a part of the PK Ranch.

In the fall of 1880, Hanna and White decided to cross the mountains to the Big Horn Basin for winter hunting. They went around by Prior's Gap and set up a small camp on Shell Creek, at the western base of the mountains. There they built a cabin and prepared to hunt buffaloes, elk, and deer, to trap beavers, and to poison wolves for their pelts.

Game was plentiful, but the wild country had attracted bands of horse thieves and other outlaws. One day in the last week of October three rough-looking men made camp a short distance below the cabin of Hanna and White. Hanna went down and talked with them, but they did not seem friendly. He felt uncomfortable about them.

That night Hanna had a hunch that he should go back to his ranch, and the next night the feeling was even stronger. On the following morning he told White that he wanted to go back to make sure that everything was all right.

[3] *Yellowstone Journal,* January 17, 1880; Oliver P. Hanna: "The Old Wild West," MS., pp. 99–108b; William T. Hornaday: *The Extermination of the American Bison,* p. 503; Granville Stuart: *Forty Years on the Frontier,* II, 103–4.

"What for?" asked White. "Why do you want to go?" Hanna said that if he did not go then, the snow in the mountains would be so deep that he would be unable to cross until June. He said he would be gone only about a week.

So Hanna packed one pony and saddled another. Following a short cut, he made the seventy-five-mile trip through the mountains in two days. At the ranch he found nothing amiss. "What a fool I was," he thought, "to let a feeling like that cause me to take that long, hard trip through the cold mountains."

Two days later Hanna started back across the Big Horns to the hunting camp. He made the trip without incident; but, on arriving, he was surprised to find the cabin abandoned. Jim White was not in evidence, and the mules and wagon were gone. Thinking it strange that White would leave in his absence, he began to look around. Under a near-by pine tree he found fresh dirt. As he scraped away the snow, he could see that something had been buried there. Could it be possible, he wondered, that those ruffians who had camped near by had killed his partner?

Hanna found an old shovel and dug through the loose dirt. About two feet down, he came to the body of White, rolled in a buffalo robe. He had been shot in the back of the head, apparently from ambush. Jim, who had downed more than sixteen thousand buffaloes, had fallen as suddenly as any of the victims of his gun.

The killers had taken everything of value—mules, wagon, bedding, buffalo robes, hides, furs, and four rifles, three of them big Sharps. About twenty-seven years later, in a blacksmith shop at Hyattville, Hanna saw an old Sharps buffalo gun standing in a corner. Examining it, he found the initial H and recognized it as his rifle that had been taken by White's murderers.

That winter of 1880–1 saw more hunters than ever on the northern ranges, principally in eastern Montana. One of the new outfits out for skins was that of George Newton and John Herbert. Newton was a youth of twenty-two, reared in Wisconsin. During the two preceding winters he had worked as a skinner for the Frazier brothers and had become adept enough to skin thirty shaggies a day. He also had acquired a Sharps .45 and had learned to use it expertly. Hunting mainly between the Musselshell and the Big Dry, he and Herbert took thirteen hundred hides during the cold weather.

Much of the killing that winter was done in the big triangle formed by three rivers—the Missouri, the Musselshell, and the Yellowstone. The skins brought an average of $2.70 at Miles City. More than two hundred thousand hides were said to have been shipped out of that region during the winter and spring. At least seventy-five thousand went down the muddy Missouri River on flat-bottomed stern-wheelers, to be transshipped by rail at Bismarck. Other hides taken in Montana were hauled by wagon to Terry or Sully Springs and loaded on freight cars.

In the late summer of 1880 either some freak of migration or the pressure of hide hunters had caused a large herd to move east into the Dakota Territory. This was the first time in years that buffaloes had been found there in large numbers. In mid-August a lieutenant of the Seventh Cavalry reported seeing myriads of them in the Cave Hill region, about a hundred miles northwest of Deadwood.

This invasion not only attracted the white hide hunters, but also brought out the Indians in large numbers. Besides hunting to satisfy their own needs for meat, robes, and hides, the warriors sold many hides to the white hunters and traders. In Wyoming, too, the Indians' hunting increased. At Fort Washakie the Shoshones and Arapahoes sold about two thousand robes and hides to the traders in the spring of 1881.

Reports that the buffaloes had returned to their former

grazing grounds in the Missouri Valley in Dakota Territory were good news to Indians at the agencies along the river. In September 1880 the Dakota Sioux at the Cheyenne River Agency sent two young scouts to check on reports and to locate the herd. They found plenty of shaggies, and soon hunting parties went out from this and other camps.

Thomas L. Riggs, a white missionary, went with a party that left the Cheyenne River Agency on the morning before Christmas. There were about sixty hunters, some of them veterans of the Custer massacre. With them were forty women to do the butchering and packing, three hundred horses, and a horde of scrawny dogs. The party left before dawn, over ground covered with snow. The hunters rode packhorses, leading their hunting mounts to save their strength. Occasionally they stopped to feed the horses twigs and shavings from the inner bark of cottonwood trees.

Soon after daybreak the party found a small herd of buffaloes huddled on the prairie. Before long they had killed fifty, allowing only one to escape. By evening they were back in camp with their hides and meat. That winter more than two thousand hides were brought back to the Cheyenne River Agency.[4]

## IV

In spite of the earlier hunting, buffaloes seemed as thick as ever on the northern plains at the start of the season of 1881–2. The Cheyenne *Leader*, on August 3, 1881, told of their abundance in northern Wyoming. "So many buffaloes are reported between Fort Fetterman and Fort McKinney and through the Little Big Horn Valley as to cause serious apprehension among the cattlemen in regard to the grazing."

[4] Hanna: op. cit.; Burdick: op. cit., pp. 13, 16; Thomas L. Riggs: The Last Buffalo Hunt." John Herbert later served as a Bismarck policeman. George Newton settled at Williston, where he became a breeder of race horses.

In eastern and central Montana they were equally plentiful. One hunter said he saw many thousands along the Big Dry, the Smoky Butte, and Timber Creek—all streams between the Missouri and the Yellowstone. But he found the largest herd in the valley of the Rosebud, south of the Yellowstone. Buffaloes whose numbers he estimated at more than fifty thousand darkened the range there for about forty miles.

Hunters and hide buyers believed that about a million buffaloes were left on the northern ranges, half of them within fifty miles of Miles City. At Fort Custer, when an approaching herd looked as if it might overwhelm the post, the commander sent out a squad of soldiers to turn it aside.

Reports of these buffaloes brought a stampede of new hunters until an estimated five thousand whites, in addition to the Indians, were shooting and skinning on the northern plains. Most of them hunted in the big triangle formed by the Missouri, the Yellowstone, and the Musselshell. Others, outfitted at Miles City or Glendive, had good luck on ranges to the southeast, between the Powder and the Little Missouri, particularly along Little Beaver and O'Fallon creeks. Dakota hunters from Bismarck found game along Cedar Creek and the Grand and Moreau rivers. For protection from the cold, the men slept in crude log cabins, dugouts, or tents made of poles and green skins.

Using methods found effective in Kansas and Texas, some of the hunters made large killings. In the winter of 1881–2, John Edwards downed seventy-five buffaloes in a single stand, and Doc Zahl eighty-five. In the Red Water country, about a hundred miles north of Miles City, one of Montana's most successful hunters, Vic Smith, was busy at the slaughter. In one stand, without shifting his position, he killed one hundred and seven in about an hour. He claimed to have killed five thousand during the season.

Along the Little Missouri, John Henderson recalled, "I

saw buffaloes lying dead on the prairie so thick that one could hardly see the ground. A man could have walked for twenty miles upon their carcasses."

Butchery so relentless and so widespread made the 1881–2 season the biggest for the region. A single Montana dealer, H. F. Douglas of Glendive, shipped more than 250,000 hides during the season. One of the Missouri River steamboat captains, Isaac P. Baker, carried down more than that number on his boats. From Custer County, which then embraced the whole southeastern corner of Montana, 180,-000 skins were said to have been shipped in 1882. In June of that year the *Rosebud*, with Baker as captain, brought 10,000 hides to Bismarck. Large quantities of buffalo meat were sold in Bismarck. The Northern Pacific hauled about 200,000 hides east from that city in 1882, nearly three times as many as the year before.

The big take of that season resulted not only from the increased number of hunters but also from the deep snow and severe cold. Drifted snow made it harder for the buffaloes to escape the marksmen with Sharps rifles. The remaining animals were being hemmed in and pushed into a smaller area. There was no avenue of escape.

The winter of 1882–3 was the last for the hide hunters. The ranges held only a fraction of the million buffaloes of a year earlier. Probably the largest herd, estimated at seventy-five thousand, had grazed northward and crossed the Yellowstone, with a ring of hunters, white and bronze, reducing its numbers. Smaller bunches were reported along the Belle Fourche and the upper Marais between the Milk River and the Bear Paw Mountains.

Between the mountains and the hide men, the buffaloes were trapped. Lieutenant J. M. T. Partello recalled that "a cordon of camps, from the upper Missouri, where it bends to the west, stretched toward the setting sun as far as the dividing line of Idaho. It completely blocked in the great ranges of the Milk River, the Musselshell, the Yellowstone, and the Marais. The hunters made it impossible for scarcely a single bison to escape through the chain of sentinel camps to the Canadian northwest. Hunters of Nebraska, Wyoming, and Colorado drove the poor hunted animals north, directly into the muzzles of the thousands of rifles ready to receive them."

Other hunters, as in earlier seasons, were at work in western Dakota and northern Wyoming. Those in Montana covered just about all of the grazing country, including the Judith Basin to the west. In the fall of 1882, John Henderson and a partner went out with a helper, a team, a spring wagon, and enough provisions to last them through the winter. They hunted along the Little Missouri, northeast of the Devil's Tower, camping with several other men. They hauled to a small trading post, where they received three dollars each for the hides and a cent a pound for the meat. "The only boots that would keep our feet warm in the sub-zero weather," recalled Henderson, "were ones made of buffalo hide. We would remove the hide from the hind legs, below the hocks. The hides were split, and the wide skin at the hocks served for heels."

Of the many hunting parties, Henderson's had set out from Miles City in October 1882. The three men went east to the badlands between the Powder River and O'Fallon Creek and stayed on the range all winter. They found the buffaloes much scarcer than they had been a year earlier, and many Indians and half-bloods out after those there were. The hunt lasted until early March. Then a chinook blew up, said Henderson, "and in a few days not a buffalo was to be seen in all that vast country. They had crossed Montana and taken refuge in the remote Milk River region along the Canadian line." The trio took only 286 hides, which they sold at $2.20 each. They also brought back some of the choicer meat, for which they received three cents a pound.

By the middle of 1883 nearly all the buffaloes were gone. Some of the hunters thought that many had migrated to Canada, but that was not true. The buffaloes in Canada had virtually been wiped out earlier than those in the United States. The largest group left was a herd of a thousand to twelve hundred in western Dakota. It was what was left of a herd of about ten thousand that had been there a year before. In October 1883 these animals were grazing between the Grand and Moreau rivers, about midway between Bismarck and the Black Hills. Then Chief Sitting Bull and nearly a thousand of his braves rode from the Standing Rock Agency and slaughtered all of them. "There was not a hoof left," said Vic Smith, who witnessed the butchering.

In the fall of 1883 some of the white hunters went out again, but they found no buffaloes. They had to kill partridges, deer, and even antelope to supply their camps with meat. There were several hundred in and around Yellowstone National Park, a few small groups in protected ravines, and an occasional lonesome bull wandering in the mountains. Except for those, the buffaloes that once numbered sixty to seventy-five million had disappeared.

A few more shipments of hides were made up from stacks still in the camps and from bales at the trading posts, but soon even those were gone. From Dickinson, in Dakota Territory, J. M. Davis made the only carload shipment of robes and hides in 1884, and that was the last. The hunters either went back to their former homes and less romantic occupations or hung their big rifles on the wall of some ranchman's cabin and started herding cattle. Thousands of Longhorns from Texas were coming into the ranges that had belonged to the buffaloes.

In time, protective measures would allow increases of

15   CAMP IN THE TEXAS PANHANDLE, 1874

16a.    DRYING HIDES AND TONGUES IN THE TEXAS
PANHANDLE, 1874

b.    HIDE YARD IN DODGE CITY, 1874

the few hundred surviving animals to several thousand. That would be enough to supply parks, zoos, and circuses, with occasionally a small surplus left for butchering. But by 1883 the day of the hide hunter had ended. All that remained was the telling of buffalo lore by the hunters and the gathering of whitened bones on the prairies.[5]

[5] Cheyenne *Leader,* August 3, 1881; Hornaday: op. cit., pp. 502–13; John Henderson, reminiscences, MS.

# 17

# SONG AND LEGEND

Stories from the campfires of buffalo hunters on the wind-swept plains could have provided grist for many a Baron Munchausen. Some of the tales were of unusual stands and big killings. Others were of narrow escapes from the charges of wounded bulls. More than a few told of finding cover in a blizzard that swept suddenly down on the open ranges. Most have been lost because neither the tellers nor the listeners bothered to put them in writing.

Of the few stories that have survived, some have grown in the telling until it is impossible to draw a sharp line between truth and fiction. More credible, as a rule, are those which hunters told of their own hardships and exploits. In one such tale, a young Texas Ranger, Drew Kirksey Taylor, described his encounter with a wounded and infuriated buffalo bull.

That was in 1876, when hide hunters were swarming over the Texas plains. Taylor, who was only nineteen, was encamped with several other Rangers in the timber along the Pease River about a hundred miles west of Graham.

One evening two green hunters drove up with two ox-drawn wagons and made camp near by. They had not brought any saddle horses, fearing that Indians would steal them; but they had two mongrel dogs.

The next day, as he had no outlaws to chase, young Taylor went out with the hunters to have a bit of sport and to show them how to kill buffaloes. In midafternoon the trio found a small herd grazing along the creek. Taylor tied his horse to the wagon, hung his six-shooters over the saddle horn, and, carrying his rifle, started walking up the creek toward the game.

The Ranger shot six or eight of the fatter animals before the others took fright and fled. Each of the wounded beasts would stagger, fall, get up, go a short distance, and then fall dead. The carcasses were scattered over about an acre of the prairie. Putting down his rifle, Taylor examined the bodies, showing the hunters the vital spot at which they should aim.

One old bull was batting his eyes, showing that he still had some life in him. When Taylor thoughtlessly kicked him in the side, the bull started to get up. The Ranger jumped onto his back and tried to hold him down; but the bull continued to rise, with Taylor astride him.

"I was sitting straight up on his hump," said Taylor. "I stuck my spurs in his sides and hung on. Right there a circus started. The old bull went kicking and bawling out across the prairie, with me hanging on for dear life. I didn't dare let go. Had I done so, he would have gored me."

Taylor had to think quickly. While gripping the sides of the buffalo with his spurs and holding to the hair of the back with one hand, he reached his other hand into his pocket and drew out his long-bladed pocketknife. He tried to stab the enraged animal, but could not reach down far enough.

When the hunters saw the plight of Taylor, they set

their dogs on the wounded buffalo. The dogs, one on each side, worried and soon slowed down the bull, weakened from loss of blood. Then Taylor was able to slide off backward. He stopped the animal by cutting his hamstrings, then put an end to him with a bullet.[1]

Charles Jesse Jones, better known as Buffalo Jones, told of a strange experience he had in western Kansas in the summer of 1872, when the plains were dotted with hunters. Jones, who had moved from Illinois in the spring of that year, had started farming and had sold buffalo hides for cash to tide his family over until he could harvest his crops. He also had roped about a dozen buffalo calves, which he sold.

Early in August, Jones, who was then twenty-eight, started off on a hunt, taking along a younger neighbor. A large herd was said to be grazing about sixty miles to the west. The day before he left, two strange men appeared, looking for work. Jones told them to come along. They could keep his camp and help with the skinning until they found steady jobs.

So the four drove west in Jones's wagon, with enough meat for three days and flour for two months. But for six days they found no game. The buffaloes had moved on to fresh grazing. The men were reduced to bread and water. In the broiling sun they suffered from the heat. On their sixth day on the flat plains, mirages began to play pranks on them. They saw beautiful lakes of clear water, their shores fringed with tall shade trees. But as the wagon approached, the lakes and trees vanished.

Finally the party came to a village of prairie dogs. Jones was about to shoot one of the small, burrowing animals for soup when he saw something that startled him. Just ahead was a small, clear lake. He was sure this one was real because he could see in it the reflection of his wagon and team.

[1] Drew Kirksey Taylor: *Taylor's Thrilling Tales of Texas*, pp. 35–8.

So he walked quickly toward it, only to have it disappear as the others had done.

By that time the water in the canteens was gone and tongues were swelling. The two strangers were becoming insolent. Jones was afraid that if he did not find water and meat soon, they might kill him and take his outfit. But all he could see was illusory lakes and groves that turned out to be weeds.

Then, as he staggered on, Jones heard a rumbling sound. Looking north, he saw six buffaloes high in the air. They were about ten times larger than normal, he said, and about five hundred feet above the ground. "They were running in space, coming directly toward me. I at once dropped to my left knee, ready to shoot. But I could not catch a bead on them. They danced around in every direction. Nearer and nearer they came, until I could hear the rattling of their hoofs.

"They must have been within forty yards of me. Then they gave a great snort as they turned eastward and bolted around me. They sailed through the air, with their legs making regular motions as though they were running on the earth. Yet they appeared circling high above and soon disappeared."

When his strange vision ended, Jones was relieved to find his gun and cartridges intact. He decided that intense thirst and exhaustion must have tricked his eyesight. He managed to struggle back to the wagon, and the party drove on until dark. Jones, who had brought along a spade, dug in a ravine for water, but found none. Finally the men heard a rifle shot and reached a hunters' camp, where they had their fill of water, hot biscuits, and fat buffalo meat. There they learned that the herd they sought had moved twenty miles to the north.[2]

[2] Charles Jesse Jones: *Buffalo Jones' Forty Years of Adventure*, compiled by Henry Inman, pp. 37–46.

## II

The lore of the camps embraced a whole series of stories about hunters who, when caught in an icy storm, found refuge for the night by rolling into a fresh hide or crawling into the carcass of a buffalo that had just been killed and was still warm. Only the most gullible historian would accept all such stories at their face value, yet only the most skeptical and arbitrary would say that none of them could be true.

In December 1847, long before the day of the commercial hunter, John Rotman, William Banta, and six of their neighbors decided to go on a buffalo hunt. All were frontiersmen living on the Texas side of the Red River, under the protection of Fort Inglish. They had heard that buffaloes were plentiful to the west, in the upper valley of the Trinity River. So, wishing for some winter sport and not averse to bringing home a load of meat, they set out. Their number would give some protection against an attack by redskins.

Besides their saddle horses, the men had a wagon, a good team, and an ample supply of bedding, provisions, guns, and ammunition. After traveling for five days, they found buffaloes and pitched their tent in a small grove near a creek. Hunting from horseback, they approached the nearest animals, which moved away and scattered over the prairie. By prearrangement, each hunter picked out a big beast and chased him. Soon they were shooting in every direction and were scattering almost as widely as the frightened buffaloes. They noticed that a sharp wind was whistling down from the north, making the air colder by the minute; but they wanted to down their game while they could.

By four o'clock in the afternoon all the men except John Rotman were back in camp and had hauled in three buffaloes they had killed. Clouds made the winter darkness come even earlier than usual. By that time the cold had increased and the wind was bringing a hard sleet. Rotman still was missing. The others kept the campfire blazing and fired their guns as signals. Still there was no sign of Rotman. About midnight the sky cleared and the cold increased. The campers kept on firing occasionally until morning, with no result.

After breakfast, four of the men went out on horseback in search of the lost hunter. About one o'clock they heard an answer to their firing and rode at full speed in the direction from which the shot had come. In a few minutes they found John Rotman on foot, cold and hungry. They put him on one of the horses, behind another hunter, and took him back to the camp, fifteen miles away.

After a warm supper, Rotman told his story. He had followed his buffalo eight or ten miles, he said, shooting at him as fast as he could. As the sky was cloudy, he couldn't tell the time. After he had killed the buffalo, he thought he would return to camp; but then he realized that he had completely lost his sense of direction. So he rode on until dark. By that time the cold wind had almost frozen him stiff. When he became so numb that he had only a little feeling in his hands, he began walking and leading his horse.

Just after dark, he related, "I came back to the dead buffalo. I decided to skin him and wrap up in the hide to keep from freezing. Finally I got the hide off. Tying my horse to a bush, I spread the green hide out, with the wool side up. I laid my gun by my side and rolled up in the hide. Then I became warm and went to sleep.

"About daybreak I was disturbed by wolves which had gathered about the carcass of the buffalo. There were so many of them, of all sizes, that the larger ones fought off the smaller ones. That caused the smaller ones to work on the hide in which I was rolled. I could see out through a small opening. When it came day and the wolves began to grit their teeth at my head, I trembled with fear.

"I could not help saying 'Sooy.' The wolves would look all around and, not seeing anything, would begin to eat again at the frozen hide. They came so close to my head that I could almost feel their teeth clipping my ears.

"In this condition I lay until about ten o'clock, when the sun thawed the hide so I could crawl out. On my release, I found my horse frozen to death. I was left to wander on foot, hungry, stiff, and alone."

A like use of a fresh hide was reported by an early Texas Ranger, N. A. Jennings, who said he heard the story from a buffalo hunter. Lawrence Criss and a fellow known as Twisted Charlie, this account says, were hunting buffaloes in the Panhandle in winter. One afternoon, after the two had killed nineteen and were skinning them, they were struck suddenly by one of the worst northers they had known.

The men piled on the fire all the wood they could find, but it wasn't enough to keep them warm. The night became so cold that, as Criss put it, "the coffee boilin' in the pot on the fire had a skim of ice on it that we had to break before we could pour the coffee out."

As a last resort, Criss took one of the green hides, wrapped himself in it, and soon was warm and comfortable. Charlie did the same, and before long both men fell asleep.

A few hours later, Criss awoke to hear a terrific howling. At first he thought Comanche scalpers must be upon them, but he discovered that the yelling was from Charlie, who was locked in his frozen hide. "Help me out!" he kept shouting.

Managing with difficulty to get out of his own hide, Criss tried to unwrap Charlie, but had no luck. Next he tried to cut the hide with a knife, but found it hard as rock. Finally he rolled the hide, with Charlie in it, over closer to the fire. Toasting one side and then the other, he thawed the hide enough for Charlie to free himself. For the rest of the night Charlie sat by the fire, unwilling to trust himself inside another hide.

Later, from Wright Mooar, came the tale of a fellow hunter's experience in western Texas. In February 1877, he said, Jim Ennis was encamped with others on Sweetwater Creek, in Scurry County. With buffaloes scarce, he went out alone on a foggy morning. After some searching, he killed a couple of bulls and stayed to skin them and roll their hides, which he left near the carcasses.

In the afternoon Ennis shot another bull, but only wounded him. The bull started walking off; but as Jim followed for another shot, the beast turned and rushed straight at him. Jim dropped his gun and ran for the nearest mesquite tree, which he climbed into with record speed. Then the bull started butting the tree. A small one, it soon snapped in two. The top of the tree, with Jim still in it, crashed down on the back of the enraged buffalo. This so rattled him that he rushed off, letting his strange load slide to the ground.

In the dense fog Jim finally found his gun, but by that time he had lost his sense of direction and had no idea of which way to head for the camp. Wandering about, he found at dusk one of the buffaloes he had killed. He built a fire and cooked some of the meat. After supper he spread the hide, rolled himself in it, and went to sleep.

During the night a blue norther froze the hide stiff. Then lobo wolves came and began tearing bits of meat from the hide. Jim couldn't understand why they seemed to prefer those bits to the whole carcass lying near by. He yelled at them, but they kept on coming. Some bit so close that they tore his clothes.

At dawn the wolves left, and about ten o'clock the sun thawed the hide enough for Jim to crawl out. When he found his way back to camp, his fellow hunters and skinners didn't recognize him. In the night his hair had turned from black to gray.[3]

## III

Other stories told of a blizzard-struck hunter's finding even warmer shelter by making use of a freshly killed buffalo bull. Henry Inman said that a party of four of his friends, all experienced hunters, had made camp in Paradise Valley early in March 1867. One afternoon, when they were out on the range stalking shaggies and had become separated from each other, a terrific blizzard hit suddenly. Three of the men made it back to camp safely; but the fourth, who was farther away, was caught in the storm. Darkness and the blinding snow kept him from finding his way. He feared he would freeze to death.

As he was beginning to become numb from cold, the lost hunter came upon an old bull that had been abandoned by the herd. Seeing a chance for shelter, he quickly killed the bull, slashed open his belly, and pulled out the viscera. Then he crawled into the cavity, which protected him from the wind and snow and was warm enough to keep him comfortable until morning.

At daybreak the storm ceased, and the sun came out brightly. But the hunter found that his shelter had become a prison. The ribs of the buffalo had frozen together and locked him inside. Wondering if he ever would get out alive, he finally heard the firing of the rifles of his companions, who had come out to look for him. When they

[3] William Banta and J. W. Caldwell, Jr.: *Twenty-Seven Years on the Frontier,* revised edition, pp. 35–7; N. A. Jennings: *A Texas Ranger,* pp. 21–3; J. Wright Mooar to J. Evetts Haley, Snyder, Texas, November 25, 1927, MS. transcript in Panhandle-Plains Historical Museum, Canyon, Texas.

came near enough, he yelled at them, and they rescued him.

Later a Kansan, Ike Lewis, told what happened to one of his Stafford County neighbors, Elijah Williamson. In the days of hide hunting, Williamson had been one of the best shots in his county, which is south of Great Bend and is drained mainly by Rattlesnake Creek. On a fall hunt, he and several others were encamped on the prairie, killing for both hides and meat. Williamson did most of the shooting, often going ahead of the skinners.

As the buffaloes had been drifting farther from the camp, Williamson decided early one afternoon to ride out and look for them. He told the other men, who were busy with skinning and butchering, to follow him that evening or early the next morning.

As Williamson struck out from camp, the air was so warm and balmy that even an ordinary coat was uncomfortable. He started out on a ridge, then decided to take a longer ride and return by moonlight. By four o'clock he was about twenty miles from camp and was still going from one ridge to another, looking for buffaloes. He found several and killed them.

Then he noticed that gray clouds were gathering on the horizon. They suggested that the unseasonably warm weather was about to end and that a norther was on the way. Williamson turned his horse and hurried back into the draw and up to the top of the next ridge toward the camp. Soon the wind was blowing like fury and was driving fine snow and peppery sleet. The air that had been so balmy turned intensely cold.

With darkness coming on, Williamson dismounted to look for shelter. When he returned, he could not see his horse. He called for the bronc, but failed to hear the usual responsive whinny.

Williamson started to walk back toward the camp, but

soon became lost in the storm. Not dressed for wintry weather, he began to suffer from the cold and the wind. His hands and feet were becoming numb. But he walked on to keep from freezing.

Before long he stumbled and fell. Realizing, even in the darkness, that he had found one of the buffalo paths that led from one draw to another, he decided to follow it. Maybe it would lead to the shelter of a hill or an embankment.

After walking on for about half an hour, becoming colder every minute, Williamson was startled by a loud "Whoof!" It was the challenging snort of a buffalo bull, which apparently had detected an unusual odor. The hunter dropped flat and waited. The bull snorted twice more, then came on up the trail. As his huge bulk loomed through the darkness, Williamson worked his numb fingers enough to aim his rifle and pull the trigger. He shot twice more to make certain that the big animal would fall.

As the bull dropped in his tracks, Williamson pulled out his sharp hunting knife. He quickly slit the hide and made an opening in the carcass from rump to shoulder. Then, with an energy born of desperation, he tore out the entrails. That done, he crawled into the bloody but welcome cavern, closing the entrance as best he could. The shelter was cramped and uncomfortable, but soon its warmth began to relieve his hands and feet of their numbness. As the wind continued to whistle outside, he felt cozy and safe.

When morning came, Williamson found that the carcass of the buffalo bull had frozen hard about him. His twisting and kicking helped to keep his blood circulating, but failed to free him. Finally his companions, who had trailed him by the buffaloes he had killed, found him and released him. Glad as he was to be out, he did not neglect to take the hide of the protecting bull.

In a story told by Frank Collinson, another sort of hazard caused a hunter to look for a buffalo for shelter. In the fall of 1875, he said, Jack Bickerdyke was hunting on the north side of Beaver Creek. That was just north of the Texas line, in the No Man's Land that later became the Oklahoma Panhandle.

Bickerdyke had killed some buffaloes a few miles above the camp one afternoon and had stayed with the skinners to help them complete their job before dark. Then he re-mounted his horse and started back toward the camp, cross-ing the Beaver and taking a short cut.

After riding about two miles, Bickerdyke found a crip-pled buffalo bull, which he killed. Thinking he would have time to skin the animal before dark, he let his horse graze and set to work with his knife. But a few minutes later he looked up the creek and saw a prairie fire sweeping down between the Beaver and Palo Duro Creek, which flows into the Beaver from the south. The grass, struck by the flames, wilted in a crackling roar. The wind was blowing strong in his direction, bringing the blaze and smoke nearer every minute. Around him were tall grass and weeds that made the spot dangerous. Bickerdyke looked for his horse, which had strayed for better grazing. But the mount was gone; frightened by the oncoming fire, he had run down the creek and was beyond reach.

By that time Bickerdyke was nearly surrounded by fire. Seeing that he could not recross Beaver Creek, he started for the Palo Duro. But the racing blaze was there ahead of him. Then, with fire all around him, he hastened back to the partly skinned buffalo. Quickly he ripped open the carcass and pulled out the entrails. Just before the fire reached him, he crawled inside, taking his rifle and pulling the skin over him as well as he could.

The blaze, leaping in the wind, singed the buffalo's hair. The heat was bad, but what bothered Bickerdyke most was the dense smoke that almost suffocated him as he lay hud-dled in his improvised shelter. After the worst of the fire had passed and the flames and smoke had subsided, he pushed up the hide and crawled out, choking with smoke and badly scared. He was so stiff and cramped that for several minutes he was unable to walk.

As soon as he could, Bickerdyke started walking back to the camp, with the charred grass blackening his boots. When he had gone about halfway, he met two of his skinners, who had come out to look for him.

"Which one of you threw that match down?" he asked. "You came near cooking me alive." [4]

## IV

Buffalo hunters were less inclined to song than were the Western cowboys, who sometimes sang to their charges on the long trail or crooned lullabies to the sleeping herd. It was hard to find anything romantic about shooting, skinning, and butchering the stinking animals. And in their camps at night, after a dinner of hump or tongue, the men usually were too tired to think of singing.

Yet occasionally a fiddle or some other musical instrument found its way into a hunters' camp. Its playing gave a bit of relief to the monotony of the wilds, and some of the hunters and skinners joined in songs they had known in earlier days. They were less likely than cowhands to make up new songs about their own experiences, yet two of the most magnificent folk songs that have come out of the West have to do with buffaloes and buffalo hunting.

Many folklorists agree with Professor George L. Kittredge of Harvard that "The Buffalo Skinners" is the greatest of the Western ballads. John A. Lomax, who did more than anyone else to popularize the song, noted that it had in its language a Homeric quality. Carl Sandburg, in whose bag

[4] Henry Inman: *The Old Santa Fe Trail*, pp. 205–6; Kansas City *Times*, April 3, 1910; Frank Collinson: "Prairie Fires."

of songs it was one of the favorite numbers, said: "It is the framework of a big, sweeping novel of real life, condensed into a few telling stanzas."

The tune of this song was old when the hide hunters began their slaughter. It appears to have been derived indirectly from an early English chantey. Ephraim Bailey, a lumberman of Hudson, Maine, was said to have joined an expedition into Canada in 1853. While there, or on his return, he wrote new words to the English sea tune. His song, "Canaday-I-O," began:

> *It happened late one season, in the fall of fifty-three,*
> *A preacher of the gospel one morning came to me.*
> *Said he, "My jolly fellow, how would you like to go*
> *To spend a pleasant winter up in Canaday-I-O?"*

Later stanzas described the hardships of that winter. "Our food the dogs would snarl at; our beds were on the snow." Later versions, one of which was called "Michigan-I-O," wove in local details. The tune was used also for a miners' song and a railroaders' song.

As is the case with most genuine folk songs, the origin of the words of "The Buffalo Skinners" cannot be traced clearly. J. E. McCauley of Seymour, Texas, attributed them to a hunter known as Buffalo Jack. One old hunter wrote to John A. Lomax, saying that he had been a member of the outfit described in the song. "It was a hell of a trip down Pease River," he added. "We fought sandstorms, flies, bedbugs, wolves, and Indians. At the end of the season, old Crego announced that he had lost money and couldn't pay us. We argued with him.

"He didn't see our side, so we shot him and left his bones to bleach where we had left so many stinking buffaloes. On the way back to Jacksboro, one of the boys started a song about the trip and the hard times and old Crego, and we all set in to help him. Before we got back to Jacksboro, we had shaped it, and the whole crowd could sing it."

The year mentioned in the song, 1873, was a bit early for hide hunting in Texas, especially out of Jacksboro. Also, the talk of providing transportation seems strange for a region in which the only transport was on horseback or in a hunter's wagon. Yet the rest of the details ring true and could have been derived from the experience of a real outfit of hunters. No one named Crego has appeared thus far in the annals of the buffalo slaughter, but such a hunter could have existed. In some versions the name is Craig. Emanuel Dubbs wrote that in the spring of 1878 he bought a log cabin on Sweetwater Creek from an old buffalo hunter named Joe Craig, who had turned squatter. But that was five years after the date in the song.

In its several versions, the song varies only slightly. One goes:

*'Twas in the town of Jacksboro, in the spring of seventy-*
*three,*
*A man by the name of Crego came stepping up to me,*
*Saying, "How do you do, young fellow, and how would you*
*like to go*
*And spend the summer pleasantly on the range of the buf-*
*falo?"*

*"It's me being out of employment," this to Crego I did say,*
*"This going out on the buffalo range depends upon the pay.*
*But if you will pay good wages, find transportation, too,*
*I think, sir, I will go with you on the range of the buffalo."*

*"Yes, I will pay good wages, give transportation, too,*
*Provided you will go with me and stay the summer through.*
*But if you should grow homesick, come back to Jacksboro,*
*I won't pay transportation from the range of the buffalo."*

It's now our outfit was complete—seven able-bodied men,
With Navy six and needle gun—our troubles did begin.
Our way it was a pleasant one, the route we had to go,
Until we crossed Pease River, on the range of the buffalo.

It's now we've crossed Pease River, our troubles have begun.
The first damned tail I went to rip, oh how I cut my thumb!
While killing the damned old stinkers, our lives they had no
  show,
For the Indians watched to pick us off while skinning the
  buffalo.

He fed us on such sorry chuck I wished myself 'most dead.
It was old jerked beef, croton coffee, and sour bread.
Pease River's as salty as hell fire—the water I could
  never go.
O God! I wished I had never come to the range of the buf-
  falo.

Our meat it was buffalo hump and iron wedge bread,
And all we had to sleep on was a buffalo robe for a bed.
The fleas and graybacks worked on us; O boys, it was not
  slow.
I tell you there's no worse hell on earth than the range of
  the buffalo.

Our hearts were cased with buffalo hocks, our souls were
  cased with steel.
And the hardships of that summer would nearly make us
  reel.
While skinning the damned old stinkers, our lives they had
  no show,
For the Indians waited to pick us off on the hills of Mexico.

The season being nearly over, old Crego he did say
The crowd had been extravagant, was in debt to him that
  day.

*We coaxed him, and we begged him; but still it was no go—*
*So we left old Crego's bones to bleach on the range of the*
*buffalo.*

*Oh, it's now we've crossed Pease River, and homeward we*
*are bound.*
*No more in that hell-fired country shall ever we be found.*
*Go home to our wives and sweethearts, tell others not to go*
*For God's forsaken the buffalo range and the damned old*
*buffalo.*

In the Southwest this ballad of the skinners had a variant, "The Hills of Mexico." The latter substituted Fort Griffin for Jacksboro and cattle herding in New Mexico for buffalo hunting on the Pease, but the outcome was the same.[5]
Buffaloes had a lesser role in another song that sprang
up at about the same time as "The Buffalo Skinners" and
became one of the most popular folk songs on the Western
ranges. It was "A Home on the Range," which started:

*Oh, give me a home where the buffaloes roam,*
*Where the deer and the antelope play,*
*Where seldom is heard a discouraging word,*
*And the skies are not cloudy all day.*

The words, which came to have many variations,
stemmed from a poem, "Western Home," which a frontier
Kansas physician, Dr. Brewster Higley, wrote in 1873 in
his dugout on a bank of West Beaver Creek, northwest of
Smith Center. The poem appeared in the Kirwin *Chief* on
March 21, 1874, and later was set to music by Daniel E.
Kelley. New stanzas were added in many parts of the West.
John R. Cook wrote that all over the Western ranges
this song was sung with as much vim as "John Brown's

[5] John A. Lomax and Alan Lomax: *Cowboy Songs*, pp. 335–8. In 1939,
when President and Mrs. Franklin D. Roosevelt brought Marian Anderson
and Alan Lomax to the White House to sing American folk songs for their
guests, the King and Queen of England, the singing of "The Buffalo Skinners" by young Lomax made one of the biggest hits.

Body." "It had a catchy tune; and, with the melody from the hunters' voices, it was beautiful and soul-inspiring." Revived by John A. Lomax in 1910, it attained a new and wider popularity; and in 1949, by legislative action, it became the state song of Kansas. Generations after the hunters had cleared the plains of their herds, school children and members of luncheon clubs still liked to sing of "where the buffaloes roam." [6]

[6] John R. Cook: *The Border and the Buffalo,* pp. 292–3; John A. Lomax and Alan Lomax: op. cit., pp. 424–8; Kirke Mechem: "Home on the Range."

# 18

# BONES ON THE

# PRAIRIE

After wolves, vultures, and decay were done with the carcasses, only the bones strewn on the ranges told where the buffaloes had been slaughtered. In places where the hunters had made stands, the bones formed a whiteness that could be seen for miles. They were a nuisance to farmers trying to break the virgin sod.

Yet even the bones were not there for long. Early settlers—fool hoe men in the eyes of the cowmen—quickly discovered that the skeletons had a cash value. For the penniless granger, beset by drought and grasshoppers and unable in some instances even to find wild game for the dinner table of his dugout or sod house, the bones were a godsend. He could load his wagon with them, drive into town, and trade his load for necessities that would last his family until the next trip. Except for the buffalo bones, many an early homesteader on the plains would have had to go back east as a failure. They enabled him to stay until he had a crop ready to sell.

The gatherers of bones did not always wait for the completion of the slaughter. Some followed closely in the wake of the hide hunters. Sometimes they even were ahead of the railroad builders, leaving their piles of bones along the right of way at points that soon would have stations.

George W. Thompson recalled that in 1870 the gathering and shipping of buffalo bones began to be big business along the Kansas Pacific Railroad. For several miles about Hays City, he said, they were piled ten feet high along the railroad sidings, awaiting shipment.

Freight trains that had carried supplies to the frontier hauled bones to carbon works in St. Louis and other cities. There the newer bones were prepared for use in refining sugar, as the calcium phosphate neutralized the acid of the cane juice. The old, weather-beaten ones were ground into meal for sale as fertilizer. A few of the choice ones went into bone china. The horns, which brought from a fraction of a cent to one and a half cents a pound in Kansas towns, provided material for buttons, combs, and knife handles.

To the south, the new Santa Fe Railroad was as interested in bones as was the Kansas Pacific. The salvaged bones, recalled L. C. Fouquet, "came in handy as the settlers hauled them to Hutchinson, where there was a firm that shipped them by carloads. The side tracks were lined with stacks of bones. They brought $2.50 to $3 a ton, and the horns $6 to $8 a ton."

About the time the rails reached Dodge City, in September 1872, a man with a two-horse team began bringing in bones and dumping them in a big pile along a siding. Some of the hide hunters poked fun at him and dubbed him Old Buffalo Bones. But he persisted and, the next year, brought out his son with a second team. In two years he shipped more than three hundred carloads of bones and made a

small fortune. He had more to show for his work than did many a hunter.

Soon Dodge City became the chief Kansas market for bones, as well as for hides. For miles east of town, bones were piled along the railroad until the Santa Fe had cars enough to load them. The homesteader who drove in with a load could always find a buyer on Front Street. Some farmers, who were busy in their fields, sold their buffalo bones to freighters at two to two and a half dollars a ton. The price in Dodge City averaged about eight dollars, sometimes ranging as high as fourteen. It became a common Kansas saying that "buffalo bones are legal tender in Dodge City."

In the dry air of western Kansas it took a great many bones to make a ton. To cause the bones to weigh more, some sellers would throw water over the load in their wagon. Others would wet those loaded in railroad cars before they were weighed.

In the winter of 1874–5, Arthur C. Bill and his cousin, each with a wagon, a yoke of oxen, and a saddle pony, gathered bones from the prairies between Dodge City and Camp Supply. They piled them along the trail where freighters for the government were glad to have a pay load on their return trip north. In Dodge the pair received seven to nine dollars a ton for bones and twelve to fifteen dollars a ton for hoofs and horns. The hoofs were used in making glue.

After making inquiries, Henry Inman estimated that, in Kansas alone, two and a half million dollars was paid for buffalo bones gathered on the prairies between 1868 and 1881. This figure was based on an average price of eight dollars a ton. On the assumption that about one hundred skeletons were required to make one ton of bones, this gathering of bones represented the slaughter of more than thirty-one million buffaloes.

Major Richard Irving Dodge, who was in close touch with the Kansas hunting and bone gathering, estimated that the Santa Fe shipped 1,135,300 pounds of bones in 1872, 2,743,100 pounds in 1873, and 6,914,950 in 1874. This, he believed, was about a third of the total for all railroads, which he estimated at 32,380,050 for the three years.

Bone gathering in Nebraska followed, on a lesser scale, the Kansas pattern. The white harvest there gave rise to Edwin Ford Piper's poem "Dry Bones," one stanza of which read:

*Springtime outran the furrowings of raw sod;*
*There must be bread; in August the bone pickers*
*Go harvesting the prairie, dragging out—*
*Rich roof for the hundred-legs and scurrying beetles—*
*From the fingers of the grass and spiderweb*
*Long curving rib and broad white shoulder blade.*

Homesteaders in eastern Colorado also sought eagerly the wasting bones. In 1874, John R. Cook saw along the Santa Fe right of way, twenty miles ahead of the track from Granada, a rick of bones twelve feet high, nearly that wide at the base, and half a mile long. Other places had similar stacks awaiting shipment, mainly to St. Louis and Philadelphia. From one Colorado station, twenty carloads of bones were shipped to St. Louis in a single week. At that time most of the bones were bringing about five dollars a ton, delivered at the railroad, though the price sometimes ran as high as nine dollars.

Later that year a Denver newspaper, the *Rocky Mountain News,* noted that the grasshopper plague had sent many frontiersmen out along the Kansas Pacific to pick up bones. One station had shipped twenty carloads to St. Louis in a fortnight. Contractors were paying five dollars a wagonload, which represented five days' work for an industrious picker. As the bones were fast disappearing, most of the gatherers had to drive thirty to forty miles from the railroad to find enough to fill their wagons. The bones were being shipped to St. Louis, Pittsburgh, and Harrisburg.[1]

## II

In Texas, as earlier in the middle plains, the gathering of buffalo bones began before the hunters had completed their slaughter. By the middle of 1877, bones were being shipped north by rail from San Antonio and other points. Some were being loaded at Galveston on coastal steamers destined for Northern markets. On November 29, 1878, the *Frontier Echo* reported that since July 1877, 3,333 tons of bones, valued at $76,599, had been shipped from San Antonio. This must have been figured at Eastern prices, for the gatherers received only six to eight dollars a ton and later, when the market was glutted, sometimes as little as four dollars.

Near his hunting camp on the plains of western Texas, Bob Parrack saw a great pile of bones brought in by one of the early gatherers. A passing freighter offered sixteen hundred dollars for them, but the owner refused the bid.

In the late 1870's, bones hauled from the Texas Panhandle, where they lay thick on the prairies, were taken north to Dodge City. Dodge still was closer than the Texas railroad points. In addition, because it was nearer to St. Louis and Eastern markets, it paid higher prices. Casimero Romero, a prosperous sheepman who moved from New Mexico to the virgin grasslands of the Canadian Valley, had a dozen big freight wagons which he used on the trail between Tascosa and Dodge. After bringing barbed wire, bacon, and other freight south, he would load the wagons

---

[1] *Rocky Mountain News*, December 3, 30, 1874; Arthur C. Bill: "The Buffalo Hunt," MS.; Richard Irving Dodge: *The Plains of the Great West*, p. 140; Edwin Ford Piper: *Barbed Wire and Wayfarers*, p. 4; John R. Cook: *The Border and the Buffalo*, p. 135; Robert M. Wright: *Dodge City: The Cowboy Capital*, pp. 156–7.

with bones for the trip north. At Dodge in this period the bones sometimes brought as much as sixteen to eighteen dollars a ton. The round trip took a month to six weeks, depending on the weather.

Some of the freighters on what remained of the Santa Fe Trail also hauled bones to Dodge or, while waiting there for freight, went out after them. Each freighter had at least one big government-type wagon, often a Studebaker, that could carry up to five tons. Usually he had one or two ordinary farm wagons fastened behind it as trailers. After filling the boxes of their wagons, the freighters would arrange the pelvic bones as pickets around the edge. This would enable them to pile the bones higher and thus carry enormous loads.

So many buffalo bones from Texas were coming into Dodge that the Santa Fe Railroad built a separate spur for loading them. It also provided special cars, which could be loaded from the top. "I saw many trainloads of bones leaving Dodge City in 1878," recalled Laban H. Records.[2]

Soon the Texas and Pacific, building west from Fort Worth, was penetrating the Texas grasslands and giving rise to new towns. Among them was Abilene, named for the Kansas cow town, which arose at a point reached by the railroad in 1880. A trainload of bones shipped from Abilene to New Orleans brought such good prices that thousands of gatherers flocked to the ranges. Prairie fires had destroyed many of the bones; but enough were left to provide a boon for those who gathered them and hauled them to the towns, and even an appreciable business for the railroads.

Baird, Abilene, Colorado City, Sweetwater, and Albany became important shipping points for bones. Tom Low

---

[2] *Daily Democratic Statesman*, June 3, 1877; *Frontier Echo*, November 29, 1878; Ralph H. Records: "At the End of the Texas Trail: Range Riding and Ranching, 1878."

and others made good money from hauling them to Sweet-water. At Colorado City in 1881, John W. Mooar, who was hauling barbed wire from the railroad there to the Quitaque section of Charles Goodnight's ranch and provisions for a Texas Ranger camp in Blanco Canyon, came back each time with a load of bones. Usually he received $12.50 a ton for them. By the time he had delivered all the wire, he had been paid more than fifteen hundred dollars for bones.

As the Texas and Pacific Railroad was built from Abilene west to Colorado City, the number of bone gatherers increased. Among them was James R. (Sheep Jim) Lewallen, of Tennessee birth. On one of his trips he was gone forty-six days. He made enough money from gathering bones to buy the initial part of his sheep ranch.

The gatherers first scoured the prairies closest to the shipping point, then worked farther out. They dumped the bones in huge heaps, each marked with a sign of ownership, until freighters could haul them to town. Seldom was any of the piles molested. At times some of the trails to railroad towns were almost filled with bone wagons. As in Kansas, some of the haulers learned to water their bones to make them heavier. One who hauled from Kent County to Colorado City always spent the night at Lone Wolf Creek, where he allowed the bones to soak while he slept. This practice increased their weight by about one fourth.

In the Texas towns the wagons stood in the streets while buyers went from one to another and offered bids on the contents. After making a sale, the driver moved on to the railroad and added his load to one of the piles along a switch. Often the heaps were six to eight feet high and several hundred yards long. Ben Middleton, one of the gatherers who sold at Abilene, recalled that a huge pile of bones usually could be seen on North First Street, just east of Pine Street. There he generally received eight dollars a ton, which meant about three dollars a load. Later, as the bones became scarce, the price rose to twenty-one and even twenty-two dollars a ton.

All through the summer and fall of 1881, Abilene dealers were busy shipping the white remainders of the vanished buffaloes. They loaded and dispatched thirty-three carloads with 465 tons in July, thirty-seven carloads with 555 tons in August, and thirty-nine carloads with 585 tons in September.

Among the bone gatherers along the advancing line of the Texas and Pacific was an Englishman, Jimmie Kilfoile. Sometimes he even piled his buffalo bones ahead of the construction crews to await the rails that would carry them east. He obtained ten to fourteen dollars a ton, clearing nine hundred dollars for the bones he had gathered on a single ranch near Big Spring.

As the bone boom along the Texas and Pacific subsided, Kilfoile operated a freighting service from Sherman and Fort Worth northwest to Mobeetie in the Texas Panhandle. On his return trips, he loaded his wagons with bones. As there were more of them than he could haul at once, he left the surplus in monster piles, marking each with the letter K, scrawled on the skull of a buffalo bull. Some of his drivers thought he was crazy to pile the bones, "but a heap crazier to put his brand on 'em as if he was afeared anybody would steal 'em."

Before the Fort Worth and Denver Railroad was completed through the Panhandle in 1887, Kilfoile abandoned his other freighting and gave all his attention to hauling bones. At every station he had huge piles, often eight or ten feet high and more than half a mile long. A buyer from St. Louis, John Young, bought all of them at six to eight dollars a ton, which brought Kilfoile more than twenty-five thousand dollars.

Although the bone boom seldom lasted more than two or three years in any one section, the gathering often continued on a smaller scale for a decade. G. N. Jowell, who moved to the western Panhandle in 1887, helped gather several wagonloads in 1888–9. "We received $8 a ton for the bones. I have seen bones stacked twelve feet high and at least half a mile long beside the railroad tracks at Amarillo. It was a great help to the settlers." As late as 1899, when Bob Parrack moved his family to the Quaker settlement at Estacado, he gathered a load of bones and hauled them to Canyon.

Texas railroads shipped more than half a million tons of buffalo bones. Even at six dollars a ton, that meant more than three million dollars for the gatherers.[3]

## III

In the spring of 1884 the gathering began on a large scale in the North. Indians, half-bloods, and whites brought out the Red River carts that had hauled many a load of robes and hides and meat and filled them with the whitening bones.

That year the gathering was especially large in Dakota Territory. "The bone business is beginning to boom in this vicinity," said the Dickinson Press on May 24. "Several loads have been brought in during the week. We understand that the business will be entered into on a large scale during the present season and will give employment to a number of men." On June 14, Beckett and Foote advertised for a thousand tons of bones. On June 28 two wagon trains came in with bones. One had twenty-seven yokes of oxen. The other, with twenty-four yokes, came from Deadwood, in the Black Hills. It was owned by Peter Bland and Arthur Johnson.

At sidings of the Northern Pacific and other railroads,

3 John Wesley Mooar Papers, MSS.; Fort Griffin Echo, January 21, 1882; Haskell Free Press, August 28, 1886; Taylor County News, February 24, 1893.

long piles of bones became a familiar sight. Often they were ten to twelve feet high and more than a quarter-mile long, containing hundreds of tons. At Minot, in northern Dakota, Fred Stoltz began buying with a free hand. From Ipswich, a hundred carloads were shipped in three weeks in the summer.

Soon the activity spread into Montana. At Miles City a single firm shipped more than two hundred tons in 1885. From this and other river towns, freighters were going as far as a hundred miles on each side of the stream to load bones and haul them to boat landings or railroad sidings. One, with eight wagons, crushed many of the bones he gathered. He sacked the meal and shipped it to a fertilizer company in Michigan, receiving eighteen dollars a ton for the crushed bones and twelve dollars a ton for the un-crushed ones.

Meanwhile, Fred Stoltz continued to buy vast quantities of bones in northern Dakota. At one time he had in stacks along the railroad tracks at Minot enough bones to fill five hundred cars. Other important shipping points, east of Minot, were Towner, Rugby, Churchs Ferry, and Devils Lake.

Indians gathered and hauled many of the buffalo bones brought into the frontier Dakota towns. Early in 1885, M. I. McCreight, a youth of twenty, arrived from Pennsylvania and began working for a small Dakota bank where one of his duties was to buy bones offered by the redskins.

In the distance, he recalled, the townsmen could see the wagon trains of the Indians as they followed the winding trails that led over the prairies toward the market. In front of each slowly moving caravan strode the chief, with his long black hair plaited in two braids and with a blanket draped over one shoulder. He was followed by a motley group of men, women, children, and dogs. Some of the tribesmen rode ponies, while others came afoot. Their approach was marked by the cracking of whips, the screeching of wooden carts in need of grease, and the yelping of dogs.

About half a mile outside the town, the visitors halted, unloaded their tepees and other equipment, and made camp. Then the chief and his councilors walked into town and inquired what price was being paid for bones. On being told that the rate was six dollars a ton, they went back to the camp and brought in their loaded carts to be weighed. From the scales they drove the carts to the railroad siding and dumped their contents. After receiving their money, the Indians swarmed into the stores to spend it. Only after their last dime was gone did the visitors break camp.

Again in 1886 travelers on the Northern Pacific saw great heaps of bones along the tracks at stations between Jamestown and Billings. That was the last season of the three-year boom on the northern plains, but the gathering and hauling continued in diminishing quantity for several years.[4]

Meanwhile, Canadian settlers did not overlook the bones on their side of the boundary. Julian Ralph, who, with a friend, traveled west over the Canadian Pacific in 1888, took note of the gathering. "We found that the bison's remains had been made the basis of a thriving industry," he said. "At the outset we saw a few bison bones dotting the grass in white specks here and there. Soon we met great trains, each with many boxcars, laden with nothing but these weatherbeaten relics. Presently we came to stations where, beside the tracks, mounds of the bones were heaped and men were swelling the heaps with wagonloads garnered far from the railroad. A great business has grown up

[4] Dickinson *Press*, May 24, 1884; W. T. Hornaday: *The Extermination of the American Bison*, p. 446; M. I. McCreight: *Buffalo Bone Days*, pamphlet, pp. 75–8.

in collecting these trophies. For years the business of cart-
ing them away has gone on."

By that time the Great Plains were almost cleared of
buffalo bones except for the Indian Territory, the last part
to be opened to white settlement. Freighters and squatters
brought hundreds of wagonloads from the Cimarron country to Wichita, Dodge City, and other Kansas towns. Some
gathered from No Man's Land, which was to become the
Oklahoma Panhandle. Among those who built sod houses
in that wind-swept country in 1886 were Oliver Nelson
and Jim Staton. One of their first actions there was to load
a wagon with bones and haul them to Dodge.

Later, said Nelson, "we made a business of gathering
bones. We hauled water along for our team and picked up
all over the high flat north of Wolf Creek. A man could pick
up a load—three thousand pounds—in about an hour,
sometimes in twenty minutes. We got $7.50 a ton. It would
spoil a week to make a trip to Dodge. About 1888 the railroad built down to Liberal, Kansas, and we hauled there.
Once the Liberal buyer offered me fifty cents a pair for all
the buffalo horns I would bring in. I drove a day and picked
up three hundred pairs of good ones. The man just lost
heart. I sold a few pairs—one for $2.50, some for $1. Later
I took the rest to my folks in Sumner County, and they gave
them away. I also brought back several pounds of bullets
I'd picked up where the carcasses lay, and brother George
melted them down." [5]

With the gathering of trainloads of buffalo bones and
the disintegration and plowing under of others, no re-
minder was left—except for an occasional wallow—of the
vast herds that had roamed the plains a dozen years earlier.
Live buffaloes became so scarce that in 1886, when the

[5] Angie Debo: *The Cowman's Southwest,* pp. 293–6. Bones left on the
prairie disintegrated within a few years.

National Museum at Washington wanted a mounted group to exhibit, it had difficulty in finding suitable specimens.

The hunters had done more than clear the plains for cattlemen and simplify the Indian problem. They had almost wiped out one of North America's most impressive animals. Fewer than a thousand head were believed left. Belated conservation measures in the United States and Canada restored the number to several times that figure, with the result that occasionally some of the animals in protected preserves had to be sold to prevent overgrazing. In 1926 there were 4,376 buffaloes in the United States and 11,957 in Canada. But hunting them long had been relegated to history and legend.

# BIBLIOGRAPHY

## MANUSCRIPTS

Bill, Arthur C.: "The Buffalo Hunt." Kansas State Historical Society, Topeka.

Bussell, Richard: "Buffalo Hunting in the Panhandle." Panhandle-Plains Historical Museum, Canyon, Texas.

Cator Papers and Letters. Panhandle-Plains Historical Museum, Canyon, Texas. Photostatic copies, University of Texas library, Austin.

Clarkson, Matthew F., diary. Mrs. William Philip, Hays, Kansas. Transcript in library of Fort Hays Kansas State College.

Collinson, Frank, reminiscences. Panhandle-Plains Historical Museum, Canyon, Texas. Collinson fought at Yellow House Draw.

Davis, Levi: "Buffalo Hunt." Denver Public Library.

Dixon, William, Papers. Panhandle-Plains Historical Museum, Canyon, Texas.

Hanna, Oliver P.: "The Old Wild West." Wyoming State Archives and Historical Department, Cheyenne.

Henderson, John, reminiscences. Mrs. Agnes Wright Spring, State Historian of Colorado, Denver.

Hughes, Joseph Atwell, account of a buffalo hunt in 1868. Kansas State Historical Society, Topeka.

Indian-Pioneer Papers. University of Oklahoma library, Norman.

Interviews with former buffalo hunters. Transcripts in Panhandle-Plains Historical Museum, Canyon, Texas.

Lockhard, F. M., reminiscences. Kansas State Historical Society, Topeka.

Maginnis, Martin, diary. Montana Historical Library, Helena.

McCombs, Joe S.: "First Buffalo Hunt Out of Griffin." University of Texas library, Austin.

McKinley, J. W., narrative. Panhandle-Plains Historical Museum, Canyon, Texas.

Mooar, John Wesley, Papers. Southwest Collection, Museum, Texas Technological College, Lubbock.

Mooar, Josiah Wright, interviews with. Transcripts in University of Texas library, Austin. Detailed reminiscences of one of the leading hunters in Kansas and Texas.

——, Papers. University of Texas library, Austin.

Mooar, Louise, Marietta, Georgia, letters to the author, 1955–7.
Raymond, H. H., diary, 1872–3. Kansas State Historical Society, To-
    peka.
Rister, Carl Coke, Papers. Southwest Collection, Museum, Texas
    Technological College, Lubbock.
Sharps Rifle Company, correspondence, 1875–84.
Spence, Clark: "Sir St. George Gore: A Celtic Nimrod in the West."
Trautwine, John Hannibal, diary of a buffalo hunt in Kansas in 1873.
    Kansas State Historical Society, Topeka.
Wilson, Wenton A., account of a buffalo hunt in 1876. Kansas State
    Historical Society, Topeka.
Withers, Mark A., reminiscences. J. Frank Dobie, Austin, Texas.

## UNPUBLISHED THESES

Burlingame, Merrill Gildea: "The Economic Importance of the Buf-
    falo in the Northern Plains Region, 1800–1890." State Univer-
    sity of Iowa, 1928.
Grant, Ben O.: "The Early History of Shackelford County." Hardin-
    Simmons University, 1936.
Grieder, Theodore G.: "The Influence of the American Bison or Buf-
    falo on Westward Expansion." State University of Iowa, 1928.
McClure, Charles Boone: "A History of Randall County and the T
    Anchor Ranch." University of Texas, 1930.
Mullings, Fred R.: "Robert Cypret Parrack: Pioneer Plainsman."
    Texas Technological College, 1946.
Thompson, Theodore G.: "Bat Masterson: The Dodge City Years."
    Fort Hays Kansas State College, 1939.

## PUBLIC RECORDS

Record Copy of the Proceedings of the Indian Peace Commission Ap-
    pointed Under the Act of Congress Approved July 20, 1867. Na-
    tional Archives, Office of Indian Affairs, Washington, D.C.

## PUBLIC DOCUMENTS

Allen, Joseph Asaph: "History of the American Bison," in Ninth An-
    nual Report of the United States Geological and Geographical
    Survey for 1875, pp. 443–587. Also published separately, Wash-
    ington: Government Printing Office; 1877.
Annual Report of the Commissioners of Indian Affairs, 1874.
Congressional Globe, 1872.
Congressional Record, Forty-third Congress, Forty-fourth Congress.

Hornaday, William T.: *The Extermination of the American Bison.* Report of the National Museum, 1887. Washington: Government Printing Office; 1889.

Message from the President of the United States, 1832. Senate Executive Documents, Twenty-second Congress, first session, Vol. II, No. 90.

Minnesota: First Annual Report of the Minnesota Commissioner of Statistics. St. Paul, 1859.

Report of the Secretary of the Interior, 1874. House Executive Documents, Forty-third Congress, second session, Vol. I, Part 5.

## NEWSPAPERS

Abilene (Texas) *Reporter-News,* February 24, 1954.

Albany (Texas) *News,* February 20, 1891.

Amarillo *Daily News,* May 2, 1940.

Amarillo *Globe-News,* August 14, 1938.

Austin *American-Statesman,* May 9, 1926.

Beatrice (Nebraska) *Express,* December 23, 1871; January 20, 1872.

*Benton Record,* Fort Benton, Montana, February 1, August 7, 1875; August 24, 1876.

Caldwell (Kansas) *Post,* 1879–83.

Cheyenne *Leader,* April 2, 1873; January 5, 1876; August 3, 1881.

Clarksville (Texas) *Standard,* May 28, 1853.

*Daily Democratic Statesman,* Austin, Texas, 1875–7.

Dallas *Daily Herald,* January 11, 1874, 1875–6.

Dallas *Morning News,* 1885–1958.

Denison (Texas) *Daily News,* 1875–6.

Detroit *Free Press,* October 16, 1871.

Dickinson *Press,* May 24, 1884.

Dodge City (Kansas) *Times,* 1876–7.

El Paso *Times,* May 4, 1913.

*Ellis County Star,* Hays, Kansas, 1876–9.

Ellsworth (Kansas) *Reporter,* 1871–4.

*Ford County Globe,* Dodge City, Kansas, August 5, 1879.

Fort Griffin (Texas) *Echo,* 1879–82.

Fort Worth *Democrat,* 1876–9.

Fort Worth *Star-Telegram,* April 29, 1928; November 30, 1934; July 15, 1938.

*Frontier Echo,* Jacksboro, Texas, 1875–8.

Galveston *News,* 1875–7.

Haskell (Texas) *Free Press,* August 28, 1886.

Hays (Kansas) *Daily News,* November 30, 1933.

Hays City (Kansas) *Railway Advance,* November 9, 21, 1867; June 23, 1868.

Houston *Telegraph and Texas Register,* May 28, 1845.

Kansas City *Journal of Commerce,* January 11, 1868; August 17, 1869; August 1871; January 14–23, 1872.

Kansas City *Star,* May 28, 1911; November 30, 1930; November 5, 1953.

Kansas City *Times,* January 3, 1950; November 9, 1951.

*Kansas Daily Commonwealth,* Topeka, January 18, 21, 1872.

*Kansas State Record,* Topeka, July 15, 1874.

*Kansas Weekly Tribune,* Topeka, November 28, 1867.

Leavenworth *Daily Conservative,* January 11, March 5, 1868.

Leavenworth *Times,* 1867–72; November 17, 1877.

Lincoln (Nebraska) *Daily State Journal,* January 16–18, 1872.

*Missouri Republican,* St. Louis, 1851–3.

New Orleans *Daily Picayune,* December 30, 1843.

New York *Times,* November 1, 1953.

*Niles Weekly Register,* Baltimore, 1842–70.

*Rocky Mountain News,* Denver, 1865–85; July 25, 1915.

San Angelo (Texas) *Standard-Times,* May 11, 1953.

*Sangamo Journal,* Springfield, Illinois, July 23, 1846.

*Scurry County Times,* Snyder, Texas, May 7, 1936.

*Semi-Weekly Farm News,* Dallas, February 28, March 6, 13, 1936.

Sioux City (Iowa) *Journal,* 1881.

Snyder (Texas) *Daily News,* October 11, 1953.

*Southwest Plainsman,* Amarillo, January 16, 1926.

*Taylor County News,* Abilene, Texas, January 30, 1891; February 24, 1893.

Topeka *Capital,* July 1, 1923.

Tulsa *Daily World,* September 19, 1952.

Wichita *Eagle,* 1872–4.

Wichita *Tribune,* May 4, 1871.

Wichita *World,* February 9, 1889.

*Yellowstone Journal,* Miles City, Montana, January 17, 1880.

## PERIODICALS

Andrews, E. N.: "A Buffalo Hunt by Rail." *Kansas Magazine,* Vol. III, No. 5 (May 1875), pp. 450–8.

Beeson, Chalkley M.: "A Royal Buffalo Hunt." *Collections,* Kansas State Historical Society, Vol. X (1907–8), pp. 574–80.

Biggers, Don H.: "Buffalo Butchery in Texas Was a National Calamity." *Farm and Ranch,* Vol. XLIV, No. 46 (November 14, 1925), pp. 28–9. Reprinted in the *Cattleman,* Vol. XII, No. 8 (January 1926), pp. 45–8.

Brown, George W.: "Life and Adventures of George W. Brown," edited by William E. Connelley. *Collections,* Kansas State Historical Society, Vol. XVII (1926–8), pp. 98–134. Detailed reminiscences.

"The Buffalo, Monarch of the Plains." *Texas Game and Fish,* Vol. I, No. 8 (July 1943), pp. 4, 16.

"The Buffalo Hunt." *Harper's Weekly,* Vol. XI, No. 549 (July 6, 1867), p. 426.

Burlingame, Merrill G.: "The Buffalo in Trade and Commerce." *North Dakota Historical Quarterly,* Vol. III, No. 4 (July 1929), pp. 262–91.

Cabe, Ernest, Jr.: "A Sketch of the Life of James Hamilton Cator." *Panhandle-Plains Historical Review,* Vol. VI (1923), pp. 13–23.

Cahill, Luke: "An Indian Campaign and Hunting with Buffalo Bill." *Colorado Magazine,* Vol. IV, No. 4 (August 1927), pp. 125–35.

Cauley, T. J.: "What the Passing of the Buffalo Meant to Texas." *Cattleman,* Vol. XIV No. 7 (December 1929), pp. 32–3.

Christie, Robert: "I Rode the Buffalo Roundup." *Saturday Evening Post,* Vol. CCXXIII, No. 46 (May 12, 1951), pp. 158–60.

Clark, J. S.: "A Pawnee Buffalo Hunt." *Chronicles of Oklahoma,* Vol. XX, No. 4 (December 1942), pp. 387–95.

Collinson, Frank: "Prairie Fires." *Ranch Romances,* Vol. CII, No. 4 (October 1941), pp. 110–11.

Crimmins, Martin L.: "Captain Nolan's Last Troop on the Staked Plains." *West Texas Historical Association Year Book,* Vol. X (1934), pp. 68–73.

Davis, Theodore R.: "The Buffalo Range." *Harper's New Monthly Magazine,* Vol. CCXXIV, No. 38 (January 1869), pp. 147–63.

Dean, Cora: "Early Fur Trading in the Red River Valley, from the Journals of Alexander Henry, Jr." *Collections,* State Historical Society of North Dakota, Vol. III (1910), pp. 350–68.

De Voto, Bernard: "The Great Medicine Road." *American Mercury,* Vol. XI, No. 41 (May 1927), pp. 109–10.

Draper, Benjamin: "Where the Buffalo Roamed." *Pacific Discovery,* Vol. III, No. 2 (March–April 1950), pp. 14–27.

Fouquet, L. C.: "Buffalo Days." *Collections,* Kansas State Historical Society, Vol. XVI (1923–5), pp. 341–7.

Fryxtell, F. M.: "The Former Range of the Bison in the Rocky Mountains." *Mammology,* Vol. IX, No. 2 (May 1928), pp. 129–39.

Gard, Wayne: "How They Killed the Buffalo." *American Heritage,* Vol. VII, No. 5 (August 1956), pp. 34–9.

———: "Hunting Buffaloes in Texas." *Cattleman,* Vol. XLII, No. 6 (November 1955), pp. 42, 65–8.

———: "On the Buffalo Range." *Texas Parade,* Vol. XV, No. 6 (November 1954), pp. 41–3.

———: "Roping Buffaloes on the Plains." *Cattleman,* Vol. XXXVIII, No. 10 (March 1952), pp. 35, 74–6.

Gard, Wayne: "Where Buffalo Roamed." *Progressive Farmer*, Texas edition, Vol. LXVIII, No. 8 (August 1953), p. 18.

Goodman, Alfred T.: "Buffalo in Ohio." *Western Reserve and Northern Ohio Historical Society Tract*, No. 36 (January 1877).

Grant, Ben O.: "Life in Old Fort Griffin." *West Texas Historical Association Year Book*, Vol. X (1934), pp. 32–41.

Green, Thomas L., editor: "Notes on a Buffalo Hunt—the Diary of Mordecai Bartram." *Nebraska History*, Vol. XXXV, No. 3 (September 1954), pp. 193–222.

Grinnell, George Bird: "The Last of the Buffalo." *Scribner's Magazine*, Vol. XII, No. 3 (September 1892), pp. 267–86.

Hadley, James Albert: "A Royal Buffalo Hunt." *Collections*, Kansas State Historical Society, Vol. X (1907–8), pp. 564–74.

Hafen, LeRoy F., editor: "With Fur Traders in Colorado, 1839–1840: The Journal of E. Willard Smith." *Colorado Magazine*, Vol. XXVII, No. 3 (July 1950), pp. 161–88.

Haley, J. Evetts, Jr.: "Adobe Walls." *Junior Historian*, Vol. VIII, No. 4 (January 1948), pp. 1–4, 22.

Hamilton, William T.: "A Trading Expedition Among the Indians in 1859, from Fort Walla Walla to the Blackfoot Country and Return." *Contributions*, Historical Society of Montana, Vol. III (1900), pp. 33–123.

Hamner, Laura V.: "Buffalo Days and Buffalo Ways." *Cattleman*, Vol. XXXII, No. 6 (November 1945), pp. 62, 64.

Hathaway, Seth: "The Adventures of a Buffalo Hunter." *Frontier Times*, Vol. IX, No. 3 (December 1931), pp. 105–12, 129–35.

Heldt, F. George, editor: "Narrative of Sir George Gore's Expedition, 1854–1856." *Contributions*, Historical Society of Montana, Vol. I (1876), pp. 128–31.

Hilger, David: "Overland Trail." *Contributions*, Historical Society of Montana, Vol. VII (1910), pp. 257–70.

Holden, W. C.: "Robert Cypret Parrack, Buffalo Hunter and Fence Cutter." *West Texas Historical Association Year Book*, Vol. XXI (1945), pp. 29–49.

Hughes, Pollyanna B.: "Adobe Walls May Rise Again." *Texas Parade*, Vol. XV, No. 5 (October 1954), pp. 34–6.

Hunter, J. Marvin, Sr.: "John W. Mooar, Successful Pioneer." *Frontier Times*, Vol. XXIX, No. 12 (September 1952), pp. 331–7. Authentic.

Jacobs, John C.: "Buffalo Hunters on the Texas Frontier." *Pioneer*, Vol. V, No. 11 (May 1925), pp. 9, 19.

Kauffman, Harlan B.: "Hunting the Buffalo." *Overland Monthly*, Vol. LXVI, No. 2 (August 1915), pp. 165–70.

Kincaid, Naomi H.: "Rath City." *West Texas Historical Association Year Book*, Vol. XXIV (1948), pp. 40–6.

Koch, Peter: "Life at Musselshell in 1869 and 1870." *Contributions,*
Historical Society of Montana, Vol. II (1896), pp. 292–303.

Kuhlhoff, Pete: "The Guns That Swept the Plains." *Argosy,* Vol.
CCCXL, No. 5 (May 1955), pp. 38–41.

Lake, Stuart N.: "The Buffalo Hunters." *Saturday Evening Post,* Vol.
CCIII, No. 17 (October 25, 1930), pp. 12–13, 81–5.

Little, Edward Campbell: "The Battle of Adobe Walls." *Pearson's
Magazine,* Vol. XIX, No. 1 (January 1908), pp. 75–85. A good
account.

McCombs, Joe S.: "On the Cattle Trail and Buffalo Range." *West
Texas Historical Association Year Book,* Vol. XI (1935), pp. 93–
101.

Mechem, Kirke: "Home on the Range." *Kansas Historical Quarterly,*
Vol. XVII, No. 4 (November 1949), pp. 313–39.

Mooar, J. Wright: "The First Buffalo Hunting in the Panhandle."
*West Texas Historical Association Year Book,* Vol. VI (1930),
pp. 109–11.

——: "Frontier Experiences." *West Texas Historical Association Year
Book,* Vol. IV (1928), pp. 89–92.

Mooar, J. Wright, as told to James Winford Hunt: "Buffalo Days."
*Holland's,* Vol. LII (January, February, March, April, May, July
1933).

Moore, Ely: "A Buffalo Hunt with the Miamis in 1854." *Collections,*
Kansas State Historical Society, Vol. X (1907–8), pp. 402–9.

Munson, Lyman E.: "Pioneer Life on the American Frontier." *Journal of American History,* Vol. I, No. 1 (January–March 1907),
pp. 97–119.

Murphy, Robert: "Tales of the Buffalo." *Saturday Evening Post,* Vol.
CCXXIV, No. 50 (June 14, 1952), pp. 47, 53–9.

"My First Buffalo Hunt." *Leisure Hour,* No. 713 (August 26, 1865),
pp. 529–31.

Nordyke, Lewis: "The Great Buffalo Roundup of 1945." *Saturday
Evening Post,* Vol. CCXVII, No. 51 (June 16, 1945), pp. 14–15,
37–9.

Records, Ralph H.: "At the End of the Texas Trail: Range Riding and
Ranching, 1878." *West Texas Historical Association Year Book,*
Vol. XIX (1943), pp. 109–20.

Richardson, Rupert Norval: "The Comanche Indians and the Adobe
Walls Fight." *Panhandle-Plains Historical Review,* Vol. IV
(1931), pp. 24–38.

Riggs, Thomas L.: "The Last Buffalo Hunt." *Independent,* Vol. LXIII,
No. 3,057 (July 4, 1907), pp. 32–8.

Rister, Carl Coke: "Indians as Buffalo Hunters." *Cattleman,* Vol. XV,
No. 3 (August 1928), pp. 17–19. Reprinted in the *Frontier
Times,* Vol. V, No. 12 (September 1928), p. 456.

Rister, Carl Coke: "The Significance of the Destruction of the Buf-
    falo in the Southwest." *Southwestern Historical Quarterly*, Vol.
    XXXIII, No. 1 (July 1929), pp. 34–49.
Roosevelt, Theodore: "Buffalo Hunting." *St. Nicholas*, Vol. XVII, No.
    2 (December 1889), pp. 136–43.
Russell, Hamlin: "The Story of the Buffalo." *Harper's Monthly Mag-
    azine*, Vol. LXXXVI, No. 515 (April 1893), pp. 795–8.
Seton, Ernest Thompson: "The American Buffalo or Bison." *Scrib-
    ner's Magazine*, Vol. XL, No. 4 (October 1906), pp. 385–405.
Smith, Honora De Busk: "Cowboy Lore in Colorado." *Southwestern
    Lore*, Publications of Texas Folklore Society, No. IX (1931), pp.
    27–44.
Smith, Joe Heflin: "Big Business on the Plains." *Cattleman*, Vol.
    XXXVI, No. 6 (November 1950), pp. 32–8.
"A Stage Ride to Colorado." *Harper's New Monthly Magazine*, Vol.
    XXXV, No. 206 (July 1867), pp. 137–50.
Strickland, Rex W., editor: "The Recollections of W. S. Glenn, Buf-
    falo Hunter." *Panhandle-Plains Historical Review*, Vol. XXII
    (1949), pp. 15–64. Glenn was in the fight at Yellow House Draw.
Tallmadge, Frank: "Buffalo Hunting with Custer." *Cavalry Journal*,
    Vol. XXXVIII, No. 154 (January 1929), pp. 6–10.
Taylor, Walter P.: "The Buffalo." *Monthly Bulletin of the Texas
    Game, Fish and Oyster Commission*, Vol. IV, No. 2 (January
    1941), pp. 2, 8.
Terrell, C. V.: "Texas Buffalo Hunt: 1876." *Southwest Review*, Vol.
    XXXIII, No. 3 (Summer 1948), pp. 233–7.
Thomas, Chauncey: "Butchering Buffalo." *Colorado Magazine*, Vol.
    V, No. 2 (April 1928), pp. 41–54.
Thompson, A. W.: "Last of the Buffalo in Texas." *Cattleman*, Vol.
    XIV, No. 11 (April 1930), pp. 29–31.
Trexler, H. A.: "The Buffalo Range in the Northwest." *Mississippi
    Valley Historical Review*, Vol. VII, No. 4 (March 1921), pp.
    348–62.
Webb, W. P.: "A Texas Buffalo Hunt." *Holland's*, Vol. XLVI, No. 10
    (October 1927), pp. 10–11, 101–2.
Wright, Robert M.: "Personal Reminiscences of Frontier Life in
    Southwest Kansas." *Collections*, Kansas State Historical Society,
    Vol. VII (1901–2), pp. 47–83.

## PAMPHLETS

[Allison, O. S.]: *Addendum to "The Life of Billy Dixon."* N.p.; n.d.
*The Buffalo and the Indian.* Denver: Denver Art Museum; 1930.
Burdick, Usher W.: *Tales from Buffalo Land: The Story of George M.
    Newton.* Baltimore: Wirth Brothers; 1939.

Collins, Henry H., Jr.: *The Unvanquished Buffalo.* Bronxville, New York: Blue Heron Press; 1952.

Earle, J. P.: *History of Clay County and Northwest Texas.* Henrietta, Texas; 1900.

Foote, Stella Adelyne: *Letters from Buffalo Bill.* Billings, Montana: Foote Publishing Company; 1954.

Hill, J. L.: *The Passing of the Indian and Buffalo.* Long Beach, California: W. Moyle Publishing Company; n.d.

Hornecker, Martin: *Buffalo Hunting on the Plains of Texas in 1877.* [Geneseo?, Illinois]; 1929.

McCreight, M. I.: *Buffalo Bone Days.* Stykesville, Pennsylvania: Nupp Printing Company; 1939. On bone gathering in Dakota.

Merriman, Robert Owen: *The Bison and the Fur Trade.* Kingston, Ontario: Queen's University Press; 1926.

*Sharps Patent Breech-Loading Metallic Cartridge Military, Creedmoor and Sporting Rifles* (catalogue). Hartford: Sharps Rifle Company; 1875.

Shoemaker, Henry Wharton: *A Pennsylvania Bison Hunt.* Middleburg, Pennsylvania: Middleburg Post Press; 1915.

Stewart, George K.: *A True Story of an Early Buffalo Hunt.* N.p.; 1948.

Williams, Oscar Waldo: *"Muddy" Wilson and the Buffalo Stampede.* Dallas: printed by the Martin Stationery Company; 1938.

## BOOKS

Allen, J. A.: *The American Bisons, Living and Extinct.* Cambridge, Massachusetts: University Press; 1876. A scientific treatise.

Baker, Inez: *Yesterday in Hall County, Texas.* Memphis, Texas: Inez Baker; 1940.

Banta, William, and J. W. Caldwell, Jr.: *Twenty-seven Years on the Frontier.* Austin: Ben C. Jones and Company; 1893. Revised edition, Council Hill, Oklahoma: L. G. Park; 1933.

Barnum, P. T.: *Struggles and Triumphs, or Forty Years' Recollections.* Revised edition. Buffalo, New York: Warren, Johnson and Company; 1871.

Batchelder, G. A.: *A Sketch of the History and Resources of Dakota Territory.* Yankton: Press Steam Power Printing Company; 1870.

Berkeley, Grantley F.: *The English Sportsman in the Western Prairies.* London: Hurst and Blackett; 1861.

Biggers, Don H.: *From Cattle Range to Cotton Patch.* Abilene, Texas: Abilene Printing Company; n.d.

———: *Shackelford County Sketches.* Albany, Texas: Albany News Office; 1908.

Birge, Julius C.: *The Awakening of the Desert*. Boston: Richard G. Badger; 1912.

Branch, E. Douglas: *The Hunting of the Buffalo*. New York: D. Appleton and Company; 1929. Best of the earlier general accounts.

Brewerton, George Douglas: *Overland with Kit Carson*. New York: Coward-McCann; 1930.

Briggs, Harold E.: *Frontiers of the Northwest*. New York: D. Appleton-Century Company; 1940.

Butcher, S. D.: *Pioneer History of Custer County*. Broken Bow, Nebraska: S. D. Butcher; 1901.

Cabeza de Baca, Fabiola: *We Fed Them Cactus*. Albuquerque: University of New Mexico Press; 1954.

Campion, J. S.: *On the Frontier: Reminiscences of Wild Sports, Personal Adventures and Strange Scenes*. London: Chapman and Hall; 1878.

Carter, Robert G.: *The Old Sergeant's Story*. New York: Frederick H. Hitchcock; 1926.

——: *On the Border with Mackenzie*. Washington: Eynon Printing Company; 1935.

Catlin, George: *Letters and Notes on the Manners, Customs, and Condition of the North American Indians*. Two volumes. London: published by the author, printed by Tosswill and Myers; 1841. New York: Wiley and Putnam; 1841. Tells of early Indian hunting.

Chittenden, Hiram M.: *The American Fur Trade of the Far West*. Three volumes. New York: Francis P. Harper; 1902.

——: *History of Early Steamboat Navigation on the Missouri River*. Two volumes. New York: Francis P. Harper; 1903.

Cody, Louisa: *Memories of Buffalo Bill*. New York and London: D. Appleton and Company; 1919.

Cody, William Frederick: *The Adventures of Buffalo Bill*. New York and London: Harper and Brothers; 1904.

Collins, Dennis: *The Indians' Last Fight, or the Dull Knife Raid*. Girard, Kansas: Press of the Appeal to Reason; 1915.

Conover, George W.: *Sixty Years in Southwest Oklahoma*. Anadarko, Oklahoma: N. T. Plummer; 1927.

Cook, James H.: *Fifty Years on the Old Frontier*. New Haven: Yale University Press; 1923. New edition, Norman: University of Oklahoma Press; 1957.

Cook, John R.: *The Border and the Buffalo*. Topeka: Crane and Company; 1907. Experiences of a hunter who fought at Yellow House Draw.

Coues, Elliott, editor: *The Expeditions of Zebulon Montgomery Pike*. Three volumes. New York: Francis P. Harper; 1895.

——: *New Light on the Early History of the Greater Northwest: The*

*Manuscript Journals of Alexander Henry and David Thompson, 1799–1814.* Three volumes. New York: Francis P. Harper; 1897.

Crawford, Samuel J.: *Kansas in the Sixties*. Chicago: A. C. McClurg and Company; 1911.

[Davies, Henry E.]: *Ten Days on the Plains*. New York: Crocker and Company; [1871]. Brief account of a hunt for sport.

Debo, Angie: *The Cowman's Southwest*. Glendale, California: Arthur H. Clark Company; 1953.

Dixon, Billy: *Life and Adventures of Billy Dixon of Adobe Walls*. Guthrie, Oklahoma: Co-operative Publishing Company; 1914. The most detailed account of the battle at Adobe Walls.

Dixon, Olive K.: *Life of Billy Dixon*. Dallas: P. L. Turner Company; 1927. Dallas: Southwest Press; 1927.

Dodge, Richard Irving: *The Plains of the Great West*. New York: G. P. Putnam's Sons; 1876. English edition, *The Hunting Grounds of the Great West*, London: Chatto and Windus; 1877.

Duncan, Bob: *Buffalo Country*. New York: E. P. Dutton and Company; 1959.

Ellsworth, Henry Leavitt: *Washington Irving on the Prairie*, edited by Stanley T. Williams and Barbara D. Simison. New York: American Book Company; 1937.

Field, Matthew C.: *Prairie and Mountain Sketches*. Norman: University of Oklahoma Press; 1957.

Flack, Captain: *A Hunter's Experiences in the Southern States of America*. London: Longmans, Green and Company; 1860.

——: *The Texan Ranger, or Real Life in the Backwoods*. London: Darton and Company; 1866.

Flint, Timothy: *Biographical Memoir of Daniel Boone*. Cincinnati: George Conclin; 1842.

Frémont, John Charles: *Memoirs of My Life*. Chicago and New York: Clarke and Company; 1887.

Frost, John: *Thrilling Adventures among the Indians*. Philadelphia: John E. Potter and Company; 1851.

Gard, Wayne: *The Chisholm Trail*. Norman: University of Oklahoma Press; 1954.

Garretson, Martin S.: *The American Bison*. New York: New York Zoological Society; 1938.

Greeley, Horace: *An Overland Journey, from New York to San Francisco, in the Summer of 1859*. New York: C.M. Saxton, Barker and Company; 1860.

Gregg, Josiah: *Commerce of the Prairies*. Two volumes. New York: Henry G. Langley; 1844.

Grinnell, George Bird: *The Fighting Cheyennes*. New York: Charles Scribner's Sons; 1915. New edition, Norman: University of Oklahoma Press; 1956.

Hafen, LeRoy P., editor: *Ruxton of the Rockies*. Norman: University of Oklahoma Press; 1950.

Haley, J. Evetts: *Charles Goodnight, Cowman and Plainsman*. Boston: Houghton Mifflin Company; 1936. New edition, Norman: University of Oklahoma Press; 1949.

——: *Fort Concho and the Texas Frontier*. San Angelo: San Angelo Standard-Times; 1952.

——: *The XIT Ranch of Texas*. Chicago: Lakeside Press; 1929. Revised edition, Norman: University of Oklahoma Press; 1953.

Hall, James: *The Romance of Western History*. Cincinnati: Applegate and Company; 1857.

Hamilton, W. T.: *My Sixty Years on the Plains*. New York: Forest and Stream Publishing Company; 1905.

Hanson, Joseph Mills: *The Conquest of the Missouri*. Chicago: A. C. McClurg Company; 1909. New York: Rinehart and Company; 1946.

Hart, John A., and others: *History of Pioneer Days in Texas and Oklahoma*. N.p.; n.d. Not reliable on Adobe Walls.

Holden, William Curry: *Alkali Trails*. Dallas: Southwest Press; 1930.

Humphrey, Seth K.: *Following the Prairie Frontier*. Minneapolis: University of Minnesota Press; 1931.

Hunter, J. Marvin, editor: *The Trail Drivers of Texas*. Nashville: Cokesbury Press; Vol. I, 1920; Vol. II, 1923. Second edition, revised, two volumes in one, 1925.

Inman, Henry: *The Old Santa Fe Trail*. New York: Macmillan Company; 1897. Topeka: Crane and Company; 1899.

Inman, Henry, and William F. Cody: *The Great Salt Lake Trail*. New York: Macmillan Company; 1898.

Innis, Harold A.: *The Fur Trade in Canada*. New Haven: Yale University Press; 1930. Revised edition, Toronto: University of Toronto Press; 1956.

Irving, Washington: *The Rocky Mountains, or Scenes, Incidents, and Adventures in the Far West*. Two volumes. Philadelphia: Carey, Lea and Blanchard; 1837. Revised as *The Adventures of Captain Bonneville, U.S.A.*, one volume. New York: George P. Putnam; 1849.

——: *A Tour on the Prairies*. London: John Murray; 1835.

Jennings, Napoleon Augustus: *A Texas Ranger*. New York: Charles Scribner's Sons; 1899. Dallas: Turner Company; 1930.

Jones, Charles Jesse: *Buffalo Jones' Forty Years of Adventure*, compiled by Henry Inman. Topeka: Crane and Company; 1899.

Keim, De B. Randolph: *Sheridan's Troopers on the Borders*. Philadelphia: David McKay; 1885.

Kennerly, William Clark, as told to Elizabeth Russell: *Persimmon Hill: A Narrative of the Far West.* Norman: University of Oklahoma Press; 1948.

Larpenteur, Charles: *Forty Years a Fur Trader on the Upper Missouri.* Two volumes. New York: Francis P. Harper; 1898.

Latrobe, Charles Joseph: *The Rambler in North America.* Two volumes. London: R. B. Seeley and W. Burnside; 1835.

Lavender, David: *Bent's Fort.* Garden City, New York: Doubleday and Company; 1954.

Linforth, James, editor: *Route from Liverpool to Great Salt Lake Valley.* Liverpool: Franklin D. Richards; 1855.

Lomax, John A., and Allan Lomax: *Cowboy Songs.* New York: The Macmillan Company; 1938.

Majors, Alexander: *Seventy Years on the Frontier.* Chicago and New York: Rand, McNally and Company; 1893.

Marcy, Randolph B.: *The Prairie Traveler.* New York: Harper and Brothers; 1859.

Matthews, Sallie Reynolds: *Interwoven.* Houston: Anson Jones Press; 1936.

Mayer, Frank H., and Charles B. Roth: *The Buffalo Harvest.* Denver: Alan Swallow; 1958.

McConnell, H. H.: *Five Years a Cavalryman.* Jacksboro, Texas: J. N. Rogers and Company; 1889.

McCoy, Joseph G.: *Historic Sketches of the Cattle Trade of the West and Southwest.* Kansas City: Ramsey, Millet and Hudson; 1874. Facsimile reprint, Washington, D.C.: Rare Book Shop; 1932. Edition with introduction and notes by Ralph P. Bieber, Glendale, California: Arthur H. Clark Company; 1940. New facsimile reprint, Columbus, Ohio: Long's College Book Company; 1951.

Monaghan, Jay: *The Great Rascal.* Boston: Little, Brown and Company; 1952.

Murphy, John Mortimer: *Sporting Adventures in the Far West.* London: Sampson, Low, Searle and Rivington; 1879.

Nelson, Bruce: *Land of the Dakotahs.* Minneapolis: University of Minnesota Press; 1946.

O'Connor, Richard: *Bat Masterson.* Garden City, New York: Doubleday and Company; 1957.

Olson, James C.: *History of Nebraska.* Lincoln: University of Nebraska Press; 1955.

Paine, Bayard Henry: *Pioneers, Indians and Buffaloes.* Curtis, Nebraska: Curtis Enterprise; 1935.

*Pioneer Days in the Southwest.* Guthrie, Oklahoma: State Capital Company; 1909. An amplification of the John A. Hart book.

Piper, Edwin Ford: *Barbed Wire and Wayfarers.* New York: The Macmillan Company; 1924.

Poe, Sophie: *Buckboard Days.* Caldwell, Idaho: Caxton Printers; 1936.

Powers, Alfred, editor: *Buffalo Adventures on the Western Plains.* Portland, Oregon: Binfords and Mort; 1945.

*Prose and Poetry of the Livestock Industry of the United States.* Denver and Kansas City: National Live Stock Association; 1905.

Read, Georgia Willis, and Ruth Gaines, editors: *Gold Rush: The Journals, Drawings, and Other Papers of J. Goldsborough Bruff.* New York: Columbia University Press; 1949.

Richardson, Albert D.: *Beyond the Mississippi.* Hartford: American Publishing Company; 1867.

Richardson, Rupert Norval: *The Comanche Barrier to South Plains Settlement.* Glendale, California: Arthur H. Clark Company; 1933.

Rister, Carl Coke: *Fort Griffin on the Texas Frontier.* Norman: University of Oklahoma Press; 1956. An excellent account of the principal outfitting point of the Texas hunters.

——: *No Man's Land.* Norman: University of Oklahoma Press; 1948.

Roe, Frank Gilbert: *The North American Buffalo: A Critical Study of the Species in Its Wild State.* Toronto: University of Toronto Press; 1951. Good on many technical details.

Root, Frank A., and William Elsey Connelley: *The Overland Stage to California.* Topeka: W. Y. Morgan; 1901. Facsimile reprint, Columbus, Ohio: Long's College Book Company; 1950.

Ross, Alexander: *The Fur Hunters of the Far West.* Two volumes. London: Smith, Elder and Company; 1855. New edition, one volume, Norman: University of Oklahoma Press; 1956.

——: *The Red River Settlement.* London: Smith, Elder and Company; 1856.

Ruxton, George Frederick: *Life in the Far West,* edited by LeRoy R. Hafen. Norman: University of Oklahoma Press; 1951.

Rye, Edgar: *The Quirt and the Spur.* Chicago: W. B. Conkey Company; 1909. Anecdotes of frontier Fort Griffin.

Sandoz, Mari: *The Buffalo Hunters.* New York: Hastings House; 1954.

Seton, Ernest Thompson: *Life-Histories of Northern Animals.* Two volumes. New York: Charles Scribner's Sons; 1909.

Smith, Winston O.: *The Sharps Rifle.* New York: William Morrow and Company; 1943.

Smithwick, Noah: *The Evolution of a State: or, Recollections of Old Texas Days,* compiled by Manna Smithwick Donaldson. Austin:

Gammel Book Company; 1900. Facsimile reprint, Austin: Steck Company; n.d.

Stevens, Hazard: *The Life of Isaac Stevens*. Two volumes. Boston and New York: Houghton Mifflin Company; 1900.

Streeter, Floyd Benjamin: *Prairie Trails and Cow Towns*. Boston: Chapman and Grimes; 1936.

Stuart, Granville: *Forty Years on the Frontier*. Two volumes. Cleveland: Arthur H. Clark Company; 1925.

Taylor, Drew Kirksey: *Taylor's Thrilling Tales of Texas*. N.p.; 1936.

Terrell, C. V.: *The Terrells*. Austin: C. V. Terrell; 1948.

*Texas in 1840, or the Emigrant's Guide to the New Republic*. New York: William W. Allen; 1840.

Thorp, Raymond W.: *Spirit Gun of the West: The Story of W. F. Carver*. Glendale, California: Arthur H. Clark Company; 1957. Carver's fantastic and unsupported claims need to be taken skeptically.

Thorpe, T. B.: *The Hive of the Bee-Hunter*. New York: D. Appleton and Company; 1854.

Thwaites, Reuben Gold, editor: *Early Western Travels*. Thirty-two volumes. New York; 1897. Cleveland: Arthur H. Clark Company; 1904-7.

——: *Original Journals of the Lewis and Clark Expedition, 1804–1806*. New York: Dodd, Mead and Company; 1904-5.

Tibbles, Thomas Henry: *Buckskin and Blanket Days*. Garden City, New York: Doubleday and Company; 1957.

Tilghman, Zoe A.: *Marshal of the Last Frontier*. Glendale, California: Arthur H. Clark Company; 1949.

——: *Quanah: The Eagle of the Comanches*. Oklahoma City: Harlow Publishing Corporation; 1938.

Townsend, J. K.: *Narrative of a Journey across the Rocky Mountains, to the Columbia River, 1834–1839*. Philadelphia: H. Perkins; 1839. Also in *Early Western Travels*, edited by Reuben Gold Thwaites, XXI, 107–369.

Vestal, Stanley: *Queen of the Cowtowns: Dodge City*. New York: Harper and Brothers; 1952.

——: *Sitting Bull*. Boston and New York: Houghton Mifflin Company; 1932. Revised edition, Norman: University of Oklahoma Press; 1957.

Wallace, Ernest, and E. Adamson Hoebel: *The Comanches: Lords of the South Plains*. Norman: University of Oklahoma Press; 1952.

Wallis, Jonnie Lockhart, editor, in association with Laurance L. Hill: *Sixty Years on the Brazos: The Life and Letters of Dr. John Washington Lockhart, 1834–1900*. Los Angeles: privately printed, Press of Dunn Brothers; 1930.

Walsh, Richard J.: *The Making of Buffalo Bill.* Indianapolis: The Bobbs-Merrill Company; 1928. The most reliable book on Cody.

Waters, L. L.: *Steel Trails to Santa Fe.* Lawrence: University of Kansas Press; 1950.

Webb, W. E.: *Buffalo Land.* Philadelphia: Hubbard Brothers; 1872.

Webb, Walter Prescott: *The Great Plains.* New York: Ginn and Company; 1931.

Wheeler, Homer W.: *Buffalo Days.* Indianapolis: The Bobbs-Merril Company; 1923.

Williams, O. W.: *Historic Review of Animal Life of Pecos County.* Dallas: printed by Martin Stationery Company; n.d.

Wislizenus, F. A.: *A Journey to the Rocky Mountains in the Year 1839.* St. Louis: Missouri Historical Society; 1912.

Wright, Robert M.: *Dodge City: The Cowboy Capital.* Wichita: Wichita Eagle Press; 1913.

Young, Harry: *Hard Knocks.* Chicago: Laird and Lee; 1915.

Zornow, William Frank: *Kansas: A History of the Jayhawk State.* Norman: University of Oklahoma Press; 1957.

# INDEX

Bent's Fort, Colo., 53–7
Bergh, Henry, 207 f., 210
Bernard, Phil, 257
Bickerdyke, Ann Ball, 241
Bickerdyke, Hiram, 241, 249, 256
Bickerdyke, Jack, 287 ff.
Biddle, Clement, 67
Big Bow, Chief, 162
Big Creek, 76, 142
Big Dry Creek, 259 f., 271
Big Horn Basin, 267
Big Horn Mountains, 260, 267 f.
Big Lake, 115
Big Spring, Tex., 229, 251, 303
Bill, Arthur C., 298
Billings, Mont., 306
Bismarck, N.D., 258 f., 266, 269,
    272, 274
bison, see buffaloes
Black Hills, 64, 201, 274, 304
Black Kettle, Chief, 78 f.
Blackfoot Crossing, 11
Blackfoot Indians, 58
Blackmore, William, 130 f.
Blanco Canyon, 234, 302
Bland, Peter, 304
blizzards, 21, 86, 92, 108 ff.,
    281–7
Blue Creek, 135
Bluff Creek, 128
Boggy Creek, 196
Bond, Orlando A. (Brick), 128 f.,
    144 f.
Bonneville, Benjamin, 5
Boone, Daniel, 20
Bow River, 11
Box Elder, Colo., 86
Brackett, A. G., 208, 212
Bradley, James H., 46
Brazos River, 158, 184, 199, 218,
    222 f., 226, 232, 234, 236 f.
Brewerton, George D., 11
Bridger, James, 44, 63
Bronson, Bill, 241
Brown, Cadmus, 251
Brown, George W., 91 f.
Brown, Joseph H., 228
Brown County, Tex., 190, 202
Brownwood, Tex., 189, 191
Buffalo, Kans., 98, 101

Buffalo, N.Y., 77, 88
buffalo chips, 24 ff.
Buffalo City, Kans., 101
Buffalo Gap, Tex., 189
buffalo hides, 90–104, 106, 108,
    115, 125 ff., 152, 200, 220, 233
buffalo meat, 22 ff., 75, 77 ff.,
    80 ff., 86, 108, 123
buffalo robes, 36 f., 43–53
buffalo stampedes, 10–13, 62
Buffalo Station, Kans., 101
buffalo wallows, 17 ff.
Buffalo Wool Company, 51
buffaloes: hunting of, 3 f., 27–
    42, 59–275; numbers of, 4–7;
    description of, 7 ff.; habits of,
    9–22; migrations of, 9 f.; leg-
    ends of, 276–94; songs about,
    289–94; gathering bones of,
    295–307
buffaloes, white, 8 f.
Bugbee, Harold D., v
Bugbee Canyon, 142
Bull Bear, Chief, 40
Bull Creek, 228, 250
Buntline, Ned, 82
Burdett, John, 91 f.
Bussell, Richard, 23, 93, 183 f.,
    195 f.
Butler County, Kans., 109
Butterfield Trail, 183

Cabeza de Vaca, Alvar Núñez,
    5, 8
Caddo Indians, 160 f.
Caddo Peaks, 189
Callahan, Jack, 94, 103, 114
Camp Alexis, Nebr., 69–72
Camp Reynolds, Tex., 232; see
    also Rath City
Camp Supply, 18, 76, 86, 108 f.,
    147 f., 196, 224, 254, 298
Campbell, Dave, 146
Campbell, Hank, 239, 241, 243–7
Canada: hunting in, 50–3, 201;
    gathering bones in, 306 f.
Canadian Pacific Railroad, 306
Canadian River, 9, 40, 128, 130,
    134 ff., 138–44, 149 f., 300
Canyon, Tex., 304

## A NOTE ON THE AUTHOR

WAYNE GARD was born in Brocton, Illinois, in 1899. He has degrees from Illinois College (Jacksonville) and Northwestern University; he did graduate work in history at Columbia University. He has lived also in Missouri, Iowa, and Kansas. His newspaper career has included work as a wire editor and foreign correspondent for the Associated Press, as an editorial writer for the Chicago *Daily News,* and as an editorial writer for the *Des Moines Register and Tribune.* Since 1933 he has been a Texan, writing editorials for the *Dallas Morning News.* For years he followed the trails of buffalo hunters across the Great Plains, gathering fresh lore for the present book. Mr. Gard has contributed to more than a score of national and regional periodicals, including *American Heritage, American Mercury,* and *Nation's Business; Reader's Digest* has reprinted four of his articles. *The Great Buffalo Hunt* is his sixth book; four of the earlier ones deal with Western history. At sixty, Mr. Gard still plays tennis and chops firewood. He is a fellow of the Texas State Historical Association and an honorary Oklahoma colonel. He was awarded an honorary doctorate of literature by Illinois College in 1959. Mr. Gard is married and has one son.

## A NOTE ON THE TYPE

THE TEXT of this book was set on the Linotype in a new face called PRIMER, designed by Rudolph Ruzicka, earlier responsible for the design of *Fairfield* and *Fairfield Medium*, Linotype faces whose virtues have for some time now been accorded wide recognition.

The complete range of sizes of *Primer* was first made available in 1954, although the pilot size of 12 point was ready as early as 1951. The design of the face makes general reference to Linotype *Century* (long a serviceable type, totally lacking in manner or frills of any kind) but brilliantly corrects the characterless quality of that face.

In the designs for *Primer*, Mr. Ruzicka has once again exemplified the truth of a statement made about him by the late W. A. Dwiggins: "His outstanding quality, as artist and person, is *sanity*. Complete esthetic equipment, all managed by good, sound judgment about ways and means, aims and purposes, utilities and 'functions'—and all this level-headed balance-mechanism added to the lively mental state that makes an artist an artist. Fortunate equipment in a disordered world . . ."

Composed, printed, and bound by Kingsport Press, Inc., Kingsport, Tennessee. Paper manufactured by S. D. Warren Company, Boston. Typography and binding designs by Vincent Torre.